Spirit
&
Matter

Spirit & Matter

New Horizons for Medicine

José Lacerda de Azevedo, M.D.

NEW FALCON PUBLICATIONS
TEMPE, ARIZONA, U.S.A.

International Standard Book Number: 1-56184-083-1

Library of Congress Catalog Card Number: 95-74972

First Edition 1997

Translated by Ivone Dreux

Our special thanks go out to Dr. Jane Mocellin
without whose invaluable assistance and dedication
this project would not have been possible.

The paper used in this publication meets the minimum requirements of
the American National Standard for Permanence of Paper for Printed
Library Materials Z39.48-1984

Address all inquiries to:
NEW FALCON PUBLICATIONS
1739 East Broadway Road Suite 1-277
Tempe, AZ 85282 U.S.A.
(or)
1209 South Casino Center
Las Vegas, NV 89104 U.S.A.

TO

MARIA EVANGELINA LACERDA DE AZEVEDO,
my mother
(who molded my physical body)

ARZELINA DE BARROS LACERDA, my maternal aunt
(who molded my spirit), and

YOLANDA LACERDA DE AZEVEDO, my wife
(to whom I owe all material and spiritual achievements),

MY GRATITUDE WITH LOVE

In Gratitude

We would like to thank the honorable presidents of the Spiritist Hospital of Porto Alegre,

Dr. CONRADO FERRARI
and
Mr. JOÃO AMADO VENÂNCIO,

both passed away. The first, was the founder of the spiritual work in the "Garden House," with the technique of Apometrics. The second one was his follower.

Today, not working for the Spiritist hospital anymore, we can well evaluate the resoluteness and the integrity of character of these leaders. With fraternal serenity, they gave us unrestricted support from the very beginning on, allowing the growing of the first seeds of the most advanced techniques in the field of mediumicity.

TABLE OF CONTENTS

Part III:
Operational Techniques 269

DEDICATION & INTRODUCTION

*THIS BOOK IS DEDICATED TO ALL THOSE WHO WORK IN THE
FIELDS OF PSYCHISM, FROM THE MEDIUMS TO THE
DOCTORS.*

A FLOWER

*It was on a cold morning, in May 1985, that I got to know Dr.
José Lacerda de Azevedo. The "Garden House" of the Spiritist
Hospital of Porto Alegre was full of people waiting to be
assisted, people of all social classes, who arrived there in the
hope of cure.*

As all the others, I waited, too.

*When my name was announced, I entered a corridor where
there were people in blue jackets walking around. I remembered
that I talked to more than one of those tranquil gray-headed
men, imagining that they would be Dr. Lacerda.*

At the end I met him. And I was surprised.

*The man, despite his height, looked humble, a sweet look,
lovably alive. He radiated faith, a luminous determination that
fluttered around in each kind gesture, in the tone of his voice, in
the contraction of his strong lips. In this first moment, I did not
realize that he was somewhere in his sixties, his grayish hair
hiding somewhat his incipient baldness. I became enchanted
with that silent sympathy behind a smile that seemed to be
always ready to open up, I was dazzled by his soft sincerity,
revealed little by little.*

*I did not know. At that moment, an undeniable veneration
together with the deepest friendship that life could offer me, was
born.*

*Slowly, in contacts that became more and more frequent, I
began to know the details of a spiritual work of enormous
importance, performed with admirable persistence, for almost a
quarter of a century. Patiently and silently, the Group led by Dr.
Lacerda was exploring the dimension of the spirit, daring to
enter universes, hidden by the limited perceptions of our senses.
Hypotheses were crystallized into laws: laws that transformed
many old mysteries into simple and natural facts, laws that
were proven and corroborated during many subsequent years.
To discuss phenomena (the old ones, as well as the new ones),
to formulate hypotheses about causes, interrelations, to reach*

15

effects and possible laws, for permanent decoding, it was necessary to study continuously. I was focused like a physicist and an astronomer, with one eye on the principles of nuclear and quantum physics and the other on the most ample horizons of philosophic thought, and as one in flight through spirit and the cosmos. A daunting task, without any doubt. But no one would ever have performed with such success, discoveries and cures, if he were not centered in the teachings of the Divine Master and if he had not deserved the assistance of the spiritual mentors of the highest evolutionary degree.

In this ample horizon opened permanently by this work, I realized that the wisdom of the ones who are eternal apprentices, was present with Dr. Lacerda and his fellows. It was as if the gigantic surprises that they were facing—decoding them—were not any different from those phenomena that they studied in the first meetings of the pioneer group, when the work was almost only restricted to reflections about the Gospels and the donation of energy fluids for the use of charitable spirits, in their Samaritan work.

Research, permanent research. Careful vigilance against prejudices, fanaticism and, mainly, against vanity. Daring experimentation: to prove, ad nauseam, *recently acquired knowledge, to give it the consistency of a diamond; considering the unknown not as something terrifying, but simply as something new that was waiting for its exploration to become known and old, one day. Having one's eyes very open, always, but immersed in eternity. Although pushing the mind to almost unthinkable limits, opening at the same time, the heart, loving everything possible, feeling in oneself the pulsing of humanity of all times in all planes of life—this is an incomplete summary of the facets that I saw in the posture of those who work in the Garden House. Charity is the base for everything. Not that unctuous, underlined and deliberately conscious charity that is contaminated by its opposite. Charity has to be limpid, luminous, natural. And consequently, humble like a violet.*

I became familiar with identical groups in Brasilia, independent, but using the techniques of the "Garden House." There Dr. Victor Ronaldo and Dr. Edson Veiga have been working for years, in silence and with the same constancy, to surprising effects. There were other groups in Pelotas. Santa Maria. Rio de Janeiro.

But if these Groups were so successful, why did they not publish this knowledge they so arduously collected to have it shining like a chandelier, to give light to everyone? Then I discovered that there was a book in its final stage, a book that would be published as soon as it was finished.

I looked for the author, Dr. Lacerda. He gave me the original of the book, still unfinished. Two thick volumes of papers, written on weekends and during the little leisure time he had away from his work as a doctor and at the "Garden House."

I read it and I liked it.

My enthusiasm was spontaneous, so much that I offered myself to help with the final proofreading. Here I could help. It was little work, but I wanted to help.

Dr. Lacerda accepted my offer. This made me very happy.

Then, I started my work as a scribe, daring to polish somebody else's text. At the beginning the responsibility scared me and I almost regretted my wanting to help. I felt that I was dealing with words that were too important, If I committed any involuntary adulteration of a basic concept, it would be difficult to redeem myself for the mistake before the author or the readers.

Several times I talked to Dr. Lacerda about my concerns. I presented exhaustive versions of the texts, being afraid even of a wrong comma, I felt foolhardy because I dared to make transpositions, cuts, and one or another synthesis. He just smiled at my feeling guilty. Usually he corroborated, but he also rejected—with the informality and spontaneity of a father. Some times we even talked, and, on the route of the definitive text, I had lessons of physics, chemistry, biology, history, medicine, pharmacology, etc., and about subjects that no book teaches. I was trying to give, but I was being enriched.

One day, when we were talking about the book that had so far neither a title nor a publisher, I asked Dr. Lacerda for the privilege of writing one or two pages as an introduction to the book. He agreed immediately, indicating that he was very happy with the idea. "But there is one detail," I said. "My name cannot appear. The text will be of an anonymous author."

Dr. Lacerda protested. But I knew that I was right, it was an immense certainty—that of knowing I was the least important in the creation of this work of which he was the invisible architect, helped by other constructors made of flesh and bone: doctors, lawyers, engineers, military officers, technicians, housewives, etc. There were also, as the cause and the fulcrum of the invisible constructors, the Superior Spirits, who orient and assist, who not only worked in concert with the Group, but also worked individually.

In effect, I did not construct anything. I was only able to polish the words, as I am a scribe. And if my work was fair, this is not my merit. I did everything for love. Love that the workers at the "Garden House," without knowing, inculcated in me, making me think what you, dear brother, will feel when you read this book.

Now, that these pages are opened, and you are ready to enjoy them, I confess that the only objective of this statement is the pleasure to offer it to you as if it were a flower. A simple and lovely flower that I want to place in your heart, as you enter into the celebration of light.

— An Anonymous Writer

OUR PRISM

*Many are the spiritists who are not interested at all in the phenomena of the soul. They even despise them either because they do not understand them, or possess an immovable selfishness. They prefer a spiritism they consider a religion. And that kind of religion is already outdated: a **nest** of transcendental certainties, where people are accommodated, make up dogmas, untouchable orthodoxies, charisma, myths...and well-delineated **limits** to investigation, even if these investigations are sound and necessary.*

Considering these people, we believe that it is convenient to say, now at the entrance of this work, that our position in relation to the theme is as important as it is complex, so that it is possible to foresee the contents of these pages.

*We believe that the basic objective of the Spiritist Doctrine is to redeem men. Redeeming them by evangelizing them, raising their feelings and thoughts, improving them in such a way that they will be in vibratory conditions that allow their spiritual evolution rapidly and safely. We can not expect from the Doctrine that it transforms everybody into scientists, since Science is not a synonym for spiritual elevation, it is only an **instrument** of the Doctrine. We know enough to say that pure and simple intellectual efforts do not take us to the **target:** pointless, without life experiences, they will only be fruitful when they are submerged in the **practice** of evangelic charity. That is why we consider of fundamental importance the increasing of the religious facet of Spiritism, by all means within our reach, because it is this that constitutes an indestructible foundation of spiritual elevation for all beings and for humanity in general.*

*We also believe that religion, joining individuals with the Creator, has to be understood and seen in its amplitude—this means, **within a cosmic context.** It has to be lived in an open way, each individual has to feel himself immersed in his own eternity, open to infinite horizons, and involved by inexorable faith—because he is always ready for enlightenment, for research and for the process of learning. Once the individual glimpses the Cosmic Christ in himself, the target is near. And it attracts him.*

We believe that the Spiritist Doctrine, in relation to its own formulations and to the ample vision of its Founder, should not follow the easy and downward route of the decadent. In this case we would be in the grip of one more static religion, limited by sectarian dogmas and infested by low particularisms and personalisms. Unfortunately, this degradation can already be seen in Spiritism—to the detriment of the spirit.

We believe that the religious intolerance and the artificial cult of doctrinal pureness are incompatible with the horizons of the Spiritual Doctrine, which is dynamic and always fresh by virtue of its own nature, and is looking for continuous progress and learning. Being limited to the past, in the name of purity, and orthodox criteria, is going backwards, to fall into the well from which Kardec and the spirits wanted to lift humanity. We must not forget: it was precisely by invoking the purity of the Mosaic Law that the Sanhedrin condemned Jesus. The medieval intolerance also invoked the purity of Christ's teachings to take thousands of people to death, in flaming bonfires and infected prisons.

Love without liberty is not possible. Love for truth is imperative.

This is our prism.

PART I

THE SCIENCE OF THE SPIRIT

GENERALITIES

The strict meaning of science[1] is the knowledge that we have about something. In a broader sense it means the knowledge we acquire by reading, studying and meditating, or it can also be the sum of the restricted pieces of knowledge that we have about a subject and the facts related to it or to a set of subjects. The knowledge of all the observed phenomena is called, generically—science. It is *systematized knowledge.*

Science can be divided into branches, according to the subject with which it deals. There are physical, economic, human, moral...and psychic sciences—the last one can be considered the most recent horizon in knowledge about human beings. Specific methods and norms guide the surveys of each one of these experimental sciences. The psychic sciences are also experimental, although, they are based on methods that we could call, with a certain right, *experimental-minds.*

PSYCHIC SCIENCES — A CHALLENGE

In all kinds of sciences—whether physical, chemical or biological—there are postulates (and the theorems which are derived from them), which are essential if we are to be able to make any equation or solution, or come to measurable results of the experiences. When we refer to transcendent levels—as those that involve the existence of a soul, for instance—the scientist feels unable to accept conclusions *a priori,* because he finds himself exploring a new and moving ground, where surveying becomes complex.

This perplexity is understandable, once this *field* is out of the prosaic domain of the five senses. Everything seems excessively vague, impalpable, *volatile*—if not fantastic.

We are sometimes afraid of mixing science and religion. The acceptance of this invisible reality is also harmed by the controversial explanations that different religions give them, explanations that in many aspects are conflicting. To make it more difficult, we have to consider that religion and metaphysics have a smell of death, ghosts, etc., reaching the atmosphere of legends and myths.

---

[1] Science: from Latin *scientia,* from *scire,* to know.

Science seems to be confused, maybe unsure, in view of these obstacles. But this attitude has its roots in the past.

THE ROOTS OF UNCERTAINTY

For centuries, science was subordinate to the dogmas of the medieval scholastic. The moment it was freed from its static and anti-experimental chains—through arduous effort—during the Renaissance, science began to employ objective research in the pursuit of liberty, and was victorious. This victorious posture is still maintained today, but it is being worm-eaten by biases that are as sticky as the dogmas that science faced in the old times. It repels, with the disdain it showed the old inquisition and the same false superiority, all those who inform us about the unknown universe that exists beyond our three-dimensional universe. For example, phenomena that make needles oscillate are not physically corroborated: this means *that they cannot exist.*

What is the face of fear today?

Science is still *juvenile,* in spite of the wrinkles of many centuries; *juvenile* because it has not seen yet its limited vein of research exhausted. Science insists in the distortion that only solids, with their Cartesian three dimensionality, are researchable. The psychic sciences, for instance, while they are concerned with the mind, restrict their objectives exclusively to *living beings,* any other ontological *reality* has been discarded by scientists—who consider these experiments unreal and unlikely because they do not see nor feel them. All those phenomena that these ontological realities provoke in human beings, are studied on living brains and they are always linked to mental activities.

It was with this untimely attitude that Science reached *now,* always in progress, but eager to solve everything that still challenges the vain, limited by Science. In the area of physics and chemistry, for example, there has been so much research, with such a volume of results and information, that in only eighty years they surpassed the scientific achievements of all human history in these fields. Thus, it was possible for man to put his feet on the moon, to probe the cosmos, and to develop technology to help industry create deadly weapons and new products.

Absorbed, now and forever, by material and immediate interests—where it places its effusion of a doughy adolescent—it is natural that science is not interested in the study of phenomena whose roots go into *fields,* considered immaterial, different *spatial dimensions* from ours, phenomena that are of unquestionable *reality,* but will not be acknowledged because we cannot smell, measure or weigh them. (These dimensions can be called *metaphysics* because they are somewhere beyond the physical plane. With this word we refer to these phenomena. Please do not think that this word indicates any clue of abstract lucubration; *meta* means "beyond"; *meta*physics, therefore, simply indicates something that is out of the physical field.)

EPPUR SI MUOVO![2]

Eppur si muovo. "Inexplicable" phenomena of growing intensity have been puzzling scientists since the middle of the 19th century. They manifest themselves in specially gifted people known as "mediums", "sensitives", "prophets", "quacks", "clairvoyants", etc. In some people, phenomena called "premonitions" happen. In other people, the phenomena of telekinesis, psychographics, psychophonics and others, happen. All of these phenomena are *already scientifically corroborated* and many of them are even embodied in the daily life of people and communities. It is difficult to accept that, in spite of the undeniable evidence, there are people who, in the name of an *adolescent* scientific attitude, try to refute them disdainfully.

This cannot happen forever. Science has been hemmed in by an avalanche of facts, pushed to confirm the existence of something that should be called "soul", "spirit" or the "site of life" (with survival after death), therefore science has been compelled to open a *relief valve.* In some way it has to satisfy the pressures that it has been undergoing since the last century: either it researches and gives a definite explanation for that waterfall of extremely important phenomena, or it confesses its blind dogmatism, its *immaturity and fear* of the manifestation of the dead.

In the past, in spite of the disastrous and unappealable decisions of the scientific *courts,* some fearless pioneers performed work of great value. At the end of the 18th century, Mesmer took care of quite a few patients, using a new method, based on animal magnetism. This provoked a large reaction in France. After him, (among others) there were Liébeault and Bernheim, who founded the School of Nancy; Charcot, in Salpetrière; and other schools. In 1872, Richet baptized the new science with the name *Metaphysics*, a science that studies the phenomena beyond psychism. The door to systematic investigation about the *reality* of the Spirit, was open.

---

[2] An exclamation of Galileo, when he was in front of the Court of Inquisition. Forced to deny his ideas about the motion of the Earth, he accepted the sentence, but he whispered to himself: *"However, it moves!"*

The neologism created (i.e., Metaphysics), dealt with unexplainable facts of that time, which were all closely bound to human psychism. Richet, who studied some sensitives with recognized mental powers over many years, defined *metaphysics* as the science which *has as an objective, the studying of mechanical or psychological phenomena, due to the forces which seem to be intelligent, or to unknown power, latent in human intelligence.* It includes, therefore, the phenomena of *cryptesthesia*, which means the ability to know about something that is occult (we do not know yet by what kind of process); *telekinesis*, or the mechanical action, that, at a certain distance, makes heavy objects move, without any human contact; and materialization of the dead, a subject that has been exhaustively studied by William Crookes (under the name of *ectoplasmics*, a word created by Richet. It is what we call now the old wrongly-named "materialization": the appearance, under special conditions, of objects and even of complete human beings—alive and intelligent—who have emerged from the parallel universe, to which we referred.)

In the modern age, Rhine introduced *parapsychology*. With new methods of investigation, mainly statistical, parapsychology is trying to find *mathematical* proofs for psychic manifestations that escape from the domain of psychology. Although, without the deepness of Richet, Rhine develops a gigantic work of laboratory research about phenomena such as telepathy, precognition, clairvoyance, and so forth. For over twenty years, he patiently observed a great number of people during his experiments, and reached mathematical conclusions that are irrefutable.

One of the reasons, nevertheless, why Rhine's work achieved status as a science, was precisely that he did not risk touching phenomena linked to spirits—for instance, ectoplasmic modeling, apparitions, psychophonics and psychographics. For some special reason, but a very significant one, the researcher did not want to get involved in any phenomena that could be attributed to the dead; nor did he try to enter the dimensional universe where they dwell. He respected the scientific *taboo*, despite its medieval stuffiness. And he was respected.

This fact exudes obvious irony. And it takes us to the following question: *Why is Science afraid of Religion?*

It seems to be dramatically necessary—and urgent—that the scientists of today remove from their shoulders that load of obsolete biases, to have this fabulous universe (although to date only a few have glimpsed it) get its charter of reality and have its scientific citizenship acknowledged. Only in this way, free from cumbersome concepts and ideas, our investigators can become the Copernicuses and Galileos we need.

There are psychics today, at the moment that this is being written, who are eagerly trying to find new paths and unveil new *worlds*. These discoverers will become enraptured by the view of the *new* that stretches out in the space that encircles the Earth, places that are invisible to earthly eyes, an unfathomable world for common people. However, everything is within the ken of those people who, gifted with sharp senses, can pick up and register uncommon electromagnetic radiation.

THE ADMIRABLE OLD NEW WORLD

There are still few people who are able to perceive dimensions, different from ours, through a narrow window that goes from 4,000 to 8,000Å^3 of the visible spectrum; through this vibratory crevice—and only through it—comes the perception of everything that surrounds us, to common people. For the sensitives, the window opens wide, and they become transported to the neighboring regions of our planet (although they are part of it), and these are places full of life and activity. They can visit the skies about which religions speak, where there are houses, buildings, temples, like those on Earth, vehicles and a great variety of appliances, all similar to ours. The inhabitants of that world are people like us. Yes, they are human beings. (There are people on Earth who even refuse to imagine that they exist.) But these individuals no longer have bodies, their bodies were left at the cemetery due to the phenomenon of death. Free from their fleshly envelopes, these people cannot be seen by us who can only see the dense form of material bodies. There in their universe, they keep their color, clothes and objects as if they were on Earth. Everything there, is as solid as in our world—this is something that should not surprise us: the perception of forms is relative; it is a *function of the spatial environment.*

THE "WHY" OF THIS BOOK

It is precisely there, in this parallel universe, that we have been operating for more than two decades. We even dared to explore it. We would like to guide investigators to this universe so they can unveil the laws, discover the beings that dwell there, and explore the influences, benign or terribly evil, that they may have upon us. (To illustrate this, we can point out, among the evil ones, many psychic diseases, already identified by physicians, but of unknown etiology for medicine.)

---

^{3} Å = angstrom, a distance. of 1×10^{-8} cm.

The objective of this book is to show a new world and indicate the means to reach it. As a matter of fact, this universe is not that new since it is as old as our planet. And "reach" might not be the right word, it really, is just a matter of perceiving it. Anyway, we can assure others that the exploration of this universe is like a trip.

A trip in this *mare tenebrosum*, however, requires a certain mental conditioning, accepting premises that apparently are unusual, along with *working hypotheses*. We would like to stress that the premises are scientifically formulated. We do not consider them dogmas of faith or religious postulates because our survey excludes any kind of proselytizing. We are stirred by the goal of finding practical and universal applications that will benefit *all* humankind, not just factions. Again, we will have the dimensional space—the seat of the actions. And it will also be the object of the survey: Man that exists beyond Man.

We mentioned that science establishes fundamental parameters and proceedings, to set up equations that correspond to the observed factors and promote the analytic relationship of the laws at stake. In the same way as it happens in mathematics, the elements that form the equation, are called *factors*.

Independent of the level on which we operate, physical or metaphysical, the development of the process follows norms, identical to the operational and laboratory methods that orient physical surveys, once the results converge to the phonemic world (this means to the visible world), due to the presence of the observed facts in this world.

As the word indicates, *phenomenon* is "that which appears"; it is a Greek word related to the verb "to appear." Everything that appears in the world is a phenomenon: it manifests itself, it becomes objective. When we deal with metaphysical phenomena, however, the *appearance* and the survey become more complex. We operate in a different dimension, reachable only through analytic processes of reasoning. If the physical world we can perceive with our senses makes the identification of its laws difficult, imagine how difficult the survey of the mind's horizon will be. In spite of this and of all obstacles, however, systematic observation of slight phenomenological manifestations (*filtered* by our dimension) have made it possible to discover valuable elements and inestimable information about this parallel universe. It is possible, therefore, to establish—in a solid way—norms of investigation that allow us to explore and prove the existence of this universe, by discovering the means of reaching it.

This *field, or universe,* has its own identity, different from the one of our universe. As for the forms, there are minor differences in relation to our world. In the more developed regions we can observe an enormous technological progress, much more advanced than ours. (We can say, without fear of error, that *all* of our scientific development comes from *there.)* But in the inferior regions, the inhabitants live in pain and suffering, because the moral laws always rule man's behavior and determine his destiny—as religions assure.

It might be surprising that the world is subordinated to the same laws that rule ours. We have realized that the Law of Gravity—of the fall of the bodies—and all the others known in physics and in chemistry exist there, too, defying the acuity of the sages.

We will offer methods and techniques to studious people to enter these boundaries. As our work follows the methodological norms used by experimental sciences, we hope not to cause any surprises because we adopt the same systematic survey and, in general, identical methods of approach.

KNOWLEDGE OF THE SPIRIT — AN EXPERIMENTAL SCIENCE

To avoid any doubt about our purpose, we would like to explain some concepts and definitions.

By "method" we mean the set of established rules, in order to have a certain subject get to know about a certain object.

From the subject's point of view there is the "deductive method" (also called the analytic or divergent method) which starts with general principles and extracts specific facts from them. (This is the method used most in philosophy and mathematics.) In contradistinction, the "inductive method" (also called the synthetic or convergent method), has, as its starting point, the fact (or a set of specific facts) and moves step by step to reach laws or general principles.

As to the object, the methods are specific and there are as many as the objects they investigate.

In our work of more than two decades, whenever there is a repeated phenomenon, we try to observe it for some time to measure its proportions and to evaluate its duration, intensity, constancy, subtle variations, spatial comprehension, repetition, etc. Once we have all this data, we try to find the Law that determines the phenomenon, since there is no phenomenon without Law. For this reason, we establish a working hypothesis: we imagine how this phenomenon works by creating a formula for it that, although arbitrary, is close to the observed reality.

From then on we observe the development of the phenomenon more attentively, as well as the hypothetical Law. If the
phenomenon acts strictly according to the imagined Law, it will
be corroborated—it is legitimate.

When we know the Law, we repeat the phenomenon as many
times as possible to confirm the exactness of the discovery.
Claude Bernard stated: *the fact suggests the idea, the idea
guides the experience, and the experience controls the
hypotheses.*

When the major Law is established, we start the observation
of minor variations of the phenomenon, because these are also
subject to minor laws that act together with the major Law,
but in an independent way. If all minor laws are determinate
and their causes are known, then the phenomenon is totally
clarified, along with its set of laws. Only then do we formulate
the general theory of the studied fact. So, we start from an
isolated fact, or we go from the particular to the general; from
one fact to the general Law that rules similar facts (or
phenomena). This is the classical method of experimental
science—the inductive one—so often used by the present
researchers and their predecessors of the nineteenth century.

We give a small example, to illustrate this.

FIRST EXPERIMENT

If a light object (e.g., a ball) is dropped a short distance from
the ground, it will fall on a determinate area on the ground,
perpendicular to the point from which it was dropped. Even if
the experience is going to be repeated several times, the point
of falling will always be the same. This is the Law of the Fall of
a Body, or better, the Law of the Free Fall, which has its origin
in the major Law of Universal Gravity.

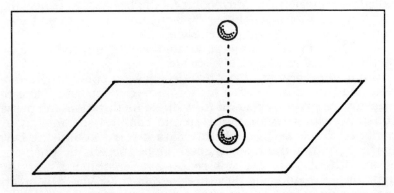

SECOND EXPERIMENT

In one of the experiments, we realized that the object suffered a deviation when it dropped, reaching a different point on the ground. After repeating the experiment we could even calculate the angle of deviation. Searching for the cause, we found that a light breeze blowing from one side and caused the deviation.

In this case a new Law works together with the first; it is independent, but strong enough to modify the result of the initial experience. This Law is called a *Minor* law or secondary law. (Natural phenomena are always accompanied by a series of secondary Laws.)

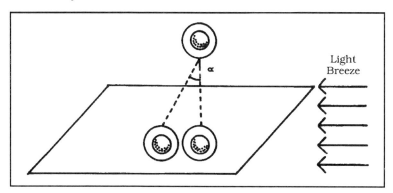

Constant observation and experiment acquired long ago are the elements that allow us to identify several laws that rule phenomena and their interactions.

* * *

With these introductory explanations, it is possible to enter systematically the work that gave us the means to penetrate the nearest parallel horizons to ours. As a matter of fact, these horizons are extremely important in understanding how everything happens. There is no danger in accepting them: none of them constitutes a dogma of faith, although it seems so. They are only *mathematical elements* that, used methodically, will take us to equations with astonishing results.

As the first and indispensable *working hypothesis*, it is necessary that we admit the reality of the spiritual world, the existence of spirits, and the *possibility* of their being real, and therefore, *legitimate phenomena*—although they elude our senses. If this *reality* is proved through experimentation, we will come to laws—bridges to the "unknown" or "occult."

Minds have to be disarmed. Barriers of scientific and religious biases have to be dropped, so that we can advance towards the new horizons. During this trip, we possibly will understand even better the reasons and objectives of this book.

There is no reason for scientific biases, because science does not defend biases; science is neutral and accepts any proven fact. Any stagnating fact is a restraint cultivated by scientists, who used to speak in the name of science to defend their positions.

If they were really scientists, they would investigate any physical or metaphysical phenomenon, with impartiality.

THE SPIRIT-MAN

Since ancient times, the Spirit-Man relationship has been the object of studies and speculations. The knowledge of our essence was a constant preoccupation of ancient peoples who were more conscious of its importance than we who are separated from them by millennia, culture, scientific conquests, and resounding technological advances.

According to what we can deduce from history, this consciousness really decreased instead of increasing, perhaps because we have been distracted through the millennia by the dangerous toys of religious bigotry and with mathematical games of constructing and destroying *what is not essential*. We were distracted, and so, too, was our science: by lack of a *scientific attitude*—a blatant paradox—science hesitates to explore and know the *vivid* reality of our *essence* (or spirit).

THE WISDOM OF THE ANCIENTS

The sages of antiquity knew the Spirit-Man much better than our modern ideation can conceive. We are still circling around whether the soul *exists or not*. They, as they accepted the reality of the spirit, were trying to take the next step: investigate the manner or process by which these two are linked.

These surveys produced many fruits of which there are some seeds left.

The comparative studies of the various conceptions about the *composition* of man—developed by the old initiate schools, philosophical schools, and several religious confessions—present well-known difficulties because they were very complex and full of confusing details. However, through all these eras (and languages underlying varied terminologies), shines one common certainty: sages and schools say basically the same thing when they refer to the vibratory stages of which man is composed.

The existence of an intermediate system between the *essence* (or pure spirit) on one side, and the physical body on the other side, is theoretically deducible by logic, and also technically imperative, since only this *vehicle* can make the actuation of Spirit or Matter possible, by organizing it. In other words, the fixation of the spirit in the body had to imply the existence of a special organ, with sufficient plasticity to adapt to the vibratory frequencies of the two—to *couple* them.

This organ—really a body—was detected by the sensitives of antiquity, it was even a subject of the *curriculum* at the initiate schools.

Through various times and among different people, denominations and details varied. In Vedic India, this mediator was called "Mana-maya-kosha"; the ancient Egyptians called it "Kha"; the Persians in the Zend-Avesta called it "Boadhas"; the Greek, "Eidolon"; for Aristotle, it was "The Subtle Body"; in the neo-Platonic school it was known as "Astroiedê" (this means "similar to the stars," because of its color); it was the "Fluidic Body of Leibnitz"; the "Perispirit" of Alan Kardec; or the "Souls" of Paul of Tarsus.

For the apostle Paul, Man is a complexity, integrated by three distinct parts—body, soul and spirit[4], where the soul has the clear function of the plastic mediator:

> *And the very God of peace sanctify you wholly; and I pray God your whole spirit and soul and body be preserved blameless unto the coming of our Lord Jesus Christ.*   — 1 Thessalonians, 5:23

In Greek history there were thinkers of primitive Christianity, mainly those from the School of Alexandria, who supported the thesis of the intermediary organ between the spirit and the body. Among them were: Athanasius, Phulgencius, Arnobius, Basilius, Origenes, Justinus, Minucius, Cirillus of Alexandria, and Saint Augustine. Other religions, such as Islam, Judaism and those that integrate present Christianity, all consider Man as a binary being: composed of a soul (or spirit) and a material body.

THE SEPTENARY — ORIGIN & IMPORTANCE

A few of the occidental religions and the large majority of the oriental religions have taught a more complex constitution of the Spirit-Man: seven interpenetrating components—the *septenary*—the more diaphanous occupying the same spatial place

---

[4] Paul distinguished between the soul and the spirit, something that the followers of both Catholicism and spiritism do not do. They confound the soul with the spirit in an unacceptable synonymy. For the spiritists, soul and spirit are the same thing, and the perispirit is the intermediary between the two planes: physical and spiritual. The comprehension of the concept makes it diffuse and excessively generic. It does not perceive the physiology of this perispirit, neither the peculiarities of the union between the perispirit and the spirit or between the perispirit and the body.

of the denser ones, perfectly defined, but *vibrating* in different spatial dimensions—where attributes, functions and manifestations are distinct.

Extremely old, this conception originated in India, from the sages who started the Vedanta Philosophy. The ancient Egyptians also taught this conception in the mysteries of Teba and Memphis. In the early Greco-Roman initiation centers, the septenary philosophy was the esoteric fundament of mediumistic cults. Theosophists, Rosicrucians, Anthroposophists, Esoterists and all the neo-spiritualist currents adopted the septenary, considering it the real structural composition of the human being.

The ancient sages studied the septenary and used their knowledge to get practical results: the treatment of sick people, psychic investigations, and manipulation of the powers of nature. By applying mental magnetic power on candidates for the initiation, they separated and detached components of the septenary (invisible bodies) to develop latent powers (e.g., clairvoyance) and dominate the powers of nature (natural magic).

Some of these techniques, of more restricted applications and results, were repeated with an extraordinary success by investigators of the last century. They could decompose the Spirit-Man in his diverse bodies, through magnetic *passes*[5] applied intensively on very sensitive beings. The experiments of Lancelin, H.P. Blavatsky, A. de Rochas and Baraduc confirmed what the ancients already knew, compelling the psychic sciences to consider the reality of the *multiple* structural *composition* of man.

These very important surveys (which, however, are not yet accepted by science) can be divided into two groups according to their being founded on the ternary or septenary.

The ternary is easy to understand—it is very simple. However, it does not explain the majority of the psychic phenomena of mediums. The septenary, more complex because it is the unfolding of the ternary—spirit-soul-body—in its fundamental elements, allows us to understand psychic phenomena more clearly. It also opens various working hypotheses in other fields of investigation,

— the survey of the causes for cures considered "miraculous" or "impossible";
— the knowledge of facts that occurred in previous lives and reminiscences fixed in the present consciousness; the erasing of annoying remembrances of disharmonic facts of previous lives.

---

[5] The purifying and enlightening of the aura.

THE SPIRITUAL BLOCKING

It is lamentable that spiritists are impeded in contributing to the progress of these investigations, because they are blocked by the Kardecist concept of the perispirit. It is necessary to broaden their knowledge about and beyond this concept to understand the function of all plastic mediators that exist between the pure spirit and the physical body.

As Theosophy has already identified and given names to the stages of the structural sequences, it would be enough if spiritists would incorporate this ancient knowledge into their marvelous doctrine—by admitting the septenary. It would not be nonsense, neither would it be a novelty: André Luiz initiated the distinction of the seven bodies, in a clear way, in the extraordinary work that Francisco Xavier psychographed. Further, Ramatis, through the psychography of Ercilio Maes, follows the oriental tradition and also adopts the septenary.

THE SEVEN BODIES — OR FIELDS, OR DIMENSIONS

According to the septenary conception, the Spirit-Man is composed of two distinct strata: the *Divine Triad,* constituted by the "Christic I," and the *"Inferior Quaternary,"* linked to the personality and which is mutable like it. In these strata, each series or body has a denomination and distinct characteristics, specific functions and manifestations limited to the field or dimension to which it is linked, since each of these bodies vibrates in a distinct dimensional universe.

Below are the structural sequences from the Spirit to the Material, in a schematic form:

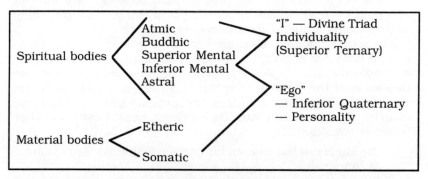

THE PHYSICAL BODY

The physical body is the fleshy outer cover (envelope) in which we live—something similar to a diving suit: heavy and almost cumbersome, which we use to act in the physical environment.

It is composed of chemical compounds that are cleverly manipulated by the phenomenon called *life*.

In fact, there is life in each of these chemical elements. Everything inside us is life. We exist with our major life *seated* in a compound of a myriad of smaller lives that organize this compound.

As our body is made of Matter, it operates with ease in the physical environment since the body and the environment belong to the same electromagnetic dimension.

THE ETHERIC BODY

As the name indicates, this body is of an extremely tenuous structure. It is invisible because it is diaphanous, of dense electromagnetic nature, but its wave length is superior to that of ultra-violet light. This is why the etheric body is easily disassociated by ultra-violet light when it is exuded by the physical body. We can say that it is quintessential, almost reaching immortality.

The physiological equilibrium reflects the harmony that prevails in the cosmos—the function of the etheric body is to establish health automatically, without interference of consciousness. While it distributes vitalizing vitamins to the physical body, this equilibrium makes sure that the vital functions stay in balance and that the corporeal set maintains its harmonic equilibrium. In this way the physiological equilibrium promotes the cicatrization of wounds, the cure of localized diseases, etc.

We should really think about the importance of the energetic structure that, although, it is not known by medicine, *Eppur si muovo.*

Functioning as a plastic mediator between the astral body (the rougher body of the spirit) and the physical body, the *body* or *etheric double* is of material nature: it belongs to the domain of the flesh-man. There are people who confound the etheric double with the astral body, calling it, simply, "double." To make the differentiation and still avoid confusion, we always add the specification "etheric" to the word "body" when we refer to the "double."

Constitution & Properties — The Ectoplasm

In normal situations, the etheric body does not separate from the somatic body of a living human being, different from the astral and mental *bodies*. The etheric body is *physical* and coupled to flesh. When it gets separated by some energy from outside the body, it is only for some moments and, in this case, at a reduced distance. In spite of this difficulty, the

French investigator of the end of last century, Colonel Aiglun de Rochas, was able to separate the etheric body from the physical body of a medium, for the first time, by means of exhaustive magnetic passes. Through this historical experience it was possible to identify the etheric body.

We know, today, that this *body* consists of material that Richet called *ectoplasm*. It is, in fact, a substance similar to plasma, a thin fluid that has the property of condensing as soon as it is exuded from the body of the giver. It gets out of the physical body through pores and natural cavities, and has been used in spiritualist sessions of "physical effects" (improperly called "materialization", because in these sessions spirits utilized the substance exuded by the medium in order to appear). The *etheric* body also has an important function in the phenomena of *teleportation*—or dissolution of objects—and in all those phenomena that require *stronger energies*. The substance is invisible in its natural state. It has its own individuality, but does not have consciousness—although it is intimately coupled with the physical body.

While the somatic body is composed of solids, liquids and gases that form cells, tissues and systems, the etheric body is constituted by the same elements and minerals; however, it is structured in such a tenuous state that it escapes totally from laboratory tests, unless the *body* is exteriorized and sufficiently condensed that it becomes visible and palpable in these abnormal conditions. Some fragments were analyzed in a laboratory, and the dominance of protein elements, similar to fleshy organs, were found.

The state of extreme fluidity is proved by the action of luminous rays. The exuded ectoplasm, when exposed to light, undergoes an immediate dispersion. This happens because the radiant energy of light is more intense than the energy of molecular cohesion of the ectoplasm, mainly when we use more intense luminous energy—of a shorter wave length—of violet and ultra-violet spectra. For this reason, the work of physical effects must start in absolute darkness until the exuded mass becomes sufficiently dense and acquires enough cohesion to make resistance to the photonic bombardment possible. Once the ectoplasm gets to a certain level of condensation, the manifesting spirit can be subjected to as much normal light as it wants.

Although it seems to be a ghost, the etheric *body* is not spiritual and dissolves a few hours after death. Sometimes it can be seen at cemeteries, in the form of a light cloud that dissolves little by little. As we have already stressed, the etheric body does not have consciousness. And it can be vital food for the lower human spirits and for the immense variety of beings living in the astral—chiefly the zoologically inferior ones and those that visit cemeteries. Clairvoyants without experience, quite often mix up the deactivated etheric doubles (crusts) with ghosts of the dead.

It seems that the astral *body* of the disincarnated—this means the lower spiritual *body*—as it is denser, carries larger or smaller masses of the etheric body. According to the evolutionary degree of its possessor, this astral *body* is less dense or more dense (i.e., lighter or heavier) and it slowly loses these material remains. It is known that the evolution of the spirit is characterized by a progressive dematerialization of its denser coverings.

Etheric Diseases

A great number of diseases that are considered settled in the human body, in reality have their seat in the anatomic substratum of the etheric organization. It is from there that they pass to the somatic body, where they appear as vital dysfunctions. This fact, only one among others, deserves the special attention of medical scientists because it opens fields for investigation which have not yet been explored by lenses and scalpels.

This research, however, does not even get the attention of spiritists, because almost all of them are tied by the excessive amplitude of the conception of "perispirit." At the moment, they do not know anything (and they are not even interested in knowing anything) about the physiology of the etheric body. It is surprising to see how close they are, in this respect, to materialists and others (including some scientists).

Knowledge of Theosophists

Besides being identified and satiating several investigators, the etheric double has already been very objectively defined and described in the book *A Study About Consciousness*, by the theosophist Annie Besant:

> *It is vitality, the constructive Energy, that coordinates the physical molecules and joins them in an organism, or better, this power of Breath of Universal Life that is taken over by the organism, during the short period of time, that we call Life.*
>
> *The designation "etheric double" expresses the nature and the constitution of the most subtle part of our physical body, this designation is, therefore, significant and easy to retain. This element, the "etheric double," is*

formed by various kinds of ether and "double" because it constitutes a duplicate of our physical body, it is its shadow.

The "etheric double" is perfectly visible to the well-trained eye of a clairvoyant, its color is kind of grayish-violet and its texture is either rough or fine, according to the correspondent quality and nature of the physical body.

It is thanks to the etheric double that the vital power—prana—circulates along our nerves, allowing them to act as transmitters of movement and sensibility of the external impressions. The faculties, the power of thought, of movement, of sensibility do not dwell in the nervous substance, neither in the physical nor in the etheric. The "ego"[6] acts in many ways, operating in the innermost bodies or vehicles; but its expression upon the physical plane is made possible by the Breath of Life that circulates along the fillets and around the nerve cells.

During the normal sleep of the ego,[7] the soul gets out of the physical body, and leaves the two parts—the rough and the etheric ones (physical body and etheric body). When death occurs, the soul also gets out of the body, and this time it is final. The soul drags the etheric double with it, and both completely abandon the physical body.

The etheric double sometimes appears in the mortuary chamber immediately after death, at a short distance from the corpse. The etheric double is also the cause of numerous appearances of ghosts that move erratically around the tomb where the physical body, which they had vitalized during life, lies.

A Bridge Between the Physical & the Astral

It is through the etheric structure that the volatile acts, desires, emotions, and any manifestation of the superior consciousness act upon the physical body, or more precisely on the physical brain.

The etheric structure promotes the necessary frequency degradation between the spiritual field of the astral and the physical field.

---

[6] By "ego" the author refers to the immortal Spirit. We prefer the more didactic expression used by Rohden: "I" to designate the eternal Spirit and "ego" when it refers to the personality. (Author Note.)

[7] The author refers again to the Spirit and confounds "soul" with "Spirit." (Author Note.)

The most spectacular actuation of the etheric double occurs during sessions of physical effects. This kind of work is quite rare, and depends on the assistant's and operator's special care and preparation.

For a spirit to become materialized—to be touched, felt, weighed, etc.—it is necessary that its spiritual form be covered by material substance. This substance—ectoplasm—comes from the etheric double of a donor medium. The ectoplasm is exuded by the pores and natural cavities. At the beginning it is a kind of heavy, dense gas, that little by little is condensed, takes a viscous, plastic form and covers the communicating spirit, until it takes the shape of the body that the spirit had when it was incarnate. With this new *body,* that is, the counterpart of its astral body, the disincarnated can remain among living beings for some minutes: it listens, speaks, walks, touches and can be touched, as if it were a common living person. In the last century, the well-known scientist William Crookes, over two consecutive years, investigated the materialization of the spirit Katie King. It was a classic case and caused justified repercussions for two reasons: the indisputable credibility of Crookes and the assent of the spirit to undergo scientific researches.

In *common* mediumistic phenomena—much less the spectacular—the importance of this mediator almost does not appear: it is not *touchable.* Without it, however, communication between the astral and the physical *fields* would be impossible because a *bridge* is missing: every communicating spirit that acts, tied to a medium, has to use this intermediary phase of frequency that permits the resounding coupling with the nervous system of the medium to the *modulation* of the spirit's thought and its expression through psychography, psychophony and other means.

The Kirlian Effect[8]

For those who prefer proofs obtained in laboratories, the *Kirlian Effect* is interesting.

A luminous irradiation and electromagnetic phenomenon known as the "Corona effect," appears around the object on which electric current of high tension and frequency has been applied. To produce this kind of current, a Tesla induction coil is generally used.

Inanimate objects (for example, metals) have a regular luminous emanation, a halo with uniform dimension, form and

---

[8] Kirlian effect—takes the name of the Russian investigator, Semyon Kirlian, from Krasnodar.

luminosity. In living beings, the halo modifies according to the conditions of the creature submitted to the electrical current.

The alterations of form and intensity reflect the vibratory dynamism of the etheric field (or body). By no means are they a *picture* of the aura or of the astral body, as some spiritists believe. These are physical manifestations because they are part of the etheric body.

Pathological conditions can modify the standard of the electric exhalation and the *Kirlian Effect* will indicate that something abnormal is going on in the organism. The reason for this is that any kind of disease affects always—and first— the energetic equilibrium of the dynamic (etheric) field (or body), altering its form—and also the effect.

THE ASTRAL BODY

In the second century of our era, Origenes, philosopher of the neo-Platonic School, taught that the spirit had a vaporous body, the "aura." In the 4th century, Saint Cyril of Jerusalem said: "The soul of the dead have subtler bodies than the terrestrial bodies. The name *spirit* is generic and common: everything that does not have a dense and heavy body is a spirit." At the same time, Saint Hilary of Poitiers stated: *"There is nothing in Nature or in Creation, be it in the sky, be it on the Earth, be it among visible things, be it among invisible things, that is not corporeal. Even the souls, be it during life, be it after death, keep some corporeal substance, because it is necessary that everything that was created, has to be in something."*

All thinkers of the primitive church made a distinction, as Saint Paul of Tarsus did, between the spirit (pneuma) and the intermediate soul (psyche) and the rough physical body, (soma). John of Thessalonica, in the second Council of Nicaea, declared: *"The angels, archangels and also the souls are really spirituals, but not deprived of a body. They are endowed with a tenuous, ethereal, igneous body."*[9]

This *soul*—of which so many authors of the past demonstrated a surprising knowledge—received the generic name, "perispirit," from Kardec. This denomination comprises several subtle bodies, even the etheric one, although it is physical. For Kardec "soul" and "spirit" are, therefore, synonyms. For us "soul" and "perispirit" should be synonyms—both expressions designate the covering set of the spirit, from the astral body to the others that are subtler bodies (with an obvious exception of the etheric body). *It is advisable to have this conceptual difference always in mind,* to avoid future distortions in the under-

---

[9] Annotation from Antonio Freire's *Of the Human Soul*, Publ. FEP.

standing of the subject of this book. Everything makes us believe that the "soul" to which these and other sages refer, is really the astral body.

Importance & Density

The *spiritual* covering nearest to Matter is called the *astral body*; it can easily be seen by clairvoyants. All spirits that embody in mediums have this subtle corporeal structure. It is as necessary for the manifestation of the spirit in the *dimension* in which it is (astral), as the body is necessary for human beings.

It is within this *body* that the spirits live in the astral *dimension;* in those that usually communicate in spiritual sessions, this vehicle is rather dense (the density is according to the evolutionary degree of the possessor). Those that do not have it anymore, because they are more developed, communicate with the mediums by mental *syntony* without embodiment.

The astral body does not have the same density in all human beings. It varies greatly in its mass. This happens in such a way, that the disincarnated man has a specific weight. In physics it is the result of the mass of a body, divided by its volume: $Ws = M/v$. This larger or smaller density makes the difference between the spirits: when we are disincarnated, we are *almost automatically* placed in the region or *vibratory band* of the spiritual world that is most compatible with our *specific weight.*

Erraticity

The spirits that are very materialized live in *erraticity,* together with the incarnated beings.

Erraticity is the existential state without any useful or objective goal, a state in which some disincarnated spirits exist. Although the primordial cause of this state is the ignorance of its own evolution and the spirit's role in the cosmic context, this anguishing *existential perplexity* gets worse with the occurrence of other factors. These include: ignorance and hopelessness about the possibility of evolution; addiction to material goods, to people, etc.; continuous revolt for considering oneself impotent to rule over nature, as the incarnated do; the natural difficulties of adapting to the environment, the distortions of evaluation, and the many personal, moral and material factors that disturb the recently disincarnated.

If these erratic spirits are not too perverse, they can easily be taken to recovery stations that exist in the astral. To do this, it is only necessary to orient them firmly.

Together with orientation, we can use a faster way to convince them. If we first treat and clean them, change their clothes, heal and cure their diseases, wounds and pains, even the most *ignorant and inflexible* ones will become hopeful and decide to develop by working and learning. This change in attitude is very understandable. Spirits without any evolution are used to remaining in the states of suffering that made them die, and so they go on living, sometimes in intense pain for many years.

When they get rid of this awful prolonging of their agony (and this can happen in only a few minutes through the use of strong jets of healing Energy as we soon will see) these poor creatures open up to love.

"Purgatory"

The zones of the inferior astral are inhabited by spirits that are guilty of constant deviations of the Cosmic Harmony. At this place, they have to drain out dense masses of inferior magnetism (this means, of low vibratory frequency) stuck to the astral body, due to the disequilibrium in which they lived. Many carry magnetic masses of others with them, as a consequence of the physical injuries they inflicted on their victims, whose blood, in that dimension, behaves as if it were a life element. Our blood, the vehicle of life, is impregnated with animal magnetism. This magnetism adheres to, and keeps on weighing on, the astral organism of the criminal (in obedience to the Law of Karma). Once disincarnated, the guilty one suffers very much because of this: he has to get rid of these negative energies. This process quite often takes years and years. It is the "purgatory" of the Catholic Church (or the Umbral, of André Luiz), well conjectured upon and described by the Fathers of the Church.

While the spirits develop, they lose their astral body little by little, becoming more and more *diaphanous* as seen by clair-voyants. After some time, undergoing evolution, they lose the astral body completely, keeping only the subtler spiritual coverings. But all the perispiritual coverings are also abandoned at a certain time, until only the Pure Spirit is left in its full Christian plenitude. In this state, spirits enjoy the "Sight of God" as all the illuminated affirm.

The Astral Mediums

André Luiz and other messengers tell us about a fact that apparently is very odd: the need of mediums *among the disincarnated inhabitants of the astral,* to get information from the superior spirits (who, through evolution, lost their denser coverings). These superior spirits can provide guidance and orientation to all those that live in astral communities. These superior entities normally cannot be seen by spirits that still have their astral body on, in the same way that human beings are not able to see spirits.

The revelation of André Luiz shocked orthodox spiritists who did not know about the reality and physiology of the soul and, therefore, this fact made many of them repudiate, as being fantasy, a whole treasury of information. However, it is a logical phenomenon and the natural consequence of the process of incarnation. As a matter of fact, incarnating implies diving into Matter, causing an increasing density of the coverings or "bodies." According to Ramatis, the worst and inexorable suffering of Jesus was not caused by the physical pain or crucifixion. The real Passion was the condensation of a spirit that was Absolute Light, until it manifested itself in the material plane: Christ endured it for approximately one thousand years, and during this time, little by little, he reclaimed all his spiritual bodies that had been abandoned millennia before. This might explain why the prophet Isaac spoke always about the "Divine Master" in the present, although he lived seven hundred years before the birth of Christ:

> *For unto us a child is born,*
> *unto us a son is given:*
> *and the government shall be upon his shoulder:*
> *and his name shall be called*
> *Wonderful, Counsellor, The mighty God,*
> *The everlasting Father, The Prince of Peace.*
> — Isaiah 9:6

Unfolding Phenomena

Under certain circumstances, artificial or natural, the astral body can separate from the physical body, by taking with it all the other coverings and even its own spirit. This normally happens while the person is asleep, when he loses consciousness and the vital functions are lowered to a minimum level necessary for metabolic exchanges.

Many sensitives can easily get out of their bodies, in spontaneous trances. But this can also happen to common people, in pathological or special occasions, as for instance, a strong emotional shock, debility due to long periods of sickness, voluminous hemorrhaging, surgical shocks and other traumatic conditions. People can go to distant places, they can describe these places, evaluate their actions and those of others, they can have physical sensations, everything in perfectly conscious conditions—thanks to the connection with the physical brain, through the *silver string.*

The Silver Cord

The spirit remains attached to the body, independently of its distance from the body, by means of the silver string. Even the Bible mentions it:

> *Or ever the silver cord be loosed,*
> *or the golden bowl be broken,*
> *or the pitcher be broken at the fountain,*
> *or the wheel broken at the cistern.*
>
> — Ecclesiastes 12:6

If it gets torn up, however, death occurs. It is irreversible.

According to the reports of spirits, when superior entities tear up this string, the moment a person dies, there is a lightning of great intensity, produced by the liberation of Energy.

This luminous and brilliant string, constituted by some form of high intensity energy, is tied to the physical body by the etheric double, in which it is rooted by the head and by a myriad of filial connections that involve the etheric structure. It could be compared to a cable of high tension if it were not inconceivably ductile; it can achieve the greatest thinness, thus allowing the spirit of a living person to escape from the physical body (and from the etheric) on astral trips of millions of kilometers. It does not break and maintain the spirit as the owner and guide of the body: through a marvelous process that has not been explained so far; all vital functions of our bodies are preserved.

Apometric Unfolding

The spirit can get away from the physical body in a more efficient way by imposition of a magnetic nature, when commanded by a trained person. This is the basis of *Apometrics*—the main subject of this book. It is a widely used technique in the treatment of incarnated and disincarnated spirits. This phenomenon, which we call *"apometric unfolding,"* opened the doors for our systematic investigations of the astral dimension, a real universe, parallel to ours.

We realized that, after some time, the sensitives trained in the apometric unfolding, acquire such consciousness of their potentialities and limitations that they move in that dimension as if they were on the physical plane. They go to other places, sometimes very far away, to work, help, assist incarnated or disincarnated spiritually sick people to whom they give inestimable aid.

Properties & Functions of the Astral Body

The ease of getting separated from the physical body is a characteristic of the astral body. It is immaterial and of magnetic nature, it does not have a *fluid* constitution as the etheric double does, neither does it form materialized objects, because its nature is completely different from Matter. However, it can easily be molded by the action of mental power. This property is helpful in treatment techniques of sick, crippled, mutilated or injured spirits, that still suffer from the diseases that caused their death. But we can affirm in advance, that all of them are recomposed in their natural form and high physiological state through the projection of healing Energy that is mentally emitted by the operator (*energetic pulses*, commanded in slow counting, usually up to seven or ten).

One of the most important functions of the astral body is sensitivity. We know that it resides in this *field* or *body;* the physical body only transmits received stimuli; the record of painful or pleasant sensations is up to the structure. Vices are of a psychic nature exactly due to this fact; their origin is in the astral: it is the astral that feels. For this reason we take our vices and passions with us when we die; if it were otherwise, there would be no reason for the disincarnated to go on suffering physical pains, or carry painful deformations with them—as has been verified in spiritual sessions.

Sensation is the roughest form of feelings. It is primary, instinctive. Emotion is much more complex, it is linked to desire; it can be exacerbated until it reaches the abnormality of *passion.* We cannot forget that sensations, like emotions, are very important states of our consciousness, since they give color and power to our acts.

Our biggest struggle—fighting against ourselves, which favors our evolution—consists precisely in restraining, controlling and dominating desires, feelings and, mainly, passions. From the instinctive and animal impulses, such as hunger, thirst, sexual desire, up to higher feelings, as for example loving our fellow creatures, solidarity, friendship, affection, tenderness, etc., or the unrestrained passions of possession, power and concupiscence, all the emotions and desires manifest themselves in the astral world. Through evolution, feelings and sentiments go from the astral to the other levels of consciousness that are peculiar to superior spirits.

Food & "Death" of the Astral Body

Our astral body constantly loses Energy, needing, therefore, an energy supply for its sustenance, similar to feeding the physical body. But the nature of this food varies very greatly; it goes from protein broth for the more materialized spirits, provided by the astral assistance stations, to quintessential energies that feed the superior spirits, which are gathered (through prayers) directly from the infinite reservoir of cosmic energy.

The spirits that inhabit the inferior astral, that are still rather brutalized (animalized), used to eat even human food. If there is a loss of energies without the necessary replenishment, which can happen due to passions, the spirit can lose its astral body and be reduced to an inactive ovoid, according to what André Luiz reports.

The normal means to lose this body, however, is through evolution; in the same way we lose our physical body when we die, we also lose the astral body. The spirits that are more evolved, and do not have this body anymore, cannot be seen by the rougher inhabitants of this plane—as we mentioned before.

In summary, evolution takes us farther and farther from the dense organizations that are a trait of Matter, until we abandon them completely. Involution, on the other hand, can also take away this body—exactly in the same way as one loses the physical body, due to vices and passions.

THE MENTAL BODY

The mental body is the vehicle that uses the cosmic "I" to manifest itself as a concrete and abstract intellect; it is in this body that the will gets transformed into action, subsequent to choosing the volitional act. It is a field of elaborated reasoning, from which the powers of mind, the phenomena of cognition, memory, and the evaluation of our acts, surge because it is the seat of the manifested active consciousness. While physical sensibility and emotions flow from the astral body, the mental vehicle can be considered the source of the intellect.

In a certain way, the mental body is still an inferior covering, because it is a consequence of these phenomena or functions that conventionally are called "intellect." Only on superior levels of consciousness—where the virtues that result from affective love for all beings are present at their highest degree— the highest spirituality, which is our essence—can manifest itself.

Concrete Mental Body & Abstract Mental Body

This *field, body* or *dimension* of the Spirit-Man can be divided in two, for a better understanding:

— *Concrete mental body,* also called the *inferior mental body:* it deals with simple, quite objective perceptions, e.g., the ones of material objects, people, houses, vehicles, etc.;

— *Abstract mental body, causal body* or *superior mental body:* it elaborates and structures principles and abstract ideas *ad infinitum;* it is the process responsible for scientific and technological advances, and also for our entire philosophic foundation.

Examples:

— *The perception of a cube through our senses (getting to know the size, color, edges, weight, smell, taste, or the sound that it makes when it drops on the floor or when it comes in contact with another object) are typical functions of the concrete mental body or inferior mental body. It registers what is outside the skin and impresses our nervous system.*

— *The evaluation of volume, area, weight and properties of this same cube, by comparing it with other similar objects or through more sophisticated methods; the formulation of geometric theories, relating symbols and laws: these are some typical functions of the superior mental body.*

The Aura — Mental Projections

The mental body has an approximately ovoid form that involves the physical body. Its peripheral portions constitute the *aura,* and the aura is of varied color and size according to the frequency of the vibratory fields generated by thoughts. It is easy for clairvoyants to perceive what is going on in the minds of people: good thoughts are of light, crystalline, brilliant colors; the inferior ones (hatred, envy, vengeance, etc.), are of dark, dense and unpleasant colors. The aura, consequently, reveals the tonic note of the mental *field* of a person. The mental Energy can be projected into Space, by means of structures known as *thought-forms.* They consist of an energy nucleus that has its form modeled by the mind that projects it, they can harm or benefit a person, according to the will of the person who creates it—consciously or unconsciously. The negative ones take the form of darts, arrows, projectiles, or turbid *fields,* for example. The positive ones, more efficient, take the form that the operator wants them to have; we can, for instance, use the mental energy also to benefit disincarnated spirits, by cleaning and dressing them and giving them food, with the objective of improving their spiritual conditions.

The natural *field* of this Energy is the mental field. When projected, this Energy normally acts first on the mental *field* or *body* of other beings, and from there it goes—already converted to psychomotor actions—to the astral end etheric *bodies* or *fields.* However, if it is projected with emotions, the lower (and more negative) the vibratory frequency of the emotions, the darker and murkier will be the magnetic masses that cover this Energy. In these cases, where the generation of thought-forms is included, the emitted mental energy will reach *first* and *directly* the astral body of the target person, from there it goes to the etheric body and then to the physical one.

Thoughts are life power—we should never forget this. The energy that they project is proportional to the potency of the mind and to the will power of the emitter.

Other Properties

The essence of the physiology of this *field, structure, dimension* or *body* that we call "mental" is not yet totally known. However, everything indicates that it is of magnetic nature, with a much higher vibratory frequency than that of the astral body. That the energy is of magnetic nature seems to be proven by experiments we have made for twelve years and from which one of our most interesting techniques for the treatment of obsession has arisen: the *depolarization* of the memory stimuli, a subject which will be discussed later.

The mental body presents specific properties and functions, besides a more powerful and penetrating action than the astral body because it belongs to its own dimensional universe. In effect, if we consider Energy as a radiant field, of any wave length, equal to Planck's Constant[10], multiplied by the length of frequency—i.e., $W = \hbar.\upsilon$—the mental body must have more propagation energy than the denser ones—such as the astral, etheric or physical bodies.

This irradiated energy is not uniform. It varies in frequency according to the quality or nature of the thought: if it is rough, if it transmits inferior interests or if it is malefic (covered by emotions of hatred, aggression or envy, for example), the frequency will be very low. In this case, the energy will be of little penetration, but the thought will consist of mass. And if this evil-doing mass reaches the astral structure of the victim, it can adhere to it (chiefly if it coincides with some lowering of the victim's tonic frequency) causing great harm. This is the case in black magic, which tends to greatly lower the vibrations of the target people, causing them to feel indefinable sufferings and anguish, discomfort, sensations of smothering, etc. On the contrary, if the thought is impregnated with kindness, compassion, love, solidarity (in short, everything that tends toward harmony) the target person will feel well, hopeful,

---

[10] Planck's equation — Quantum Physics:
    W = energy;
    $\hbar$ = Planck´s Constant $(6.6128273 \times 10^{-27}$ erg/s$)$
    υ = frequency

happy, with a sensation of extreme lightness. This is explained by the emission frequency, because vibrations that are superior to the person's tonic make him feel well; if they are inferior, the effect will be the opposite.

We can conclude, therefore, that the thought can be creative or destructive.

If the tonic note of a person's personality is of high frequency, the negative thought-forms do not have the right conditions to adhere to the astral body: they are automatically repelled. Nothing fastens to people's corporeal-spiritual structure if kindness and pureness are their dominant characteristics; malefic thought-forms only affect people who are at a compatible vibratory band.

Mental Resonance

The mental body is much or little refined, according to the degree of mental and intellectual development. When we think, the "I" imparts specific vibrations to the mental field or structure, causing the spreading of the vibratory state in all directions—as it used to happen in phenomena pertinent to physics. When they receive this energy with a fixed length wave, all the mental *fields* or *structures* (bodies) that are at the same frequency or in harmony with it, start a vibratory resonance.

If the thought is of high nature, the tuned-in beings will vibrate at this tonic note, strengthening the initial wave. The same happens with malefic or low-leveled thoughts. Therefore, it is easy to understand the importance of keeping the highly praised mental hygiene and good thoughts, the *pureness of heart recommended by initiated masters and spirits, who are evolved in all areas.* We used to live stuck in environments of a low vibratory level, where passionate emanations and base material and immediate interests predominate—an ocean of low frequencies. If we cultivate attitudes and thoughts of a high level moral standard, these inferior emanations will not affect us. But if we proceed in the opposite direction, we will be synthesizing these negative bands, lowering our vibratory mental tones and, consequently, we will sink into this inferior process which implies suffering, conflicts and diseases.

The "Noures"

Pietro Ubaldi calls the thought waves *noures*—"currents" of thought. The superior *noures* are of creative aspects because, when they happen to harmonic and receptive beings, they can arouse the same thoughts that these beings have in mind. They act in a fruitful way; there is a great similarity with outer factors that awake and generate the life that a seed contains. For example: if a wave of mystic thought reaches a materialist (for whom devotion is something worthless or even unknown), it can awake in him ideas about religion, something curious about a certain abstraction, or a similar phenomenon. *Noures* cause related waves; once they are emitted, they can make thought or devotion vibrate, stimulating devotion; but the object of this devotion can be different, according to the mental body of each receptor. In short, the mental wave transmits the thread of thought. But the tissue and its color are due to the mental body of the receptor.

Although we addressed the mental field in a form to transmit notions (and, therefore, superficial) the reader must have understood the essential part: thought is Life Power. And this is enough, for the time being.

What Does the Study of the Mental Body Reserve for Us?

We have analytic elements to demonstrate that the mental plane vibrates in another dimension, situated beyond Time and Space. It is the seat of all the phenomena of clairvoyance, telepathy and precognition. As it transcends the Cartesian dimensions, to which other inferior bodies are subordinated (astral, etheric and somatic bodies), it is possible for a sensitive to project himself to this dimension and know precise details about past facts, predict the future, and guess the thoughts of the people present.

Man, still living in narrow, atavistic patterns, a result of millennia of his evolution (which limits him to a materialistic way of life), has not awakened yet to know about these new horizons, and that is why he does not know, neither does he believe, in these possibilities. In the same way, he does not know (or does not believe) about the dimensional universe of the astral plane, a fact that makes him deny his reality—and the spirits milling around us. Under these conditions, he only "knows" the simpler and more immediate things of his life on the physical plane and thinks that only manifestations related to this plane constitute reality.

For this reason, a philosopher stated: "Man only knows and understands what the natural order of things allow, besides this, he cannot and does not know anything else."

However, inside himself, on inaccessible levels to the common mortal, there are unsuspected things, and powers not realized yet, still unknown, although they exist.

It is possible, then to assume that these secrets of nature, still unrevealed to the large crowd of profane, can be disclosed to those that "...have eyes to see."

Time & Space Do Not Exist in the Mental Dimension

Man lives coupled to the atavistic forms of the mechanism of thinking and reacting to stimuli, a result of millennia of biological evolution. Therefore, his psychism is extremely dull in relation to the psychic realities, this means that he did not develop his inherent faculties. Although nature gave him the ability to evolve naturally, with a rather developed central nervous system, he did not learn how to use his astral and mental prosencephalon. This is why he limits his existence to a life confined to the immediate answers given by the stimuli of the environment. Even his reasoning, or the evaluation of his values that his living here on Earth provides, is limited to materially leveled psychism, precisely because he does not know (and does not believe) in another kind of psychism.

The human being lives tied and blocked by the three Cartesian dimensions where the values of Space and Time are dominant. He is weakened by these barriers, unable to attempt larger leaps beyond the parameters of Space-Time, leaps that would be perfectly possible for him, in adventures that would open his astonished eyes to new horizons, full of extraordinary possibilities, such as glimpsing the past or knowing in advance about the future.

Does man even suspect the possibility of jumping out of these material dimensions of Space and Time? If this would happen, the past and the future would be present, since Time and Space are two existential conditions that dominate our physic-mental world, and apparently it is difficult to get rid of this natural tyranny.

This adventure can be undertaken by all those who want to. There are people (very few) among the human population, who have been able to predict the future with exactness, centuries before the events happened. There are people, as well, who could see events that were happening at distant places.

The possession of these qualities has always been a mystery, and those people were either victims of religious persecution or were made divine by the anonymous crowd.

They, themselves, the sensitives who had these powers, could not explain these capacities. However, when we study these phenomena better, we come to the conclusion that they are nothing other than manifestations of the dimensional horizon of the mental body. When a being is able to be *transported* to this dimension and totally penetrates its parameters, he has the possibility to scrutinize the pigeonholes of time, and see facts that are beyond the present time.

Prophecies are founded on these possibilities.

Man lacks appropriate techniques that will yield or allow for these possibilities. He also lacks sufficient or accurate training to try to see what he wants to see at a given moment.

We intend to delimit the field of these possibilities, determining the greatness of this field, so that future investigators dispose of more precise referential conditions, for broader systematic investigations in these dimensions, that transcends Space and Time. Free of the present limitations, men and women of the future will be able to penetrate these horizons, using powers that will make him the owner of immense constructive powers which contribute to improving his life.

THE BUDDHIC BODY

There is almost nothing to be said about the vibratory structure (or *field, body* or *dimension),* closest to the spirit. This body is so distant from our physical standards, and from our means of expression, that it is not possible to compare it by describing it. It is possible to say that *buddhi* is the perispirit according to the etymological acceptance of the word: it is the first vibratory structure that, by involving the spirit, demonstrates it in an active way.

However, a short time ago, we were allowed to discover an interesting property of this structure that can be used, and in a very practical way, in the treatment of the incarnated and disincarnated (since both are, first of all, spirits).

As this body is timeless (as the superior mental body is, too), we used the technique to reach this superior *dimension* of people, as a starting point to scrutinize their pasts. In this way we could detect anomalous situations, very painful events, deeply rooted in time, in the extremely tenuous stratum of a hidden past that happened at very remote times.

We said extremely tenuous stratum; but this does not mean that it is *inactive.*

According to the Cosmic Law—as enunciated in the sentence: *"...your sin will find you out."* (Numbers 32:23)—any kind of disharmony provoked by a conscious being will vibrate in the transgressor's consciousness until the abnormality—including both the causes and the consequences—is totally dissolved. As any disharmonic act has life power, the psychic environment of the agent of the perturbation presents the tonic note of disharmony.

As we have already exhaustively observed, in such cases the person loses the greatest good of the spirit—PEACE. He suffers quite a lot, he considers himself an unpardonable sufferer, a sensation that denotes a deep rooting of the *consciousness disease* that, quite often, has affected numerous existences.

This kind of deep suffering can only be relieved or solved through the dissolution of the disharmonic foci. And this, as far as we know, can be achieved in two ways. One is the spiritual elevation of the transgressor, awakening to a life full of love and being good to those next to one; the other one is the use of specific techniques, with the projection of manipulated energies by capable operators.

THE ATMIC BODY OR THE ESSENCE-SPIRIT

Is there any way to define *That Thing* which, by definition, transcends symbols and words?

Through millennia and successive civilizations, any attempt to describe what we designate by "spirit" is considered incomplete because of the inefficacy of words.

The concepts of Vedic Philosophy continue to be enlightening due to their transparency. According to the Vedas, the One and Universal Being—Brahma (The Non-manifested), transcendent and eternal—becomes immanent in his temporary action, when he manifests himself. The beings that he emanates, contain his essence, in the same way as the thinker is in his thoughts. The absolute, the universal, is manifested in each individualized being, even in the very small ones, exactly because it is absolute, and, therefore, escapes human understanding, it *transcends* whatever exists.

This omnipresent absolute, manifested and *manifesting* in each being, is called *Atman* or *Spirit*. The pure atmic "body" or "Spirit," this *Cosmic I* constitutes the Divine *Essence* in each created being. We are all identical to God in the sense of Being (Essence), but different from Him in the sense of "exist": *God does not "exist"; God Is* eternally present.

It could not have been for any other reason that Jesus said; *"You are Gods."*

Once a guru taught his disciple, who was feeling depressed facing the difficulties of existence, the following:

> *You have to see yourself as you really are: a spirit with terrestrial clothes. The real person, the 'I' that you are, is not your body, in the same way as I am not in my body—that is something fragile and suffering.* **We are immortal and divine spirits.** *Strong and indestructible. Always trying to get better, to improve, to purify our qualities. At the moment we are on mission here on Earth; we do not know what the mission is, but it will undoubtedly be for our best.*

HUMAN CONSTITUTION

Plane	Esoteric	Buddhist Terminology	Function	Irradiates	Causal Structure	Grouping
Divine Plane	Pure Spirit Atma Cosmic I	Light	Fundamental Principle coordinating the aggregated cellular physique, the intermediate spiritual bodies and their link with the Divine Plane.	The Divine Principle of Pure Thought.	Arupa (without form)	Superior Ternary Cosmic I Individuality
	Superior plane of the soul	Buddhic	Synthesizing Consciousness Focus of the spirit's manifested individuality. Creative Power Principle.	Creative Thought—The Verb.* The spiritual soul, intuitive and moral.	Spiritual Body	
Spiritual Plane	Abstract Mental	Superior Manas	Vehicle of the volitive manifestations.	Intelligence that models the structure of the other more inferior bodies.	Causal Body	
	Concrete Mental	Inferior Manas	Soul of simple perceptions of consciousness.	Concrete Thought.	Mental Body	
Intermediate Plane	Astral (the most inferior body of the spirit)	Kama Rupa	Instinctive animal Soul, where the transformations of the physical power into psychic power happens. Organism of sensations.	The soul of the active power. Emotions.	Astral Body	Inferior Quaternary Ego Personality
	Double Etheric	Linga-sharira	Coordinator of vitality and its distribution to all cells. Excitation, nervous irritability, 'prana' are coordinated by these physiological organizations. Intermediate between the dense body & the astral plane.	Vitalization for the physical body; health.	Etheric Body	
Physical Plane	Physical Body	Stula-sharira	Material support of the incarnated spirit. The means it uses to act upon material.	Activity through psycho-motor action. Physiological Vitality.	Physical Body	

* In Portuguese, "The Verb" : From the Bible, the word from the Lord.

NOHTIXON — THE THOUGHT AS THE SPIRIT'S WORK[11]

According to Descartes, thought is the spirit's essential attribution. Extended to the material, it is the process through which the soul (spirit) becomes conscious of itself, constituting the basis of our **mental life.** *In a broader sense, we understand by "thought" the set of ideas, sensations, volition, etc., and any reflected, elaborated and organized knowledge.*

Before a thought manifests itself concretely, it bases its action on a phenomenon of volition: it depends on the thinker's wanting and willing.

It is known that thought can act directly on dense material, without the cooperation of the psychomotor action that normally serves as a **bridge.** *It is already accepted in the scientific area that thought/volition acts on object, without the help of the hands or any other part of the body.* **Telekinesis** *(as this phenomenon is conventionally called) has been ascertained in some gifted sensitives, as for instance, the Russian Nina Kulagina, who was able to move light objects (toothpicks, match boxes and others) at a distance of some meters.*

Ineluctably, it is a **power** *that surges* **through** *the physical structure of an incarnated person, from the set of bones, muscles, tendons, organs and nerves of the body. Therefore, if it is Energy, it must be possible to explain it mathematically. Searching for this formulation we find equations that, perhaps, decipher the action of thought at a* **physical** *or material level.*

To make the understanding of the equation easier, we would like to clarify that we started from the evidence, that thought constitutes the conjugation of a kind of quintessentialized Energy (not measurable) and spiritual—in the formula $(\Psi^{V}{\rightarrow}{\infty})$— with the Energy of the physical skeleton. This Spiritual Energy acts on the electric sets, neurons and efferent nerves—which provided measurable electric charge, the $(\text{Volt} \times 10^{-x})n$ of the formula that excites the muscle and provokes its contraction. This is normal **psychomotor action**; *but we would like to repeat: Energy also acts* **directly**, *without the intermediation of the physical body.*

---

[11] From the Greek. According to the author's meaning, it should be understood as "thought as developed by the work conducted by the spirit." (Editor's note.)

EQUATIONS
LIFE

I) $W_{N\pi} = \{(\text{Volt} \times 10^{-x})1 \bullet (\Psi^{\nu=1})\}\,\Pi$ = protozoan or equivalent

II) $W_{NZ} = \{(\text{Volt} \times 10^{-x})n \bullet (\Psi^{\nu>1})\}\,Z$ = zoon, animal, metazoan

III) $W_{NA} = \{(\text{Volt} \times 10^{-x})n \bullet (\Psi^{\nu\to\infty})\}\,A$ = (antropos) Man

Physical body	Soul
Electric energy at physical level	Mental energy at astral level

ν = (nu) mind. For man it tends to the infinite

Ψ = (psi), psychism, psychic elaboration

$\nu^{=1} = 1$ = unity of mental power

W = Energy

N = Number of neurons or fixing unities and/or electron conductors

n = Number of electric units of the animal being studied

The formula can be simplified at the human level. Using the equation:

$$E = \text{Volt} \times 10^{-x}$$

to quantify the energy of a neuron associated to psychism, we will have:

$$W_{NA} = En\,\Psi^{\nu\to\infty} \qquad W_{NA} = En\,\lim_{\nu\to\infty}\Psi^{\nu}$$

From which we can deduce the following Law that rules thought as an **operation of the Spirit:** *"THE ENERGY OF THOUGHT MANIFESTED IN THE PHYSICAL FIELD EQUALS THE PRODUCT OF NEURONIC ELECTRIC ENERGY (En) TIMES THE PSYCHIC ENERGY (of the soul)—Ψ IN POTENCY ν WHEN ν TENDS TO THE INFINITE."*

When mental energy is applied in the astral world, dealing with disincarnated spirits, it produces spectacular results.

We, the incarnated, can transform neuronic energy, that is somatic electric current (the vector Z, as we will see shortly) and uniting it to cosmic energy (vector K) through the spiritual mind, projecting it to the astral or physical dimension according to our wish.

In the physical world, the psychomotor act is the normal manifestation. When it is projected in the astral plane (having in view the incarnated or disincarnated spirit), it produces surprising results—although it depends on what we could call density of the environment.

It is common to meet hypnotists and magnetizers who act upon the audience as if they were puppets, making them behave according to their wills. In these cases, the result of the energies, the vector ($\vec{\Sigma}$), acts directly upon the astral dimension of the target people, dominating them to such a point that they change their behavior, doing things that are out of character.

It is important to realize that this phenomenon is a constant in almost all kinds of obsessions. The mind moves live powers.

THE CHAKRAS

The word chakra comes from Sanskrit and means "wheel."

The chakras are power centers, real vortices through which the dynamic magnetic fields are linked to the physical body. The seat of the chakras is in the etheric double, but their origin is in superior structures; these energies in vortices are of a cosmic nature and spiritually feed the being that manifests the phenomenon **life**. *Always rotating, they have more or less angular velocity, depending on their location in superior or inferior areas of the body. The chakras which control spiritual life— located in the head and other superior parts—have higher velocity than the chakras which control vegetative life (physiological activities)—situated in the lower parts of the body trunk.*

The activity of these vortices is increased by the evolution of a person or by energy projected from outside, especially with this objective. When stirred up, the acceleration of the chakras corresponds to a spiritual development, with great benefit to the person, who becomes more active and vitalized; if the superior chakras are activated, the psychic powers rise.

Chakras are organs which belong to the transcendental physiology of the human being. They are fulcrums of power actively animated, and continuously receive fluxes of cosmic and other energies from outside the body. These energies are transformed by the chakras, lowering the frequency, according to the type of chakra. After the energies have been duly modulated, they are distributed in the areas or fields where the chakras act.

Each of these vortexes, organs, or power centers, has their own specific frequency and color. The seven chakras are distributed in the following way:

Chakra	Name in Sanskrit	Location
1. Base	Muladhara	Base of the spinal column
2. Splenic	Svdhisthâna	On the spleen
3. Umbilical	Manipura	On the navel (the solar plexus)
4. Cardiac	Anahata	On the heart
5. Laryngeal	Vishuddha	On the thyroid
6. Frontal	Ajna	On the forehead
7. Coronal	Sahashara	At the top of the head

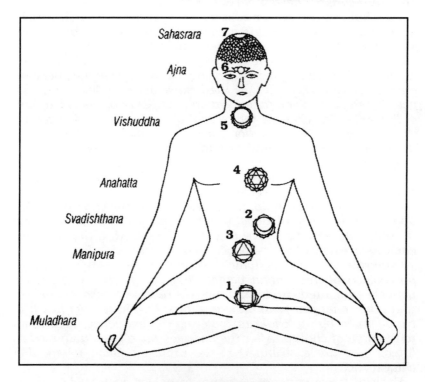

THE CHAKRAS

THE BASE CHAKRA & KUNDALINI

This chakra is located on the base of the spinal column in the coccygeal region. According to clairvoyants, this chakra—the most primitive of all—is formed by four colored rays, where red is predominant. It is a vital chakra par excellence, and, when activated (i.e., when it is energized), the red color becomes more intense and gets **livelier***.*

In this chakra is the seat of an Energy called "Serpentine Fire" or "Kundalini," due to the snakelike form it takes when it goes up the body to vitalize other chakras. It is a vital primary power that animates **incarnated** *life; each being receives the quantity of it that is compatible with his characteristics of frequency, amplitude and volume.*

When the Kundalini energizes the higher chakras, it also increases their frequencies according to the levels of the different vibratory planes: etheric, astral, mental or buddhic.

The sudden or impulsive activation of this chakra is inadvisable. As it controls the more primary genetic functions, any change in its function can cause great danger and annoyance. We should never forget that this powerful Energy is linked to the telluric powers generated by the magnetism of our planet.

THE SPLENIC CHAKRA

This chakra is located on the spleen. The vitality it distributes, concerning the level of frequency, is superior to that of the basic chakra. It is the chakra of vegetative life and is compounded of seven rays which are more brilliant than those of the basic chakra; and their colors vary. This chakra is of great importance to mediumistic phenomena because it is due to its magnetic field that spirits are able to embody in mediums.

The splenic chakra is naturally activated by Kundalini, in an intensity compatible with its physiology. When it is energized in a spontaneous and uncontrolled way, we say that the chakra "is open." This can give rise to unwanted spirit embodiments that can cause trouble. In these cases it is necessary to reduce the activity to its normal level: we have to close the vortex and reduce the vibratory frequency through passes.

THE UMBILICAL CHAKRA

This chakra is situated on the navel and has ten rays, also called "petals." Their colors go from reddish to greenish. The umbilical chakra is linked to the physiology of the soul, to the field of primary emotions and sentiments, and also to the nervous system. That is why violent emotions paralyze digestion and affect the liver.

THE CARDIAC CHAKRA

This chakra is located on the heart. It is of a shiny golden color and is divided into twelve parts or rays. The cardiac (heart) chakra is linked to higher emotions, affections and sentiments. There reside, for example, kindness, fondness, sympathy and even hatred; in other words, volatile emotions. The violent and uncontrolled emotions directly affect the physiology of the heart, and can even stop it, causing death.

THE LARYNGEAL CHAKRA

Situated on the throat in front of the thyroid cartilage, this chakra has energetic frequency bands distributed along the sixteen rays of which it is composed. It is silvery and brilliant; the shine of the vortex shows that it is of a higher vibratory frequency.

The spiritual-physiological function of the laryngeal chakra is to transmit ideas through speaking. It is, therefore, of great importance to **psychophony** (i.e., verbal communication by a spirit through a medium). When there is difficulty with the communication of the embodied spirit, we activate this chakra until it produces sympathy with the spirit's frequency and an adequate opening of the communication channel. (The process is easy: it is enough to project energy by counting, until speech is clear—it usually takes only moments, as we will see.)

THE FRONTAL CHAKRA

The frontal chakra—the third eye—is located in the forehead, between the eyebrows. It is composed of forty-eight rays, divided into two parts.

It is the chakra of the higher spirituality. In mediumistic phenomena, it is possible to provoke the embodiment of any disincarnated spirit (or incarnated that is unfolded from the physical body) by touching the medium's area of this chakra, with a finger, and at the same time projecting energy to **syntonize** (i.e., establish contact) with the communicating spirit.

THE CORONAL CHAKRA

The "lotus of the thousand petals," according to oriental terminology, is at the top of the head, with colors of different shades and of extremely intensive activity. The decreasing of its luminosity in a normal human being shows lowering of the vibratory tones and can indicate a victim of obsession or black magic.

THE PLEXUSES

Plexuses are magnetic centers that coincide with the chakras, but are related to the nervous system of vegetative life—the sympathetic and parasympathetic systems—and also to specific ganglia.

Thus, the basic chakra relates to the spinal ganglia that correspond to the sacral region called the "coccygeal plexus."

The "splenic plexus" corresponds to the splenic chakra. To the umbilical chakra corresponds the "solar plexus." To the cardiac corresponds the "cardiac plexus." And, finally, there is the "carotid plexus" located on the frontal chakra.

THE BUDDHIC WEB OR THE ETHERIC WEB

Between the astral and the etheric body there is one of the most important protective organs of the physical human body, still unknown to most people. It is the "buddhic web" that avoids the predatory action of malefic spirits upon the physical body of human beings. Of magnetic nature, this web gives an extremely compact magnetism to the spirit's astral body in order to prevent their perpetrating damages into their victim's astral and physical organism. However, if they succeed in passing through this magnetic barrier—by means of evolved techniques and pertinacious persecution—the victim will be defeated and die from it, if this is what his persecutors want. This fact happens quite often in relation to black magic; bulky foci of ominous and penetrating energy are applied over consecutive months on the victim, provoking cancer, incurable diseases and all kinds of evil deeds. Once the buddhic web is torn, incarnated operators normally are not able to redo it. Only superior spirits can reconstruct it, due to the vibratory frequency of their energy.

When the incarnated spirit contacts other spirits during sleep, the barrier of this web impedes the remembrance of this encounter. Obsession is also quite held back by this barrier, because the obsessor, usually, can only act indirectly upon the incarnated enemy by means of simple or hypnotic suggestion, by induction, or by involvement in negative magnetic fields.

MEDICINE & THE SPIRIT-MAN

The frontispiece of the temple of Delphi in ancient Greece had the inscription *Gnoth Seautón*[12], showing how much the ancient thinkers worried about Man's major problem. This concern had been present for centuries, maybe since the dawn of our consciousness. It would go on into our own times. And, we can prophesize that it will continue into our future.

For centuries, man has been surveying the universe that surrounds us; always with increasing patience and meticulousness, we deepened the knowledge that gave birth to the sciences. By penetrating to the innermost part of Matter, we discovered the sub-atomic particles—the last detectable components—a fact that certifies the efficiency of our research and explains our rapid technological advances. However, all this knowledge has not helped us to better understand the reality of the immortal beings that we are. We go blindly, groping around in relation to our own innermost part. In short, we learned how to know. But we did not learn how to know ourselves.

Through the eras, and with the nuances of every historical moment, unsolved questions have always challenged the sharpness of the sages and the explanations of religion. Problems such as the origin of Man, his objectives on Earth, his unknown destiny, continue to be wrapped up in legendary mists, with their translation and decoding hampered by prejudices.

During the Renaissance we could see the medieval mentality shaken up by gusts of new ideas. Although those of the Renaissance swept away the old medieval miasma, they did not solve our fundamental problems. It is true that their unrestrained search for the beautiful revived the arts; with their creative fecundity they prepared for the beginnings of Science—that saw its basic directives growing, with an increase in pursuit of material interest. Their *wanting to know* had to be coupled to knowing *how to do;* and so, the roads to the present technological development were formed. There was even more to it: together with the results of the application of

---

[12] Get to know yourself.

the rational principles in the production processes, came the lavish profits that are the basis of capitalism.

In a natural escalation, science stretched its domain to the abstractions of philosophy. Exceedingly objective, its methods eased access to the secret mysteries of nature, making everybody interested in the richness of its fruits. Later on, always based on empirical observation, science induced laws that rule phenomena. And so, it built up the basis for modern knowledge, getting rid of mistakes, superstitions and medieval dogmas.

During that time, man was not yet prepared to understand, in all its depth, the dynamics of his interior world. The knowledge of the soul, although announced as being fundamental, was nothing other than inconsistent fluffs of primary concepts, coupled to eternal pain and destitute of disclosure— and, therefore, incompatible with the new scientific conquests.

Between an immaterial world, presented as being excessively distant, and the rich source representing the touchable and objective universe that is at his disposal, man, of course, turned to the latter. In a helter-skelter way, grew the tendency to repudiate as archaic the whole skeleton of creeds and religions, considering them inefficacious because they did not offer any logical explanation for natural phenomena.

This distancing from the religious exegesis made science drop into the opposite end—into the web of exclusively materialistic interpretations. This happened even with their approach to phenomena that clearly related to another dimensional universe, as for instance those that refer to the soul. In other words, our investigations and our science got rid of religious prejudices only to become entangled in other dogmas—this time materialistic—but just as untouchable as those before.

Let us examine the situation of medicine.

At the beginning of the nineteenth century, using the conquests of chemistry and making meticulous investigations in the field of physiology, medicine made a leap of enormous importance—and so, today, highly sophisticated surgical techniques allow complex and spectacular transplants of organs. As medicine became liberated from the legends of a dim past, it became transformed into an almost exact science, eminently objective and rational.

But if the advance was enormous—and it certainly was—in relation to the unveiling of the physical body's secrets, the same did not happen in relation to the phenomena of the mind's abstract world. In spite of the ingenious conceptions of Freud and his followers (who introduced the study of mental diseases at the universities), the problem of mental diseases continues to challenge studious people today.

Here is one among many questions without answers; who, for example, is able to say what the innermost nature of schizophrenia is? Another one: how can we explain the periodicity of a manic-depressive psychosis?

Electroshocks, psychotropics, techniques of psychotherapy, either do not solve the pathologic problem or fail completely as therapeutics: they just slightly touch the surface of the problem without healing the inexorable intimate sufferings. On the other hand, *complexes, frustrations, repression* and other phenomena mentioned by Freud have not yet explained—or solved—the mysteries that involve the illnesses of the mind, with their destabilization of the personality. To reach the essence—to decipher the mental pathological processes—a big leap will be necessary; the real *quantum* leap of psychiatry: medicine must get out of its present limitations; it must acknowledge and explore the universe of the immaterial beings, the world of spirits, acknowledging its existence.

If the non-acknowledgment of this reality persists, our therapeutic techniques will go on considering the physical body more than the natural substance of the disease: the spirit. Sedatives, and the whole panoply of medicaments, will go on having effects on the brain, distant from the real translation of the soul's problems. Even analytic psychotherapy, which should already have solved our problems, will go on, tied to the flesh-man, only touching an entanglement of causes that are rooted in remote times (as, for instance, occult people: occult because they are invisible, but alive and *active).*

In short, if the spirit is not acknowledged as *existing and real*, psychiatrists will only pay attention to effects. They will be impeded from divining the root causes and will never cure effectively through their clumsy and cross-eyed therapeutics.

Independent of the theories we will elaborate (and how many we have already invented!), not being aware of the reality of the Spirit implies remaining where we are: suffering from artificial techniques and treatments, divorced from the real etiology of ailments.

Since the beginning, there has been no justification for this stagnation. But today it is even worse. The field is open—it is necessary to advance. New theories—with *solid experimental foundations*—point at the spirit, illuminating and unveiling. But we need courage, not only to acknowledge these theories, but also to examine them, as happened in other less luminous times.

SPIRITISM

In spite of all the lights accumulated in millennia of civilization, there was no attempt until the middle of the nineteenth century, based on scientific methods, to establish a bridge linking physical science the non-physicality of the spirit. In 1857 the Spiritist Doctrine arose, codified by Allan Kardec, based on messages from spirits. With this Doctrine, founded on experimental bases, quite advanced conceptions were definitely established, conceptions referring to the existence of a universe (or dimension) different from ours, a world of thrilling life. Kardec's work and investigations took us further: they made the exchange between our world or dimension and this other one possible—based on the fact that the inhabitants of one and of the other one are the same people, different only in their apparel—fleshly or *immaterial.*

As the first bridge between the two universes, Kardec made the study and a better understanding of man in his double aspect—material and spiritual, possible. Laws were revealed, illuminating the "know yourself." And many of man's mysteries were deciphered, seen as a *continuum of Time and Space,* together with a series of implications. As a result, new conceptions came up and evangelic lessons made the dust of altars into a philosophy of life.

Opposite to science, it is in the field of the soul that the Spiritist Doctrine (or Doctrine of the Spirits) builds the comprehension of man and, with it, the rational therapeutic of the mind's disturbances. Obsession, the most common of these disturbances, is brilliantly equated by spiritual therapy—much more logical and effective—with results that satisfy totally the anxiety of the sick and the obsessed ones.

It is lamentable that medicine has not yet allowed (at least not officially) the use of spiritual treatment techniques in hospitals for insane people. This makes the recovery of the sick more difficult—or even impossible. The immortal Spirit-Man, who exists before the cradle and survives the tomb, needs more accurate techniques (based on concepts that transcend time) and treatments that include the spirit, mainly in cases where the detected illnesses are derived directly from the spirit itself. This kind of attitude should be acceptable according to the elementary principle of logic: if there is a spirit and it is the sick one, the indicated treatment obviously has to be *spiritual;* treating the mind and the spirit with therapeutics for the physical body is more than illogical, it is absurd.

Nevertheless, this is exactly what medicine does.

The acceptance of the Spirit-Man, as taught by the spiritual Doctrines and by Spiritism, would illuminate the horizons of our Species. But the Spiritual Doctrine goes further. It shows the possibility of an exchange with the inhabitants of that parallel dimension: *people* who do not have a fleshly body, yet keep their mind and emotions; people who can, under certain conditions, interfere positively or negatively with our existence.

Similar to the oriental philosophic currents, Spiritism is based on the principle of *Palingenesis* (resurrection) or *Reincarnation*, through which we explain the Law of Evolution. It also embodies the lessons of the ancient (and brahmanic) Law of Karma, or Law of Personal Responsibility, according to which debts and moral deviations are paid along multiple existences, where one also acquires positive values, indispensable to the improvement of our *immortal being*.

But nothing is accepted by science, although this heap of principles and laws constitute a doctrine that is *practical* and illuminates—very well—the causes of the phenomena of immaterial nature (*psychogenic diseases*, for example). Spiritism shows that most illnesses, psychic or physical, are of the spirit; therefore, they need *spiritual treatment*—with specific techniques.

The book is precisely about this kind of treatment. It is not at all a classic therapy. But it is up to date. It is *more* than up to date: we are sure that it is the therapy of the future.

THE USELESS CONFLICT OF THE SPIRIT

Psychology is not much concerned about the soul anymore. It restricts its care to what it considers material manifestations— which are rather narrow-minded and limited to the physical body. Phenomena of the mind—imagination, ideas, sensations, perceptions, desires, emotions; even consciousness and the act of thinking—everything was discarded in favor of compartmentalized reactions. Because they are "measurable," they are the only ones considered worthy of being compared and of undergoing *experimental* investigations.

This is understandable. Since the beginning of this century there has been an irresistible scientific iconoclasm in relation to concepts considered theistic. An almost absolute materialistic predominance took over, able to embrace everything from the philosophical foundations of political actions up to the pigeonholes of the scientists of life.

When John Broadus Watson, professor at Johns Hopkins University (Baltimore, Maryland, U.S.A.), published his book *Behaviorism* in 1913, the first great blow against classic psychology and the future sciences of the spirit was given— because they necessarily had to be based on Behaviorism. Together with Psychoanalysis (Freud) and Reflexology (Pavlov),

Behaviorism became the dominant doctrine in the processes and methods of all the sciences of life. It is true that there was a propitious atmosphere for this, supported by historical, cultural, political, and religious facts. Due to this, materialistic concepts grew like an epidemic, with such an impetus that even today it continues spreading all over the world, becoming deeper and deeper.

The cultural and ethical consequences of this phenomenon, however, have been of such a baleful order, that we are sunk in oceanic anguishes and uncertainties, although constant religious preaching goes on debating spiritual themes that become inefficacious before the overwhelming materialistic preoccupation that characterizes "modern times." And we keep on, without any light in front of us.

This reduction of the phenomena of the soul to mere cerebral manifestations (the cerebrum is considered as the *causal center)* was more harmful to humanity than the abandonment in biology of the old vitalist theory of the origins of life. While the vitalists considered the origin of life *spiritual,* being only a causal and static factor, the materialistic theory of behaviorism rejected any dynamic manifestation of the spirit, since it reduces its activities to a reactive process of blind answers to determined stimuli. All this, at a *level* where everything, apparently, is measurable: the human body.

The Behaviorism of Watson, and the Neo-Behaviorism of Hull and Skinner, instrumentalized and invented this *behavioral psychology,* where manifestations of the mind and consciousness do not have a chance: the soul does not exist because it cannot exist!

> *Psychology has as its only objective the prognosis and the control of behavior; introspection cannot be part of its method.* — *Behaviorism,* J. Watson

(These ideas are well suited to an era where man tends to be seen—mainly—as a unit of production or consumption.)

If psychology became impregnated with materialism, the biological sciences were not left behind. They were also *intoxicated,* all of them, for such a long time and in such an intense manner, that intoxication, probably has become chronic.

The old mysticism of Moses (when Jehovah created the light on the first day and afterwards constructed, part by part, the whole of Creation) and the scientific vitalism of the eighteenth century gave room to the theories that were more attuned to modern man and times. This was more conducive to the pondering of experimental analysis and the measurement of facts. All are characteristics of modern times.

Brilliant and laborious explanations, based on laboratory experiments, try to explain the origin of life through complex physical-chemical theories in the attempt to identify them as a mere result of physical and chemical reactions of Matter. If these reactions had been repeated over the millennia, they would take Matter to a state of such a dynamic and transcendent order that it would become alive; in other words, it would reach this *set of special conditions,* different from its original state, an indefinable state that we call *Life.* This Life would be, therefore, inherent to Matter and it would have grown out of this matter, due to *propitious conditions.*

Loeb, a representative of the classic Mechanism, affirms:

> *Live organisms are chemical machines that are mainly constituted by colloidal matter, have the property of maintaining and reproducing themselves. The essential difference between live matter and inert matter is that the cell synthesizes its own specific matter complex, based on simple compounds, indifferent or not specific, that it takes from the surrounding environment...*
> — *The Organism As A Whole,* J. Loeb

J. Haldane and A.I. Oparin described the indispensable conditions for the first vital manifestations that the planet should have, in order to have something individualize them, make them move by themselves, make them grow and reproduce, etc. It would be necessary to have a warm broth, composed of simple proteins in the form of primary components—the amino acids—that function as real bricks, setting up protein chains. (*It is not by accident* that proteins are the main constituents of the cells of living being's physical bodies.) These chemical compounds, indispensable to life, probably formed *spontaneously,* through the interaction of ambient physical conditions during the never-ending series of *experiences*—produced by chance, by nature.

Urey intended to repeat those natural experiences indispensable to life at the beginning of the planet. He joined, in a closed container, several simple substances such as water vapor, oxygen, hydrogen, and ammonia, subjected them to appropriate temperatures and electric sparks of high tension. After a time they noticed that a synthesis had occurred. New substances were present, including carboxyl acids, tiny amounts of aldehydes and...amino acids.

The presence of amino acids in the artificial *warm broth* gave new perspectives to the experience, making it extremely valuable. (The presence of amino acids is indispensable to the creation of protein molecules.) However, in spite of the brilliant experience, the phenomenon *Life* could not be explained; we only learned a possible way of forming a material organic substrate to which it is linked.

Although Mechanism is still predominant, reactions came up from time to time. Bergson, for example, exclaimed:

> *The world is a process of infinite growth in time; evolution is not a mere mechanical process, but it is Life itself, a cosmic Life that embraces everything. What constitutes Life, the supreme goodness, will always be present, because it is the most spontaneous and natural being.*
> — *La Evolución Creadora*, H. Bergson

More modern authors such as F.C. Northrop, H.S. Burr and others, also reacted through Neo-Vitalism, to explain, in a logical way, life, morphogenesis, etc.

As a matter of fact, it would be enough to admit the reality of the Spirit to get close to our essential problem. Life, although it animates Matter, does not belong to Matter; it vibrates in different dimensions. Life makes use of Matter through the Spirit, and stays there as long as the Spirit stays there, too. When the Spirit leaves, Matter and Organism decompose: it is death.

Our conviction is that Life came together with the Spirit, and it is in the Spirit. When the warm broth at the early dawn of times, rich in mineral salts and amino acids, had propitious conditions, the Spirit fecundated Life. At the beginning it was primitive, embryonic. But it evolved into the complex forms of the superior animals.

> *In the beginning was the Word,*
> *and the Word was with God,*
> *and the Word was God.*
> *The same was in the beginning with God.*
> *All things were made by him;*
> *and without him was not any thing made*
> *that was made.*
> *In him was life...*
> — John 1:1-4

KNOWLEDGE TOWARDS THE ABSOLUTE

Science informs us that creation, in its totality, is composed of Energy. This Energy is distributed through several vibratory levels that embrace the whole visible and invisible universe; from the material state limited by the three Cartesian dimensions, up to the immaterial dimensions explored by religion. Matter is the roughest state because it is formed by condensed Energy. The most rarefied Energy we can imagine—perhaps the most primary of the cosmos—is the most profound strata of creation.

THE ATOM, YESTERDAY & TODAY

Since ancient Greece (400 B.C.) humanity has known the foundations of physics in the field of the "infinitely small." Leucipos and Democritus foresaw the existence of the smallest particle of material—a particle, basically immutable and inde-structible (*a* + *tomus*: "that which cannot be cut"). For more than two thousand years, nothing new was added to this subject besides the idea of Descartes who saw the tiniest portions of material as a "whirlwind in motion" (an expression that could fit the electron of today).

In our century, however, the theories of quantum physics and relativity caused a deep change that marked the beginning of a new understanding, more advanced than the basic ideas of the ancients. Matter began to be considered *another form of Energy*. Elementary material can be created artificially, through the transformative synthesis of an infinity of chemical compounds; it can also be "destroyed" by the transformation of expansive energy (atomic fission).

The total quantity of energy, however, seems to be always the same—a fact that confirms the thesis that the entire universe was created without any possibility of energy loss: The First Law of Thermodynamics—Conservation of Energy.

The postulate of classic physics was the famous "Second Law of Thermodynamics," according to which the universe will become exhausted like a watch without the mainspring; dissi-pating its energy continuously as it used to be at the begin-ning: in the "Emptiness of Nothing," which Genesis refers to. However, (as we know today) any loss is compensated by an individuation in other form of energy, *ad infinitum.*

The atom of Democritus underwent, therefore, profound changes which ranged from the way of conceiving the atom to the knowledge about its structural constitution. Vast fields of investigation opened up and brought light to the subject. Physics introduced the study of atoms which led to the study of energies and particles of this microcosm. And Quantum Theory came to revolutionize the concepts of Matter and Energy, no longer stagnant, but interchangeable, constituting, therefore, an indissoluble whole.

CHASING THE PRIMORDIAL ENERGY

When the material mass disappears, by means of atomic disintegration, it gets transformed into *equivalent energy*; i.e., there is a radiant mass that corresponds to the material mass, always maintaining the same total weight in any of the forms that it assumes, according to Einstein's Equation:

$$E = m \cdot c^2$$

(This equation revolutionized the modern world, caused political instabilities, and to the afflicted civilization, meant the horror of destruction through atomic means.)

In the ceaseless search for the basic Energy of the universe, the elementary particles of which the atom is constituted were identified. Its old indivisibility—proposed by Democritus and Leucipus—disintegrated as soon as the stable proton and electron were known. Later on even smaller particles were discovered, but they are extremely unstable.

Today, physicists are challenged by the fact that even these tiny particles of energy cannot be considered elementary anymore. We are closer and closer to discovering the primary Energy of the cosmos, a kind of energy that, for the time being, appears in the depth of the already known particles: mesons, photons, neutrinos, antineutrinos, leptons, baryons, etc. Soon, scientists will face basic energy, because that is the inexorable direction of the "Great Unmanifested Agent," the cause of the existence of the universe. This is rather paradoxical, considering that science will reach Him in spite of the materialism on which science, at the present time, is founded.

THOUGHT, OUR MOST OBVIOUS ENERGY

In the universe where we exist—relative, prone to phenomena, manifested—numberless forms of energy are already known, interacting and in constant transformation, according to natural laws. We have to admit, by an elementary principle of logic, that there is a basic component of energy (or something that gets transformed into it), a real source of whatever exists, subtler, therefore, than anything that is known.

Everything that is relative can be considered as a disturbance to this absolute state, any kind of energy, even the most unfathomable. The energy of thought, for instance, also has to be a manifestation of this primary state.

The unique and absolute source of all forms of Energy includes, in a universal set, even the tiniest ones that escape from the most sophisticated devices that science uses; as an example we have the energy of thought, so obvious that we use it almost automatically. Being a phenomenon, thought can only be explained as a product of a kind of energy, that we use on the physical plane to manifest, individually as well as collectively, all the problems of our civilization: philosophical, scientific and religious achievements, the arts and the most sublime or profound conceptions we have already formulated.

The transmission of thoughts over large distances has been proven scientifically in countless cases. It constitutes a pheno-menon that, although not generalized, confirms the energetic nature of our *mental emissions*. It is believed that this kind of power, due to its very high frequency and an extremely short wave length (because it is radiant energy), propagates as the known electromagnetic radiation—and it seems that this really happens; therefore, it has to be very close to the sensitive threshold of the manifestation of the Absolute Causal Being.

GOD ON THE HORIZON

Going on in this direction, science is going to find out that the Absolute Being is more than a scientific hypothesis, since we will see later that there really exists a cause for this most primary Energy; consequently, it causes everything that exists. To accept this premise is a mere matter of time for science.

The day might seem to be distant when physicists dare to proclaim the existence of the Absolute Being, infinitely vibrat-ing beyond the extreme limit of the primordial Energy. This day may be long arriving, maybe longer than we want, but all of us are able to experience direct contact with this marvelous spiritual reality, the Source of Life. With deeper knowledge of beings and things, chiefly when we will penetrate into the inferior part of the astral body (or dimension or field, where the quintessential Matter of the etheric body is in conjunction with the boundaries of the astral body), then we will be in a condi-tion to understand more clearly the foundations of creation.

The spiritualized science of the third millennium will certain-ly reach this point. The physicists of the future are convinced that the Absolute Being presides over the laws of science, although he transcends everything. Until then, and on this last journey, we can go on the venture of living, to the always near presence of the Source manifested-Unmanifested. Living per-manently linked to this source of life, is assimilating, instant by instant, the transcendent energy that spurts from it, over-flowing with happiness and interior treasures.

One of the simplest ways to make this living real, would be to go on teaching ourselves the lessons of the illuminated of all religions. We should not worry: we are our own synthesis; our essence includes everything, from the largest galaxies to the least perceivable energies, passing by our brothers of the same species and their achievements. Fraternity, therefore, should not be considered as an empty abstraction—it is imperatively cosmic, actuating in each one's consciousness.

MATTER — ENERGY — SPACE
(AN INTERCHANGEABLE TRINOMIAL)

According to quantum physics, Matter gets dissolved in Energy and Energy gets dissolved in something unknown. This *something unknown*, however, is nothing else than...Space!

Space is the last consequence, the last stage of energetic degradation on matter's way to an apparent "nothing." On the other hand, if we want to start from "nothing" towards Matter, our starting point would be Space—repository of everything that exists—up to the heavy metals, in a long and complex process of slow condensing. Matter is, therefore, in the final analysis, the condensation of *Space*. And Energy, with its vast number of vibratory bands, is the intermediate stage between Space and Matter. This intermediate stage is formed by the *deformation of Space*, in a state of tension.

THE ORIGIN OF MATTER

Temporarily deformed and in a *state of tension*, Space frees power with an intensity proportional to the degree of formation. In the segment of affected Space, a dynamic state arises, because "power" or "energy" imply dynamism, potency and work. When the energy of this tension reaches a certain degree of dynamism, it gets naturally condensed, through the ever-increasing movement in vortices that get smaller and smaller. Large "masses" of Space have their size reduced to get dense in the first and most simple, stable and measurable manifestation of Matter according to the equation:

$$\frac{\hbar \cdot \nu_\gamma}{c^2} = M_{\bar{e}}$$

Or:

$$\frac{(6.612873143 \times 10^{-27}\ \text{erg/s}) \times (1.23777 \times 10^{20}\ \text{cycles/s})}{8.987764166 \times 10^{20}\ \text{cm/s}} = M_{\bar{e}}$$

M = 0.91070027179 x 10^{-27} g (mass of electron)
$\hbar$ = 6.6128273143 x 10^{-27} erg (Planck's Universal Constant)
ν_γ = 1.23777 x 10^{20} cycles/sec (frequency of gamma rays)
c^2 = 8.987764166 x 10^{20} cm/sec^2 (square of the speed of light)

75

By this equation we see that Energy gives rise to Matter.

THE BIRTH OF THE PHOTON

To compute the equation above we have to solve a stage before the *condensation* in which the spatial dynamism—at the highest energy—produces an infinitely small vortex from which results a certain value—still more elementary—which is still unknown to physics. The value of the gamma photon has not been verified and measured by even the most sophisticated devices we have. That is why we say that the photon does not have mass. We could call it "quantum mass", or *dynamic mass,* with a value of $0.73578882342 \times 10^{-47}$g theoretically determined by mathematics.

The value of the gamma photon, basis for the appearance of the electron, is given by the following equation:

$$\frac{\hbar}{c^2} = M_0$$

$$M = \frac{6.6128273143 \times 10^{-27} \text{ erg/sec}}{8.9877764166 \times 10^{20} \text{ cm}^2/\text{sec}^2} = 0.73578882342 \times 10^{-47} \text{ g}$$

M_0 stands for the quantum mass of the photon

$\hbar$ = Planck's Constant (called the "Quantum" of energy) indicates the energy necessary for the jump of the electron from its original orbit to another, more external, one. When it is divided by the square of the velocity of light, Planck's Constant materializes the gamma photon.

PHOTON — ELECTRON

Interesting: the product of this value multiplied by the frequency of the same gamma ray equals the mass of the electron!

Let us consider the following:

$$(0.73578882342 \times 10^{-47} \text{ g}) \times (1.23777 \times 10^{20} \text{ cycles/s})$$
$$= 0.910700271707 \times 10^{-27} \text{ g}$$

When the photon (that in reality, is a *concentration* of energy), or another particle of very tiny mass and of great energy lightly touches the atomic nucleus of a heavy metal, it is converted into an electron and a positron (an electron with positive charge). The opposite happens when an electron and a positron meet: they destroy each other—their masses are transformed into *gamma rays* of high intensity energy.

According to Manuel Dopacio these infinitesimal particles, projected into Space, at the velocity of light, trace a vectorial trajectory. When they touch a heavy metal their rectilinear motion brakes, and, at the same time, they start rotating, acquiring mass; so the electrons are born: energetic clouds with a diameter of 5.6356×10^{-13} cm.

(This allows us to understand better the mysterious origin of the electric current in dynamos. The photon of the magnetic field is transformed into an electron of spiral motion and by the effect of this movement, is impelled along the conductors.)

MOMENT OF INERTIA — UNITARY MASS OF MAGNETISM?

If we take the "quantum" of Planck's energy—the constant $\hbar$—and divide it by the velocity of light, we will have:

$$\frac{6.6128273143 \times 10^{-27} \, \text{erg/s}}{22.99796 \times 10^{10} \, \text{cm}} = 2.205775698 \times 10^{-37} \, \text{erg}$$

Or:

$$\frac{\hbar}{c} = M$$

But this same value of "M" is obtained as the product of the theoretical mass of the gamma photon multiplied by the velocity of light.

$$M_0 \cdot c = M$$

$$(0.735758882342 \times 10^{-47} \, \text{g}) \times (2.99796 \times 10^{10} \, \text{cm})$$
$$= 2.2057756989 \times 10^{-37} \, \text{g}$$

As we can see, both results, indicate a particle of an infinitely small mass: 10^{-37} g. It is possible that it represents the unitary mass of magnetism. This makes sense, because if we divide this value by the mass of the electron, we will have:

$$\frac{M}{M_{\bar{e}}} = \lambda_\gamma$$

$$\lambda_\gamma = \frac{2.2057756989 \times 10^{-37} \, \text{g}}{0.9107002717 \times 10^{-27} \, \text{g}} = 2.4220654 \times 10^{-10} \, \text{cm}$$

This is the value of the wave length of the gamma ray. The frequency of this same ray, multiplied by the theoretical mass of the gamma photon, will be the mass of the electron (as we have already seen):

$$M_0 \cdot \lambda_\gamma = M_{\bar{e}}$$

Consequently, if we divide M by the wave length of the gamma ray, we also have to obtain, the value of the electron:

$$\frac{M}{\lambda_\gamma} = M\bar{e}$$

$$\frac{2.2057756989 \times 10^{-37}\ \text{g}}{2.4220654 \times 10^{-10}\ \text{cm}} = 0.91970002717 \times 10^{-27}\ \text{g}$$

(This value M, the quotient of Planck's Constant times the velocity of light:

$$M = \frac{\hbar}{c}$$

is called the *moment of inertia*. It was conceived by Euler in 1765 as the product of the mass and the square of the distance.)

On the other hand, the product of the mass of an electron times the wave length of the gamma ray (that is, a measure of distance) results in the value of the *moment of inertia:*

$$M\bar{e} \cdot \lambda_\gamma = M$$

$$(0.9107002717 \times 10^{-27}\ \text{g}) \times (2.4220654 \times 10^{-10}\ \text{cm})$$
$$= 2.2057756989 \times 10^{-37}$$

By these equations we can see the reversibility between Matter and Energy.

SPACE, RESERVOIR OF INFINITE ENERGY

We were going about the fundamental binomial of physics—Matter and Energy—and we would like to add (for further reasons) that it is not really a binomial, but a *trinomial:* Matter, Energy and *Space.* We live and breathe Space, it surrounds us, and penetrates the innermost part of our being; it is present in the three dimensions of our physical body—as well as in the other, invisible ones of the spiritual world. Everything is Space. We are, as an ultimate consequence, manifested Space: *Space that has become a phenomenon.*

Space, therefore, is God's first manifestation. It is for this reason, considering its greatness, that Space gets merged with God in the infinitude of extension.

To illustrate this fact, and to give us conditions to perceive the equivalence between Matter and free energy, we will establish an easy comparison by means of Einstein's equation.

Let us transform the mass of a man of eighty-five kilograms into pure energy by $E = m \cdot c^2$. (The measurement system used is CGS.)

m = 85.000g (mass)

$c^2 = 8.987764161 \times 10^{20} cm^2/s^2$ (square of the velocity of light)

3.6×10^{13} = The factor to convert ergs to kilowatt hours [Kwh]; as the erg is a very small measurement, we convert the results into Kwh, the usual measurement for electric current) and,

E = energy

We have:

$$E = 85.000\,g \cdot (9.987764161 \times 10^{20}) = 7.6395995 \times 10^{25}\ \text{erg}$$

Or in Kwh:

$$\frac{7.6395995 \times 10^{25}}{3.6 \times 10^{13}} = 2.1221110 \times 10^{12}\ \text{Kwh}$$

Let us now compare the total of pure energy, freed by a man who weighs 85 kg, with the electric energy produced by large power plants.

In January 1985 the State of Rio Grande do Sul produced 1.5 million Kwh. In a year the production would be:

$$(1.5 \times 10^6)\,24\,\text{hours} = 3.6 \times 10^7\ \text{Kwh}$$
$$(3.6 \times 10^7)\,365\,\text{days} = 1.314 \times 10^{10}\ \text{Kwh}$$

If we divide the energy that results from a man of 85 kg by the annual consumption of Rio Grande do Sul, the result will be:

$$\frac{2.1221110 \times 10^{12}\ \text{Kwh}}{1.314 \times 10^{10}\ \text{Kwh}} = 161.5\,\text{years}^{[13]}$$

This means that Rio Grande do Sul would have to furnish all the energy that it produces for *one hundred sixty and a half years,* to form a man of only 85 kg, or, the reciprocal: the energy released by the material contained in a man of 85 kg would be sufficient to furnish energy to Rio Grande do Sul for 161.5 years.

Therefore, we see how immense the condensed energetic potential in Matter is. And, on the other hand, what an immense, unimaginable potential of free energy *Space is.*[14]

---

[13] These equations are from a work by Manuel Dopacio, contemporary Argentinean physicist.

[14] The theory about Space is from Dino Kraspedon.

THE ENIGMA OF SPACE

Besides the micro-particles that integrate the atom, under the infinitely small universes with which everything that exists, is manifested there, in addition to the primordial Energy, there is something indefinable, that escapes from our understanding. It is not Matter, neither is it Energy. However it *is* an Absolute Being in a state of *potential existence*. From this state of pure existence, not yet manifested, derives the whole of creation; it is the ultimate substrate of existence.

Essence is relative; the Absolute contains infinite potential. A Unique Being, eternal and unmanifest, he is transformed into all kinds of life and is in everything that exists, by creating continuously. As a consequence, he is the ultimate—and eternal—scientific reality, the *omega* of science.

The space that surrounds us gives us an idea of this reality. When we look at the sky we feel the vertigo caused by incommensurable grandeur; millions of stars, constellations, galaxies, universes follow each other in the infinities of Time and Space in such a way that we are unable to conceive the macrocosmic greatness. On the other hand, if we lower our eyes to infinite smallness, we will feel the same vertigo; Space opens up, micro worlds evolve, constellations of energy, subatomic *universes.*

Where then, are the limits of Space?

If it is in the interior of the atom, and among the galaxies, what kind of *thing* is it? Which is its unitary particle—its atom—if it really has one? Should it be only the immeasurable emptiness of which Lao-Tsé speaks, merging with God? Or could it be the *primary unity* with which the universe was created?

In this last case, Space would have been the first manifestation of the Absolute.

As a matter of fact, it has greatness, consequently it exists. It is immeasurable in its vastness, it does not only involve, but it also penetrates everything that is manifested—in a compulsory and omnipotent immanence. On the other hand this great emptiness transcends the Cartesian dimensions, since it is present, and with the same characteristics that we know, in the world of the spirits.

There, in the same way as here, it penetrates molecules and atoms of the astral bodies (that we already know well); it certainly is also among the subtler bodies; as well as in the higher planes, in the coverings that are more internal and closer to the Divine Flame—Absolute in us.

SCIENCE WITHOUT SPACE

According to its immanence, transcendence and infinitude, this emptiness resembles God. Nevertheless, it is *something*. Something so important for its immanence in creation that for this reason alone, it would deserve a special place in science. Unfortunately, however, that is not what is happening. It seems as if men have never realized what an inexhaustible barn of cosmic energy is permanently at their disposal.

Not knowing the endless richness of infinite Space, we go on looking for the mechanical energy of waterfalls, or of the fossil energy of petroleum. We do not perceive (perhaps because it is too obvious): Space can be manipulated, twisted, deformed, condensed; all its free energy can be used; the entire, incommensurable Space is at man's disposal, and its exploration depends only on appropriate techniques.

The most tenuous forms of energy are stored in inconceivable quantities in the sidereal space and can be perfectly handled though the mind. Yes, our mind: it is the most adequate tool to use in the spatial world, because it is there that our thoughts are propagated. Therefore, we can condense great energetic currents and project them to long distances for any purpose that we have in mind.

It is lamentable that our science almost does not have 'space' for Space; however, that is not surprising. Science sees like a microscope: continuously increasing the magnification, but, thereby, limiting the visual field. In this way it produces more and more specialists who each know more about nothing. They know almost everything about man but his essence. They are so versed in analysis that they do not know how to elaborate a synthesis anymore. Intoxicated by old and new details, our scientists tend to despise philosophers, exactly because they conceive synthesis. However, we *need* synthesis, to benefit even science. Broken and split, degraded in its humanistic purposes (because it is linked to immediacy of its materialistic foundations), science, quite often, blurs our sight of the horizon, when it compels us to a myopic objectivity that only sees what is very near and what is in reach of our senses.

* * *

We made this very short digression through the fields of Matter and Energy, because all our spiritual work and, consequently, all the content of this book, are subjects relative to Energy and its use.

KARMA, THE GREAT COSMIC LAW

INTRODUCTION

Karma is the *Law of Action* through which the work created by God emanates from His nature.

At the beginning there was just the Absolute, the Unmanifest, in all His potential plenitude. When He started creating, He projected everything that exists, from His own divine nature; for this reason we are sons of God in the purest sense of the word. God is present in us: this is called *immanence*. By His infinitude, however, God transcends to the created work. "You are Gods," said Jesus.

Karma is the great Law that presides over creation. It rules the absolute harmony of the cosmos, in its lowest details. If there is disharmony in any corner of Space, this great Law suffers the interference of another one—secondary, but independent: the Law of Reaction. This law obliges everything to go back to its place, in an immense process of a harmonic readjustment. Coupled, these two cosmic laws constitute the "Principle of Evolution," that can be compared with the eternal "come-to-be" of Heraclitus. This principle rules the manifestations of the unmanifested, His permanence in the Space-Time continuum and His glorious return to the Creator. This is the synthesis of all the phenomena of the Cosmos.

When Man deviates from the Cosmic Harmonic Law, he becomes satanic; through his antagonism to the Harmonic Law, he spreads the chaos within himself and around him. The Law of Reaction, then, obligates him to reestablish harmony unconditionally, in the same degree of the perturbation. The re-ordination will fatally happen, not only in the interior of the person, but also in the portion of Space he disorganized (including all beings who were involved in the chaos).

All beings are subject to this great process of karmic readjustment. The total sum of the readjustments, small or large, will give the being in evolution the experience and knowledge to take him from ignorance to wisdom, from Darkness to Light.

KARMIC REDEMPTION

In the redemption of the karmic disharmonies there are four[15] well-defined stages:

KNOWLEDGE OF THE PRODUCED DISHARMONY

The "debt" (the bad action done to other beings or to the own doer), has to be redeemed up to the last "cent." The owner has to know the value of the debt, in order to pay it off.

The evolutionary process unfolds during this time and the being goes through several successive incarnated stages, in which he loses the remembrance of his past. How, then, can he know about the quantity and the value of the mistakes he did, chiefly if they were made in a remote past?

Such questions, although logical, show ignorance about the perfecting process directed by the Principle of Evolution. Everything we obtain by a volitional act (i.e., by a conscious effort) we do not lose: it is stored in our essence, in the immortal spirit. In other words, the negative or positive experiences (be they harmonic or disharmonic) will be magnetically printed into the memory bank of the spiritual brain of the person. For this reason, any incarnated human being knows perfectly about all the mistakes he made at any time in his conscious life. His physical brain does not know what he did in past incarnations, but the spirit knows everything; this explains the diversity of temperaments, and bad or good tendencies, that man shows from early childhood on.

Men are different from one another because they *inherit* from themselves the temperaments that give them unique characteristics. They develop a predominant and distinct character. A patrimony acquired through experiences lived through successive lifetimes, an immutable temperament which characterizes each human being. The only thing that varies in this temperament is the character, which is enriched or impoverished by new values or experiences, by the abrasion of educational processes of each incarnated stage.

ACQUIESCENCE IN REDEEMING THE DEBT

Every being craves for peace, for harmony, for happiness. The fear of death, or pain, of suffering is an atavistic constant, inherent in man in his inferior stages of evolution. Therefore, there is the need to evolve, to have peace, to look for happiness even by being foolish. At the beginning we think that we can achieve this venture by getting material goods: it is the phase when man runs after money. In this childish stage of evolu-

---

[15] Edgar Armond.

tion, man is a predator: he uses aggression, he hurts whoever dares to set limits on his possessive actions. By doing so, he spreads more disharmony than benefits around him. The negative balance accumulated by these follies, will make him feel, later on in other incarnations, that nothing useful was left of all the perturbations he caused, except for the anathema of those he made suffer, and whose pain is going to burn in his consciousness. In a new incarnation he will be an internally embittered person, because evil generates evil.

At a certain moment of his evolution, man feels the need to get intimately harmonized: a negative charge piled up in his spiritual memory obligates him to feel an urgent need for a change in the direction of his life; he becomes conscious that the values to be acquired have to be different—not the material ones. In this phase, he is in condition to face the adversities that he himself provoked, with stoicism and without revolt. He acquiesces, therefore, to redeem his mistakes.

But how do we know that a person is willing to redeem his mistakes?

This can be recognized by the resignation with which the person faces sufferings that sometimes come unexpectedly. Those who are in conformance with irreversible situations, such as physical or moral pain, show their disposition in redeeming similar adversities that they themselves caused to the destiny of other people in a distant past.

Those who revolt against suffering and rail against Divinity, proclaiming the injustices they are undergoing, do not want, nor can they redeem, anything, because they do not consider themselves debtors. Therefore, they are not yet at the point where their consciousness awakes. Only the repetition of the experience in disharmonic bands will make their consciousness open up.

THE VALUE OF DISHARMONY

All kinds of disharmony that beings have to struggle through, constitute a passive suffering, by which they get to know the karmic process and the debts they have to redeem during their existence.

Usually we think that it is through suffering that man redeems the evils he did in his remote past. This is a big mistake! Suffering only shows the extent of the mistakes he made; it never means money for the payment of any kind of guilt. What kind of logic is it to think that the suffering of the culprit could be the payment for guilt. Would God be sadistic?

It really would be very strange that a suffering which is passively accepted—a put-out eye, for example—could be used to restore the put-out eye of an enemy of a previous incarnation. It is inconceivable that Divine Justice be that primary. We would have the consecration of the Law of Talion, such as, "an eye for an eye and a tooth for a tooth" being perpetuated with the money of God for the readjustments of guilt.

In effect God—who is absolute justice, goodness in the superlative form, purity without flaw—must have other means to apply His infinite justice. In Absolute Harmony we cannot include pain—that is contrary to His nature.

Pain is a mere indicator. It only shows the "quantum" of disharmony practiced: through it the human being learns that he must not hurt his fellow creatures. Suffering, consequently, is educational: it serves as an experience to prevent the repetition of mistakes. In other words, pain teaches us love.

INDEMNIFICATION

By indemnification we understand the payment of debts. *And there is only one kind of money in the Universe for the payment of any debt: love.*

Love is the magic money that corrects mistakes and elevates individuals. Only by loving others—and whatever else exists—is the individual glorified. When Paul of Tarsus said: "It is not me anymore who lives; it is Christ who lives in me," he was entering the plenitude of divine love.

Questions & Answers

Q—What happens to a person who is able to get rid of all of his karmic debts, or of his sufferings?
A—*He will be able to make his payment.*
Q—Knowing that the person feels relieved and, as if he were born again, because he is so happy that he is free of the circle of sufferings, we repeat: what happens to him?
A—*He will be in conditions to redeem, with ease, his karmic debts.*
Q—What is karma?
A—*Karma is the Law by which the Creator manifests his absolute nature in all the creation.*
Q—Are the Laws of Karma—the Law of Action and the Law of Reaction—by any chance, antagonistic?
A—*They are never antagonistic, they complement each other, they are almost independent from each other. The great Law of Action implies in the Law of Reaction, which is the karmic readjustment; that always tends to goodness and harmony, since goodness only exists in the divine work. God could never create the evil that is contrary to His own nature. Although the evil can last for consecutive millennia, it is always relative and*

transitory. In reality, all evil is a degeneration of goodness, in the same way as disharmony is a perturbation of harmony. Harmony and disharmony also are complementary states, reversible between themselves, they are called antagonistic, only because they represent the opposite poles of a state. When the evil integrates in goodness, only goodness exists. When disharmony vanishes in harmony, only harmony exists.

The good and the evil walk together, but he who chooses one of these two roads will hardly ever trail the other one, says a very old Egyptian proverb. In our life harmony and disharmony walk together. As disharmony is the act or energy that disturbs harmony, the harmonization of disharmony is the action through which we can integrate disharmony in harmony (using even disharmonic energies for this purpose). As they are neither independent nor opposed, but always complementary, one cannot substitute the other completely because, if there were a plenitude of one of them, man would be absolute in one of the poles, equaling the Creator.

As a corollary, we conclude that the existence of absolute evil in the devil is entirely impossible because, if it were so, Satan's power would be like God's—*Absolute*—though in the opposite sense.

The apostle Paul said this about the inherent duality:

> *For the good that I would I do not: but the evil which I would not, that I do... But I see another law in my members, warring against the law of my mind, and bringing me into captivity to the law of sin which is in my members. O wretched man that I am! who shall deliver me from the body of this death?*
>
> — Romans 7:19-24

MAN'S LIFE — THE FIELD FOR THE KARMIC LAWS

When we study man—the unique living being that has a conscious capacity to choose solutions in a continuous and sequential manner—we come upon a terrible duality in which he has been struggling, without being able to equalize it: *ignorance and suffering.*

When we speak about ignorance, we do not refer only to the intellectual kind. This type of ignorance is of rather secondary value if we reflect about the spiritual ignorance in which we have been living and in which we *persist in living,* even today.

The spiritual crisis generated and experienced by humanity at the end of this civilization includes all secondary crises with which we have been struggling: worldwide economic crises, unsolved political crises, and moral crises together with the consequent decadence of social and moral norms. These crises are common to all civilizations at their end. Despite the incredible means of entertainment, enjoyment, easy communication, and comfort that we have, an existential crisis occurs and we are mired in disharmony and materialistic unrest.

Responsible action for the spiritual crisis can only be solved with the amelioration of each person. The sum of the renewed people's actions would improve society as an automatic consequence. It is possible that, by this way, that we would reach the ideal society without classes, a goal that has been a dream from Plato to the historical materialists of our day.

There is no redemption-halo, affirms Rohden; i.e., redemption does not come from man's outer side. Our salvation comes from *inside;* it emerges from the innermost part of our body. It is, therefore, an auto-redemption. Modifications imposed by external agents do not alter people in their essence. This is the reason for the failure of governments: they will never solve the anguishing problems that afflict all social classes. Society, at the end of this century, eager for helpful solutions, has forgotten the lesson that history taught us: people do not see that the solutions to all their problems are within themselves.

Let us look around us and *inside us.* Almost all of us live by looking for any shortcut. We have strayed, we are lost in labyrinths that we ourselves created. It has been always this way, in spite of the radiant luminosity of the laws taught by the Envoy.

After all, why all this?

The explanation was already given to us by the apostle Paul, nineteen centuries ago:

> *But the natural man receiveth not the things of the Spirit of God: for they are foolishness unto him: neither can he know them, because they are spiritually discerned.*
> — I Corinthians 2:14

We have had the perfect formula for our salvation for two thousand years. It is simple and within our reach in the immutable Cosmic Laws of the Gospel. Although we know these Laws, for centuries we have insisted on transgressing them. The historians of the future probably will say that this was the biggest, the most long-lasting, and the most catastrophic collective mistake of our species.

LIFE COMES FROM GOD

Everything that exists has its origin in God and, after a long evolution, it returns to God.[16]

From God—the Absolute—through the Law of Actions (karma) acting as a centrifugal force, emanates space and something that the Hindus call *Prana*—vital power—with the rising of energy or something similar. By the phenomenon of interaction, it becomes denser until it constitutes more and more dynamic vortices. In determined stages of intensity, these vortices, through the condensation of a gamma photon, constitute the free electron, as we have already seen.

In a more advanced stage, while motion is intensifying, energy also increases (and consequently, so does temperature), causing the emergence of stable nuclear elements: the atomic nucleus with protons, neutrons and, in the periphery, electrons. And so the first element of *The Periodic Table of the Elements*—hydrogen—is born. It is constituted of one proton and one electron in orbits of an inconceivable velocity. Thus, we have the first stable, defined and individualized particle. Due to continuous cooling, the other elements are formed.

The spiritual principle is nested in Matter. It does not have its origin in Matter, as materialists affirm. When the molecular combinations of mineral salts, water, oxygen, nitrogen, appropriate heat, electrical ionization—in short, when everything becomes compatible with the primary biological stage—then the fundamental amino acids from which will be the sustaining substrate so the spiritual principle can become organized and fixed in what will be the first alive primary particle. Life, then, is born the way we know it: alive, this particle reproduces and evolves into more complex forms. And, finally, there is man.

The spiritual principle is Life; therefore, it comes from God. Matter is only the substrate to which it becomes linked to form the living beings of our dimensional universe.

---

[16] Philosophical concept of the Irish monk John Scot Erigena, 9th century. A transitory place in the inferior astral, for evil spirits, so called by André Luiz, which can be compared to the Purgatory of the Catholic Church.

APOMETRICS

GENERALITIES

The term *Apometrics* is composed of the Greek word *apo*, which means "beyond" and *metron*, "measurement." It indicates spiritual unfolding or bilocation, a subject that has been studied intensively by several classic authors (e.g., Bozzano). The unfolding is essentially the separation of the astral (or mental) body from the physical body.

The unfolding is relatively easy: over a lifetime it occurs once in a while in a spontaneous way (without *conscious* volition). It usually happens during sleep, or in a hypnotic sleep (induced by magnetic passes or suggestion) or, during mystic ecstasy; it can also occur when there are great emotional or circulatory shocks: fainting, coma, convalescence of serious diseases, physical traumas; it can also be the consequence of the use of narcotics, and it also happens during mediumistic trances; less often, it can happen spontaneously to very sensitive individuals when they are in a state of vigil. (For illustrations, see *Classic Cases of Unfolding*, transcribed from the book *Unfolding, Phenomena Of Bilocation*, by Ernesto Bozzano.)

ORIGINS OF APOMETRICS

Apometrics refers to the unfolding of the astral or mental body, apparently unknown to classic authors; nor are there any reports about it in the publications of scientists or those who study psychism. It is an animistic[17] technique, with no relation to mediumistics.

In 1965 a man showed up at the Spiritist Hospital of Porto Alegre, saying that he had a technique for medical treatment, totally different from official medicine: he used the service of disincarnated doctors who indicated the therapeutics for the illnesses of sick people. The man was called Luiz Rodrigues, from Puerto Rico; he had been living for many years in Rio de Janeiro. At first sight, his technique did not seem to be any different from the mediumistic processes of Kardecian Spiritism, although he insisted he was not a follower of this

---

[17] Animistics: The philosophical system of the animists; pertaining to the soul; the attribution of a living soul to inanimate objects. *The New Aurélio Dictionary* First Issue, Eleventh Printing.

Doctrine. But it was different, yes. And very much: instead of the disincarnated doctors coming to the patient, *it was the patient who, unfolded,* went to the doctors of the astral, to get his diagnosis and therapeutics.

Mr. Rodrigues called his technique *hypnometrics.* This term did not seem appropriate to us since he did not use any kind of sleep, nor did he try to induce it. He simply used a slow, regressive counting, starting with the number corresponding to the age of the patient. When the counting was done, the patient was out of his body.

We ascertained that the technique *worked.* But the cause of success was not known even to Mr. Rodrigues.

We attended two hypnometric sessions and, we suspected after the first one, that in this technique there had to be the use of magnetic power-fields, since there has to be some kind of energy to have the unfolding of a body. In fact, the counting probably projected a succession of energetic impulses on the patient's astral or mental body and that caused the unfolding.

This is what we could prove, right at the beginning, in a series of experiences. And so we abandoned the designation *hypnometrics* and substituted for it *Apometrics.* That seemed more appropriate, since the technique did not have any association to sleep.

The technique of apometric unfolding proved to be applicable to any kind of person independent of age, health, mental state, or even the resistance that the person could offer. Once the acting energy comes from outside, it does not depend on the person's will. Easy to apply, Apometrics is of unquestionable efficiency and is *not* mediumistic.

Hypnotic techniques of unfolding (or the ones that use magnetic passes), are always limited because they can only be used for certain types of patients. On the other hand, Apometrics always presents positive results in everybody, even with oligophrenic patients of almost zero rationality, not reachable by hypnosis.

USEFULNESS OF APOMETRICS

The greatest success of Apometrics is in its application to mediums who achieve easier contact with the spiritual world.

In our work we use clairvoyant mediums who can see when they are unfolded in the astral field. (Common people, without clairvoyance, do not even believe that they are unfolded.) On the other hand, experienced mediums can see and hear spirits during the trances of unfolding. In addition, they can move in Space where they visit astral colonies, perform efficient work to redeem suffering spirits, and participate in organized aid caravans in that dimension; they also visit incarnated sick people in their homes, integrating spiritual groups whose objective is the cleansing of homes.

To assist a sick person we use unfolded mediums in contact with the doctors of the astral. Next, we unfold the sick person, too, who is then, in his astral body, assisted by the disincarnated doctors in the presence of the unfolded mediums. These, then, relate everything that is going on while the doctors take care of the sick—diagnostics, astral surgeries, details of the patients problems—with the elucidation of the disease and practical orientations for the consolidation of the cure. Unfolded, the patients are assisted with more efficiency, depth, and speed by the disincarnated doctors. The diagnostics used are very detailed and precise; in astral surgeries, it is common to use high techniques and sophisticated equipment in hospitals of the superior astral.

This description—dead doctors treating the sick astral body, mediums and patients visits to invisible hospitals, with surgery rooms and advanced equipment (and, of course, buildings, gardens, vehicles, etc.)—all seems to be fanciful imagination, as if it were scientific fiction.

But it is not.

For more that twenty years, dozens of mediums have unfolded at the Love and Charity Hospital, the astral institution that helps us in our spiritual work. During all this time different mediums (first separately, and then in groups) and on different days, contributed much to our careful investigation, giving identical descriptions of the gardens where they rested, of the building, the rooms, the surgical centers, allowing us an accurate examination of the surgical techniques.

The astral trips of our sensitives were always the object of very attentive observation. Besides the detailed description of the visited places, we are very much interested in the diagnoses and prognoses of the patients assisted at a distance, practiced by the astral groups accompanied by our mediums.

According to *all the experiences we went through*, there is no way to escape the evidence that, through Apometrics, the therapeutic process becomes amplified and diversified. It offers a special kind of medicine to the spirit, performed by disincarnated doctors together with incarnated doctors. Besides this, it allows the regression of incarnated and disincarnated spirits to previous lives; when it shows the remote past of the sick—unveiling their karmic connection with other spirits—arousing not only the investigation of the effect of the Law of Karma, but also the profound treatment of diseases, of naturally enduring effects.

CARE. SPIRITUAL ASSISTANCE

Although the technique is quite easy, there is a series of correlated circumstances (ruled by special laws) that hampers its application, making it complex. The practice of this technique requires special care, with constant attention to the details of the phenomenon. *That is why we recommend that people who would like to learn how to apply and use the Apometric technique of treatment take a six month internship with our group.*

First, as a primordial and indispensable condition, the work must include, and be protected by, the spiritual plane—and this plane has to be of high level; without this assistance nothing will be achieved. Failure will also be certain if mediums and investigators—the physical level of the work—are not devoted to goodness. If the participants, incarnated and disincarnated, do not maintain a high ethical level, work can become counterproductive in both planes—the physical and the spiritual.

Simple curiosity and trifling application without any serious objective also constitute negative factors that condemn any spiritual task to failure. In this field of activity, where we work in free horizons outside the fleshly covering, the harmony of all the components of the group is absolutely indispensable. And not only is harmony indispensable, it is necessary, too, that each participant keeps the best possible mental hygiene to avoid the interference of negative currents and heavy vibratory fields which make the movement of the mediums in the astral world very difficult.

THE TREATMENT

Once the assistance of the astral plane is guaranteed by repeated contacts of the mediums with the disincarnated operators who follow the medium's orders (the operators are responsible for the success of the work), we put the sick in trances to unfold them, using the same technique utilized for the unfolding of mediums. Afterwards, we transport the patients, one by one, to the hospital designated for them in the astral. There they are checked, treated, advised, subjected to surgeries, etc.—all these activities following a working plan ruled by order, equilibrium, and advanced scientific concepts.

Usually the sick do not register anything. They do not see anything, nor do they feel anything that could be classified as abnormal. Sometimes, however, we observe phenomena such as dizziness, drowsiness, feeling of lightness and, sometimes, in sensitives or trained mediums, even a complete sight of the plane where they are. After a few minutes the treatment given by the astral groups is over and the patient is connected back to his physical body. We always care very much about a perfect coupling between the astral and the physical body; otherwise, the patient can feel dizziness, a sensation of void, indisposition, or even headaches for some hours.

THE OBSESSORS. APOMETRIC DE-OBSESSION

Almost without exception, patients come followed by a group of obsessors: the *spiritual agents* of their diseases. We have to assist, first, these unhappy spirits, some of whom are in great suffering and have been magnetized to the sick for a long time. They do not limit themselves to persecuting their victims all the time: they try to harm them in all possible forms; their vengeance is blind. Usually they are enemies who had been victims of *their* present victims in former incarnations.

The obsessors act individually, in small groups, or in large gangs—it depends on the magnetization they have with the victim, their degree of peril, the astral means they have, their intelligence and mental potentiality. In any event, they are terrifying. We need much good will to serve God's work to give them love and assistance. Once they are gathered, they have to be taken to specialized hospitals in the astral or to the regions the Guiding Spirits send them according to the vibratory standard of each sufferer. Giving them love offers them an understanding of hatred and its dark consequences.

We learned that we can never leave an obsessor free. They seldom have their behavior and attitudes modified in Spiritist sessions which use only dialectics to enlighten them. Usually only one session is not enough to convince them. They cannot easily change the cruel behavior they are used to, particularly if they are evildoers working for incarnated or disincarnated entities who are interested in the destruction of a person.

THE "NEW" SYNDROMES

In the haste and desire to harm, obsessors use highly refined techniques of torture to harass their victims. They put all kinds of instruments on the victim's bodies—ropes, chains, lacerating fetters, etc.—to weaken them and cause continuous suffering. Therefore, mysterious illnesses occur, with baffling symptoms, that mislead medical diagnoses. Among the many new syndromes that Apometrics allowed us to discover, we can cite the diseases caused by parasitic devices fixed in the nervous system of the astral body of the sick. This syndrome, for its importance, could stand beside the classic syndromes of medicine; however it is provoked by technicians of darkness, interested in harming people physically and mentally.

Apometrics causes real "miracles" in the treatment of de-obsession. Not only do those being obsessed receive treatment, the obsessors also are given treatment, either individually or in small groups. This subject will be discussed in detail later.

CLASSIC CASES OF UNFOLDING

Case #1: Unfolding During Surgery.
Patient: Mrs. J. P., University Professor.
Reported: In the *Journal of American S. P. R.*, 1908.

When I was 24 years old, I was subjected to an anesthesia to undergo a surgery. When I was coming back I had the feeling of being free in the room: I felt perfectly well but I was without my body. I had the feeling that I was transformed into a spirit and that I had reached, through pain, the so-desired peace. I looked down at my inanimate body in bed. In this room were the two sisters of my mother-in-law; one was sitting beside the bed, warming up my hands, and the other was standing on the other side of the bed, observing us. At that I had the impression that the evidence needed for proof of the situation was imminent. Things that, however, I cannot remember, but I understood that they were part of the plot. I absolutely did not want to go back to my body but, unfortunately, I felt that I was forced to do so.

The most curious thing about my experience was that, as soon as I woke up, I asked: "Where is Mrs. K?" And my mother-in-law answered: "How do you know that she was here?" In fact, Mrs. K. was not present before I was anesthetized. She arrived afterwards, when I was already asleep and with my eyes closed. I answered: "I noticed her standing over there." I did not want to add anything else as I was afraid of sounding silly narrating the experience I just had. Until that moment I was never able to understand what people meant when they said there was a future life.

Case #2: Unfolding During Surgery. Contact with the grandmother who had already died.
Patient: Mrs. V.D.S. from New Jersey, U.S.A.
Reported: By Sylvian J. Muldoon in *Projection of the Astral Body.*

When I was sick in the big hospital of Pittsburgh, I underwent a serious surgery. For the first time in my life I had anesthesia. I was just starting to inhale it, when I experienced a marvelous sensation of well-being and blessedness. But to my great surprise I saw together with the doctor and the nurse, in front of me, my body, lying on the surgery table, inert and lifeless. I saw medicine and surgical equipment on a table on one side. I even observed that the nurse's cap was on backwards, a fact that amused me.

I looked upwards and saw my dear grandmother coming through the ceiling; she had died 10 years before. She came close to me, took my hand, saying that we had to go quickly because we were short of time. We immediately passed through the ceiling as easily as if we had gone through a curtain of smoke. Then we were in the luminous atmosphere, and my grandmother called my attention to the landscape that looked familiar to me. She showed me the house where I lived, surrounded by beautiful trees. When I began to get enraptured with the sight, my grandmother said: "We do not have time anymore. It is necessary that you go back to your body!" And, before I could answer her, I woke in my bed, and saw the nurse curved anxiously over me...

This is what I had to relate about the experience of unfolding I had. That was a powerful revelation for me: if what happened to me is going to be repeated in the moment of death, then there is no use in fearing death.

Case #3: Unfolding During an Accident.

Patient: Dr. Overend G. Rose, physician.

Reported: In the magazine Light, 1932, Dr. Rose describes an accident he had when he was riding a horse; he was thrown violently from the horse and was unconscious for five hours.

During my unconsciousness, I saw my own body lying on the ground and the two men who picked me up. I heard them whispering that I was dead and I observed my body being taken to a house nearby. Soon afterwards two doctors arrived. They tried everything to wake me and, during the long hours that passed until they succeeded, I was always watching the scene. I hovered above my body in a warm, radiant atmosphere. There are no words to express the feeling of peace, of well-being, that invaded me. Then, suddenly, I heard a voice—I do not know where from—telling me that I had to get ready to reintegrate into my body and, as soon as I reentered it, I told the doctors that I would certainly be fine in a short time...

The most important facts about this strange experience are the following: First, I had never seen the two men who picked me up. They were strangers who were just passing by when the accident happened. However, I described their faces, clothes, horses and the cloaks they threw on a fence before they came running to help me. Second, even having been unconscious, I told the doctors about the difficulties the people had carrying me to the nearby house; and I could describe the seriousness of my

*injuries. And all this because my conscious personality was out-
side the body, and could observe things better than if I had been
in my body.*

*I declare that this extraordinary happening gave me an expe-
riential certainty that there is life beyond the tomb, where it is
not necessary to have a fleshy body to see, hear, and think; a
life where we keep our terrestrial personality.*

Case #4: Unfolding in Antiquity.
> **Patient:** Basilius, Egyptian.
> **Reported:** By Tacitus in *History—Book IV* and cited by
> Allan Kardec, in the book *The Book of the Mediums.*

*Over the months that Vespasianus spent in Alexandria waiting
for the season and the seasonal winds in which the sea offered
safety, many wonders happened through which were manifested the protection of heaven and the interest the gods had in
the prince...*

*These wonders doubled the prince's desire to visit the sacred
dwelling of God, to ask him about things concerning the Empire.
He ordered that the temple be closed to everybody while he was
there to hear what the oracle would say. Suddenly he realized
that behind him was one of the most eminent Egyptians, called
Basilius, who he knew was sick in a very distant place from
Alexandria. He asked the priests if Basilius had come to the
temple that day; he also asked the people outside the temple if
Basilius had been in the city that day. Finally, he decided to
send some of his men by horse to get news from Basilius.
Vespasianus learned that at the time he saw Basilius in the
temple he was at a distance of eighty miles. Since then he never
doubted that the apparition was supernatural and the name of
Basilius became a kind of oracle to him.*

Case #5: Unfolding With Movement & Embodiment in a
Medium together with the phenomenon of psychography.
> **Patient:** Sofia Swoboda.
> **Related:** By Alexander Aksakof in *Animism and Spiritism.*

*On July 20, 1858 a girl, Sofia Swoboda, was sitting at the table
with her family, having some punch to celebrate a special family
event; she was well-humored, calm and happy although a little
tired of her daily duties. Suddenly she remembered that she
had not done one of her homework assignments, a translation of
a text from French into German; it was supposed to be ready for
the coming morning. It was too late to do anything now: it was
11 o'clock. Besides this, she was very tired.*

Worried about her lapse, the young Swoboda left her family and went to the next room, thinking of her forgetfulness. She lamented even more because she liked her teacher very much. Then, without realizing the unusualness of the event and without showing surprise, Sofia persuaded herself that she was in front of the teacher, Mrs. W., and told her about her grief. Suddenly the apparition disappears and Sofia, relaxed, goes back to the family meeting telling them what happened.

The following day, Mrs. W. arrived at the due time and immediately told Sofia that she knew that her homework was not ready, and narrated the following in front of Sofia's mother: the night before, at ten o'clock she got her pencil to communicate with her ceased husband by means of automatic writing, as she was used to do, but this time, instead of tracing the desired name, the pencil started to formulate words in German, in a handwriting similar to Sofia's; there were nice words with which Sofia expressed her unhappiness about the homework she had not done because of her forgetfulness. Mrs. W. showed the paper and Sofia was convinced, not only that it was her handwriting, but that the words were the same she used in her imaginary conversation with the teacher. The young Sofia Swoboda attested that Mrs. W. was a person of great sincerity, unable to tell a lie. (Psychische Studien, 1789)

> ...We found another example of mediumistic writing executed by Sofia Swoboda's spirit in a session held in Moedling while Sofia was sleeping in Vienna...

On May 21, 1866—Pentecost Day—Sofia (she was living in Vienna at this time) had spent the morning at the Fair of Agriculture in Práter; she went home very tired and with a headache; after having a fast meal she went to her room to rest. When she went to bed it was 3 o'clock in the afternoon. Before she fell asleep she felt like getting unfolded, i.e., "leave her body and get independent from it." Her eyelids closed heavily and she was immediately transported to a room she knew very well: it belonged to a person that she also knew very well. She saw the person and tried to make this person see her, but she did not succeed. Sofia then went back to her room, but as she still felt quite well, she had the idea to go to her sister's father-in-law's house—Mr. Stratil—with the intention of making him a nice surprise. With the speed of a thought, feeling herself free, she had a quick look at Vienna and at the Wienerberg and then found herself in the beautiful country surrounding Moedling; there she was in Mr. Stratil's private office. In front of her were Mr. Stratil and Mr. Gustav B. who she liked very much and to whom she wanted very much to give a palpable, independent *activity of the spirit, since he had always shown a skeptical attitude towards this subject.*

She was absorbed with the impressions of her vertiginous transportation, and at the same time, she was feeling a kind of pleasant humor. Indeed, she was feeling admirably well, without any uneasiness or depression...

She spoke directly to Mr. B. in a happy tone when she suddenly woke up (in Vienna), due to yelling from the room next to hers, where her nieces and nephews were sleeping. She opened her eyes extremely annoyed. Very little was left of the conversation in Moedling which was suddenly interrupted.

Fortunately, Mr. B. had written down the whole dialog. Mr. Stratil added this to the collection of spirit communications. The conversation with Sofia, therefore, presented the graphic symbols of a spirit communication given by a medium.

Case #6: Frequent and Spontaneous Unfolding.
Patient: Miss Emilie Sagée.
Reported: By the same Alexander Aksakof, in *Animism and Spiritism.*

The Apparition of the Double to the Young Emilie Sagée

In 1845 there was an institution for noble girls in Livonia (and it still is there) called the "College of Neuwelck." It was situated approximately 36 English miles from Riga, one league from the little town of Volmar. At that time, Mr. Buch was the dean of the institution.

There were forty-two students, almost all of them from noble Livonian families; among them was the thirteen year old, second daughter of the Baron from Güldenstubbe.

Among the teachers was a French woman, the young Emilie Sagée, born in Dijon. She was of the Nordic type: blond, blue eyes, chestnut brown hair, with a beautiful appearance. She was slender, of good height, pleasant temperament, kind and happy, but a little bit shy, nervous and excitable. She was of very good health and during the year and a half she was in Neuwelck she did not have more than one or two light indispositions. She was intelligent and very well educated. The directors were always very satisfied with her teaching and her aptitudes during the time she worked there. She was thirty-two years old.

A few weeks after she entered the institution strange gossip about her began to spread among the students. When one student said she had seen Emilie in a certain part of the building, frequently another one affirmed that she had met her in a different place at the same time, saying: "This is not possible, because I just saw her passing by those stairs," or even affirm-

ing that she had seen Emilie in a far away corridor. At the beginning the students thought that there was a mistake, but the experience was repeated and repeated. After some time the girls thought that something strange was going on and told the other teachers.

Though the teachers had been informed what was going on, they declared, either by ignorance or by intention, that all this did not make sense, and that there was no reason to give the fact any importance.

But things got more complicated and there was no possibility of fantasy or a mistake. One day Emilie Sagée was giving a lesson to thirteen girls, among them the young girl de Güldenstubbe. To make her demonstration more understandable, the teacher wrote the passage on the blackboard; the students saw suddenly, with great terror, two young Sagées, one beside the other. They looked exactly alike and they were making the same gestures. Only the real person had a piece of chalk in her hand and was really writing, while the other one did not have any chalk and was just imitating the movements of the one who was writing.

This caused a great sensation in the institution, chiefly because all the girls, without exception, had seen the second form and their description of the phenomenon was identical.

A short time after this one of the students, Antoinette de Wrangel, was allowed to go to a nearby party with some of her colleagues. She was busy with her "toilette" and Miss Sagée, with her habitual bonhomie and kindness, was helping her to button the back of her dress. When the girl turned around, she saw two Emilie Sagées in the mirror, both busy with her dress. The girl felt so terrified with this sudden apparition that she fainted.

Months went by and similar phenomena happened several times. Once in a while the students saw her standing behind herself while she was having dinner, imitating her movements without fork and knife and food. Students and servants witnessed these facts in the same way.

However, the double did not always imitate the movements of the real person. Sometimes when Emilie got up from the chair, they could see the double sitting on the chair. One day when Emilie had the flu, the young Wrangel decided to read to her. Suddenly she saw Emilie getting pale and contorting as if she would faint; the girl got scared and asked if she was feeling worse. Emilie said "no" in a very weak voice. A little later the girl went back to Emilie's room and saw very clearly the double of the sick teacher striding across the room. This time the girl controlled herself and did not say anything to the sick Emilie. A *short time after she left the room she went down stairs and, very pale, told the others what she had witnessed.*

The most notorious case, however, of this activity, the indepen-dent apparition of two forms, is certainly the following:

One day all forty-two girls were in the same room, busy with their embroidering. It was a big room on the ground floor of the main building. There were four large windows in this room, or better four large glass doors that opened directly to the stair landing and to a very large garden. In the middle of the room was a big table where the different groups of students met to do their needlework and other activities.

On this day the girls were all sitting at the table and could see perfectly what was going on in the garden. While they were working they saw Miss Sagée, busy in the garden, picking flowers near the building—one of her favorite activities. At one end of the table a teacher was sitting in a green Moroccan leather armchair, supervising the tasks. At a certain moment this lady left the room and the armchair was empty. But only for a short time, because the girls could suddenly see the form of the young Sagée sitting there. Immediately they turned their eyes to the garden and saw Miss Sagée picking flowers, only her movements were slower, heavier, similar to those of a drowsy or exhausted person. Again they looked at the armchair where the double was sitting, silent, motionless, but seeming so real that if they had not seen Miss Sagée in the garden and did not know that the double was sitting in the armchair without having entered the room, they would believe that it was the teacher herself sitting there. Nevertheless, two of the more courageous girls, convinced that it was a real person and not being used to this kind of extraordinary apparition, went near the armchair and touched the apparition. They believed that they were feeling a kind of resistance, comparable to what they would have felt if they had touched some light fabric of muslin or crepe. One of them even walked in front of the armchair, passing through a part of the form. In spite of this the double remained there for some time; and then it dissolved gradually. Immediately, the girls noticed that Miss Sagée had restarted collecting flowers with her habitual liveliness. The forty-two students verified the phenomenon in the same way.

Afterwards, some of the girls asked the young Sagée if, at that moment, she had not experienced something peculiar; she an-swered that she only remembered having thought the following while she was in front of the empty armchair: "I wish the teacher had not left the room; certainly these girls are going to waste time and do some naughty things."

These curious phenomena lasted, with some variants, for approximately eighteen months; i.e., the time the young Sagée had her job at Neuwelck (during part of the years 1845-1846). There were some spells of one or two weeks when everything was calm. These manifestations happened chiefly when she was very busy or expending a lot of effort in the fulfillment of her duties. It was noticed that the clearer and more consistent the double became, the more rigid and weakened became Miss Sagée, and reciprocally, the more dissolved the double got, the stronger became the corporeal being. She herself was not conscious of what was going on, and only came to know about the phenomena when other people told her; usually the eyes of the present people advised her, but she never had the opportunity to see the apparition of her double, neither did she feel the rigidity and the inertia that took over her when the double was seen by other people.

Over the eighteen months in which the Baroness Julia de Güldenstubbe had the chance to witness and hear about these phenomena, there was never a case in which the apparition was at a great distance—many miles—from the corporeal person. Sometimes the double appeared when Miss Sagée was walking in the neighborhood, but the distance was not very big. Usually it happened inside the building. All the inhabitants of the institution had seen her, The double was visible to everybody without distinction of sex or age.

Such extraordinary phenomena could not go on for over a year in an institution of this kind without causing harm. Since the apparition of the young Sagée's double was confirmed, first in the classroom and later throughout the institution, the fact reached the parent's ears. Some of the more timid students became very excited and agitated each time they witnessed such a strange and unexplainable event. Obviously, parents started to have reservations about having their daughters under such strange influences, and many of the students who went on vacation did not come back. At the end of eighteen months there were only twelve students left of the forty-two. In spite of the reluctance they felt, the board of directors had to dismiss Emilie Sagée.

When she was dismissed, Emilie, desperate, exclaimed in the presence of Julia de Güldenstubbe: "Oh! It happens already for the nineteenth time. It is hard to stand it!"

When asked what she meant by this, she answered that wherever she has been—since the beginning of her career as a teacher at the age of eighteen (she had already taught at eighteen places before she went to Neuwelck)—the same phenomena occurred resulting in her dismissal. Because the boards of directors of these institutions had always been very satisfied with her job, they gave her very good recommendations. But, each time, she had to look for a new job as far as possible from the previous one.

After she left Neuwelck she lived nearby in the company of a sister-in-law who had many young children. The young baroness Julia de Güldenstubbe visited her and got to know that the three and four year old children knew about the peculiar unfolding of her aunt, and they were used to saying that they had two aunts Emilie.

Later on Emilie Sagée went to the countryside in Russia and the young Julia did not hear of her anymore.

I received information about the details through the young Julia de Güldenstubbe, who authorized me to publish them with the indication of names, places and dates; she was one of the students who remained at the institution of Neuwelck all during the time that Sagée taught there; nobody else could give a more exact report of the facts with all details.

In this preceding case, we have to exclude any possibility of illusion or hallucination. It seems to be difficult to admit that the numerous students, teachers and directors of nineteen institutions underwent the same hallucinatory influence caused by the same person. Consequently, there is no doubt that it really was a case of apparition in the exact meaning of the word: a real unfolding of a corporeal being that was even more evident because the double, in many cases, was doing something different than the person herself was doing.

APPLIED APOMETRICS

THE POWER OF MIND

Free in the reservoir of Space, the infinite cosmic energy is permanently at our disposal. However, in spite of the availability that makes her virtually our domain, almost all of us live ignoring it: we refuse to acknowledge its existence just because it is not in a *state* with which we are acquainted. In fact, it does not have the characteristics of the energies identified in other forces. And *if it is not electromagnetic, neither does it have a definite wave length, it cannot exist—we think.*

In spite of this fact, this inexhaustible energy constitutes a force in a potential state, an infinite field of something that escapes from our understanding: energy *in its resting state*[18],

---

[18] According to neurophysiology, thoughts and other messages are transmitted through nervous impulses using neuron structures in which electrical activity occurs. This electrical activity manifests itself as resting potential and action potential.

highly moldable, sensitive to forces that act upon her. And the mind, the mind under the action of the will is the operative tool that moves, molds and directs—with unlimited power—the energy of this infinite ocean.

If the operator, in conscious volitional action, mentally commands the agglutination of this energy, there will be a moment when there is an accumulation or intensification of this potentiality (generating a state of disequilibrium in relation to the environment) and *the energy is ready to be projected, molded, or manipulated* in any form we want, so that things can be *created.* If, for instance, we want to create food to sate a hungry spirit, it is enough to project the thought on the infinite ocean of energy and take out "something" that, *condensed* by the will, is going to transform it into the fanciest food we want to serve.

It is in this way—exactly like this—that superior spirits build houses, make furniture, vehicles, etc., in the astral world. It takes few hours to do this, sometimes even less using material taken from the cosmic source. We, on the physical plane, would take months or even years to construct equivalent things: starting the project, preparation of the land, etc.

The mind, the spirit's instrument of expression and *consciousness* (consequently *our* mode of expression, as we are spirits even if we do not admit it), has conditions for operating in the astral world, with all possibilities of success, according to the will of the operator and the released mental energy. The modeling power or the desegregating power that we have in this dimension is similar to the one we have in the physical world while we are incarnated. Thus, we act in this world that surrounds us, and transform it according to our will: we mold, create, construct, destroy within our present physical, volatile, ambient and energetic conditions. But we have to observe that all these achievements originated in our minds; everything is always, at first, the result of our imagination, and becomes concretized according to an act of will. Although this seems obvious, if we were permanently conscious of this reality our world would be much different. And, perhaps, we would not use only 20% of our mental capacity as we now do.

The *Open Sesame* for the world of the spirits, the magic key to actuate this dimension parallel to ours, is mental energy impelled by an act of will, by a firm and objective *will* that is transformed into *power.* We must realize that it is the same volitional act that actuates and gives us power over the physical world, an act that is in the origin of the conquests of every civilization and of the destruction of Hiroshima. The action of mental energy is not significantly different in the incarnated or disincarnated spirit. The alteration seems to be only a factor of time. In the physical world, everything takes more time to be constructed, since it is necessary to overcome the matter and the inertia of the mass. In the astral world, everything is faster.

This acknowledgment and the constant practical exploration of these open possibilities, in dealing with the spirits, constitute the secrets of the success that we have had so far in assisting them. To the spirits this is not new, since André Luiz, an eminent disincarnated doctor, wrote about this subject in his book *The Laborer of the Eternal Life*. In the chapter "The Sublime Visitor" he describes the formation of an artificial landscape in a big bubble of a transparent vitreous substance, where a spirit coming from the Christic dimension was going to get materialized (in the astral). In the description we can see the difficulties that André Luiz and two fellows of his faced when they participated in the creation of the landscape. We are going to reproduce this passage, because we consider it extraordinarily clarifying:

> *To another class of observers, the Instructor Cornélio could seem excessively methodical and rigorous; however, not to us, who could feel his profound sincerity and the deeply-rooted love for sacred things.*
>
> *After a long interval, designated to our mental preparation, he went on, without any affectation:*
>
>> *We will project our mental forces on the crystalline screen. The picture that is going to be formed will consist of a symbolic landscape, where gentle waters, personifying peace, feed a vigorous tree that represents life. I will assume the responsibility of the creation of the trunk, while the leaders of the missions intertwine the creative energies to make the lake tranquil.*
>
> *And addressing us especially, the more humble collaborators, he added:*
>
>> *You will form the covering of the tree and the vegetation that is going to surround the serene waters, as well as the part of the firmament that is going to cover the mental picture.*
>
> *After a short pause, he concluded:*
>
>> *This is the picture that we are going to offer to the exceptional visitor who is going to talk to us in a short time. Let us heed to the signals.*
>
> *Two helpers were posted beside the small camera, at attention, and when the harmonious signal sounded, we*

all entered in profound concentration, emitting the potential of our innermost forces.

I felt, due to the pressure of my own effort, that my mind was moving towards the crystal compartment, I imagined that I was entering it, placing bunches of grass beside the drawing of the lake to come... Using the vigorous energies of imagination, I remembered the kind of plant I wanted in this temporary creation, bringing it from the terrestrial past for this sublime hour. I structured all the details of the roots, leaves and flowers, and I worked, intensively, in my innermost I was reviving remembrances and placing them on the picture, with all possible fidelity.

When the signal of interruption was given, I retook the normal position of someone who was observing in order to examine the results of the experience, and I contemplated it. Oh! What a marvel!... There was the fundamental compartment totally transformed. Waters of indefinable beauty and an admirable sky-blue color reflected a corner of the firmament, watering the roots of the venerable tree whose trunk was telling silently of its own grandeur. Wonderful miniatures of cumulus and nimbus clouds were parked in the sky, apparently hovering very far from us... The borders of the lake, however, were almost nude and the branches of the tree were only scarcely covered.

The Instructor addressed us firmly:

> *My friends, your obligation was not integrally fulfilled. Pay attention to the incomplete details and demonstrate your power with the necessary efficiency. You still have fifteen minutes to complete the task.*

We understood, without any major explanation, what he wanted to say and again we became focused to consolidate the details that were missing in the landscape.

I tried to give more energy to my mental creativity, and with more readiness I got small flowers from little boughs remembering my functions as a gardener, in my beloved home that I left on Earth. I prayed, I asked Jesus to teach me how to accomplish the duties of those who wanted the blessings of his divine love in that Sanctuary and, when the signal sounded again, I confess I cried.

COUNTING: ENERGY IN PULSES

In our work in the "Garden House" we are used to handling great quantities of undifferentiated "raw-material" of the cosmic source in benefit of the sick. We create, for example, clean clothes for vagrant spirits; we offer tables full of food to the hungry crowd. With these energies we also treat the repugnant wounds of the spirits, of the disincarnated in deplorable conditions, who still have the sore spots they had when they were incarnated (due to scarce spiritual evolution, joined to the ignorance of the things of the spirit).

The free energy of the cosmos is extremely plastic: it condenses and agglutinates in obedience to a firm and experienced will. The *agglutination happens slowly*, according to the counting; each number, pronounced, is an energetic pulse designed to produce a segment of what we intend to create; so, going on with the counting, 1...2...3...4...5..., slowly part by part, we reach the final result—which is so fast that it amazes people. At the end of the counting or of the forming pulses, we see what we wanted to create.

In a few seconds—a maximum of fifteen—we reconstitute an arm, or a member that was amputated in an accident or for any other reason, and because of which the disincarnated patient still suffers terrible pain. At the end of the counting, when we visualized strongly the reconstruction of the injured part, we ask the spirit to palpate this part. To his surprise, the member is on its proper place and in *perfect condition.*

We believe that here is the highlight of this technique. In spite of the surprising effects, we cannot call these reports fables because we have been observing these facts for more than twenty years, there are witnesses to these results that are not only impalpable spirits, thankful and surprised with the wonderful gifts that literally fell "from heaven." There are the mediums too, that witnessed the successes of these creations in the astral plane, chiefly because they participated in these creations. And, of course, there are the patients themselves.

There is no mystery in this form of operating mental and cosmic energy, and *there cannot be* any mystery. The counting only gives the rhythm to the flux of the energetic impulses or *pulses.* There is no mystery about the number seven or about the tone of the voice or the acts and gestures of the operator. We have to discard any idea about rituals or ritualization of the volitional act, it is a simple and lovely wanting based on the certainty that whatever we *want* will happen or will be obtained. In all these facts we saw *phenomena.* Phenomena that, for this reason obey well-defined laws, so much that we can establish enunciations for most of them.

ADVANTAGES OF THE APOMETRIC TECHNIQUE

If seen from the scientific point of view, the technique is basically simple. It is so transparently simple that we ask those thousands of workers who help in our charity sessions, at Spiritist centers, to pay attention to it.

Usually in these sessions we intend to treat the obsessed through dialectics. We try to show the incorporated spirit that he does not have his physical body anymore. We try to convince him that, "now," he has to live as a spirit in an environment of spirits. Among other petty things, we even tell the suffering spirit that a spirit "does not have a body."

Let us examine the reactions of these poor spirits, comparing them to ours. How much would we care, for example, about explanations telling us that Matter does not exist, that it is constituted of pure Energy, if we are suffering from the terrible pains of a burning? It is obvious that before we hear about the truth of physics—and even understand it—we have to relieve our pains. And it is also obvious that the suffering spirits need this, too. It is a *pressing* and immediate need that by no means is achieved by naive dialectics, even if it is well-meant. When they hear that the spirit "does not have a body," they probably will misunderstand it; it might even sound like mockery to them. For them the astral body is as palpable as the physical one is for us.

Due to all the benefits, uses and advantages of Apometrics, it would be advisable that the use of its techniques be multiplied in order to involve the maximum number of spiritual workers, or, at least all those who are able to apply the technique. We know that there are many of them. And, by experience, we know that the use will only be complicated if the candidates and operators—due to lack of interior preparation—act like the sorcerer's apprentice and get lost in the trap of vanity. This book offers everyone everything we have learned. And this is not only because we are interested in serving, but is also due to the determination of our spiritual mentors.

In the "Garden House" we have been healing people through Apometrics for decades. Cripples, vagrant, exhausted spirits, real errant skeletons, have been brought to us to receive the vital energies they needed. We—all the participants of the works—provided what they needed in large amounts, healing and relieving their pains. There are also those, as we mentioned before, who, extremely hungry and thirsty, eat and drink as much as they can, of what is on the tables full of food, blessing the unexpected adventure that is offered.

Then they are oriented. We show them the goodness of Jesus, the opportunity and the possibility of progress they will have, from that moment on, in better astral regions where they will be taken after the meal. We clarify, we give them the light of Good-News. And they follow it.

In this way, with the palpable benefits that they can feel, the so-called indoctrination becomes powerful, since our words only reinforce the positive effects they feel. Therefore, they easily can be conducted in masses, on a kind of conveyor belt, to be installed in large buildings of the astral colonies, specialized in recovering entities of this kind.

We would like to make clear that the work is greatly facilitated because the mediums are apometrically unfolded. Outside of their physical body they are always with the sufferers, helping the spiritual workers guide them to the places where they get assistance, and—*what has always been extremely important to us*—they give detailed information about the operation of redemption.

When we assist obsessors we do not care only about them. As we have already mentioned (and now do again to emphasize the fact), we also take care of their accomplices, because they never act by themselves—they usually are in the company of spirits of the same level of evolution. If we helped only the obsessor, we believe that our work would be incomplete, since we would leave an indefinite number (sometimes a very large number) of suffering and needy entities without assistance. If we take care of all of them, the work of de-obsession will be more efficient and profitable once the number of benefited spirits becomes enlarged. This will cause obvious and excellent results with respect to the incarnated who started the assistance, as we can well imagine.

APOMETRICS VERSUS BLACK MAGIC

If we use the apometric technique and the inexhaustible provision of cosmic energy, we can hold back, with much more efficiency, the thrust of the black sorcerers and the spirits that are prone to ominous tasks. We keep them in powerful fields-of-force and separate them from the incarnated they harm. At the same time, we try to locate the astral line bases where they are sheltered; these are sometimes real fortresses, where, with great safety, they supply themselves with energy and plan and execute their malefic actions against living people. Once they are located and dimensioned, it is easy to de-activate them.

One technique of de-activation involves preparing mediums and supplying them with special equipment: protective body-suits, instruments and other tools that may be necessary, created through mental force upon the reservoir of cosmic energy. Unfolded by Apometrics and well-equipped, the mediums make raids in which they use charges of high explosive power to demolish the buildings, power plants, prisons, laboratories, etc., that these institutions have and that are turned to evil. This kind of technique, used to de-activate the bases of the "Umbral,"[19] has been used for more than twelve consecutive years, with total success. During these years, one of the groups that work for the "Garden House" deactivated over a thousand of these bases.

According to these results we can easily evaluate the importance and the value of Apometrics. We would like to emphasize that it allows us, the incarnated, to penetrate with absolute safety, in the cracked and indescribable depths of the inferior astral, in these fortresses armed against the harmony and well-being of the inhabitants of the surface of this planet. It gives us conditions to mine these fortifications—so we can right them afterwards—and observe the explosions that destroy everything (when we are safely re-coupled to our bodies), commanded by the operator.

GOLDEN RULES FOR APOMETRICS

Here, however, we have to trumpet a vigorous alert to those who are enthusiastic about the subject. At the foundation of all this work—as it should be with any spiritual work as a matter of fact—there must be LOVE. Love is the foundation. Always.

The techniques that we indicated are efficient, without any doubt. We recognize that the control of these subtle energies is fascinating—once we also suffered from this fascination. But if everything is not impregnated with *charity,* there is no use doing it. And there is more to it: besides charity, and as a natural consequence of it, humility must also always be present, as well as the disposition to help anonymously. If there is a lack of love and a disposition to *serve just for the pleasure of it,* there is danger of a misapplication of the techniques—as well as of the source of cosmic energy—which can become satanic due to their disagreement with universal harmony. We would like to give this advice: only through obedience to the evangelic commandments, can experimenters and operators enjoy safe conditions to penetrate the secret mysteries of nature, with the adequate use of these "unknown forces."

---

[19] See the chapter, "Matter — Energy — Space."

THE FORCES USED IN APOMETRICS

THE MENTAL FORCE

We have been discussing the use of the free, potential cosmic energy that corresponds to the *process of Space condensation*. We also showed that the mind is the operative tool that molds, moves and directs, with unlimited power, this energy of the infinite cosmic ocean.

The mind is, therefore, one of the forces that the apometric technique uses. Or better, it is a power *plant*. It produces a kind of energy different from the one we commonly use, of which we can identify certain characteristics such as frequency, wave length, reflection, refraction, chemical or photoelectric action, etc. But there is no doubt that the energy of mind is of radiant nature once the thought is able to transmit at a certain distance. And it can be captured, almost integrally, by individuals gifted with a special sensitivity. It can also act on solids, a phenomenon largely studied in Parapsychology ("psycho-kinetic effects" or "PE").

If thought is radiant energy—a wave in propagation—it has to be ruled by the same laws that rule electromagnetic energy. We know that an electromagnetic wave is composed of two energetic beams (or waves, or fluxes), which cross in two planes at an angle of 90°, that maintain the same axis of propagation. (See the Magnetic Flux diagram below.) Consequently, mental energy has a flux vector, thought has direction and a point of application—that is the object of thought. This flux acts on free cosmic energy, molding it.

THE ZETA FORCE

But besides these energies—the cosmic and the mental that are so subtle that they are compatible with the spiritual fields or dimensions (mainly the astral)—there is another one, as subtle and important as the other two, that also actuates in our work of Apometrics.

It is the energy from our physical bodies, this prosaic, but extraordinary energetic source. Constituted of Matter, our bodies are, in reality, a condensation of energy, that when released, would be sufficient to supply energy to the whole state of Rio Grande do Sul for over one hundred and sixty years.[20] It is a fantastic force, but is repressed in our atoms and molecules, dispersed in our magnetic fields, a kind of *energy, that certainly moves and is directed by the acts of our volition.* With this energy at his disposal (because it is in his

---

[20] See the section *Space, Reservoir of Infinite Energy* in the chapter "Matter — Energy — Space."

own body), the apometric operator can form powerful magnetic fields-of-force to hold back rebellious or demented spirits and crowds of astral evildoers. As another example we can point out the supply of this physical energy to unfolded mediums, impelling them on astral trips, when they are on duty fulfilling their missions.

ENERGIES IN ACTION

According to everything we have observed and experimented with along our work, we could solidify an understanding, from a scientific point of view, about the *mode* these phenomena are processed.

When the *cosmic plasma* gets condensed (perhaps this is the best definition for the undifferentiated cosmic energy), a lowering of frequency happens in its mass so that this plasma, now already transformed in radiant energy by the action of the rough energy *let off* by the physical body through an act of volition, functions as the bearing wave; it becomes a continuous flux under the command of the mind oriented by volition. As it is a flux of vectorial form, it has to behave in the same way as the Poynting vector. Everything indicates that the cosmic plasma (which we call K, kappa) behaves as a magnetic vector of a very high standard of energy, joining the vector of the vital force Z, that must function as the heavier electric flux of the Poynting equation:

$$\vec{\Sigma} = \vec{K}.\vec{Z}$$

Where $\vec{\Sigma}$ (sigma) represents the active Poynting vector.

We can see that the equation is the same that we have in physics. And its application to this kind of phenomena, although it might be strange to excessively spiritualized brains, has shown efficacy as a formula that makes an explanation possible.

Any direct action of the vector $\vec{\Sigma}$ on Matter has to be considered a rare exception. It appears in very rare cases, probably due to the predominance of the vector Z in the equation. An example of this can be seen in the sensitive donors of etheric energy (ectoplasmics).

Each time the volition of the apometric operator commands and gives the rhythm, by counting in a high voice (1... 2... 3... 4... 5... 6... 7) the projection of mental energy that helps the condensation, beams and gives direction to the energies of these two main sources, the Z (animal energy of the physical body), the resultant vector, $\vec{\Sigma}$, and the equation:

$\vec{K}.\vec{Z} = \vec{\Sigma}$ are responsible for the apparent "miracles."

We will give another example—it may look commonplace, but is taken from our routine works: a supply of energy.

We sent a group of mediums, unfolded by Apometrics, to a city 2 or 10 Km distant to assist a person who asked us for help. The command to project the group to that city was given and, when the mediums finished the counting, they complained about being unable to penetrate into the house; all of them had the feeling they "did not have fuel anymore" to go ahead. We repeated the counting (1...2...3...4...5 6...7) and Σ̄, the flux vector, is applied to the group and fulfills its function: the mediums enter the house and assist the patient. If the group asks for a cleansing of the place or a projection of light to keep away the astral Darkness, we command the accomplishment of what they are asking for and, with a new counting, K̄, Z̄, and Σ̄ they clean and illuminate exactly as they wanted. We repeat: there are no mysteries, numerological mystics, taboos or rituals. Everything is clear, absolutely rational and has resisted to the precise scientific testing in experiences that have lasted for a quarter of a century.

QUANTUM MECHANICS VERSUS BLACK MAGIC

To see the reasons of our conviction clearly (and as the theory is confirmed by practical experience), we report another case, among the thousands that we have assisted.

End of 1984.
In the "Garden House" of the Spiritist Hospital of Porto Alegre, during an exhaustive assistance of a large number of sick people, we had to face an obsessor that had the terrible characteristics of a black sorcerer. He did not manifest violence, neither did he show hatred. He smiled, very sure of his power, with the serenity of one who knows in advance that he is the winner.

*In front of such reactions, the experience makes us foresee that we will have a great and laborious challenge for our capacity of helping. These spirits—black sorcerers—are able to accumulate great knowledge about sorcery and its techniques, which they handle very well; sometimes they are also masters in the art of torturing people. In addition they know much about transcendental physics, and above all, about magnetism. It is not in vain that they show superiority, polite and calm manners with which they mock those that challenge them. They are really fearful. It is very difficult to hold them back because they protect themselves with a variety of expedients: sophisticated fields-of-force, sacred amulets they got when they were initiated in a temple in past times (and which they go on wearing in the astral), and even **gigantic atomic plants** (that is right: **atomic**)* sited in their well-organized bases in the inferior astral, guarded by an unimaginable retinue of guards and helpers. As they used to know, very deeply, advanced techniques to manipulate vital human energy, they are extremely dangerous. Once they are embodied, they suck the vital energies of the mediums while they are speaking. This obliges us to double our attention to the changes, even the least and subtlest ones, that the mediums can present—as, for example, sudden weaknesses, or light indispositions. With the black sorcerers our proceeding has to be direct, very objective. Prolonging dialectics, even if it is a very nice talk, only makes them laugh at us, mocking at our naiveté, as we can observe in kardecist sessions. To annul them we have to annul the initiation they had received (this is equivalent to a dis-initiation), by deactivating their magnetic powers which they have abused rampantly, sometimes for millennia. The normal and correct procedure is to conduct them immediately to the past, to the temples where they received the initiation, and withdraw from there any objects that helped them to get power, destroying them immediately: chalices of sacred oils, knives for sacrifices, prayers, registration of their names in the temple, in addition to bracelets, scepters, rings, amulets—anything that contributes to or was used during their priesthood which they are not honoring anymore, because now they serve evil.

But let us go back to that morning in 1984, when we learned an even more objective way to deal with them.

The sorcerer smiles in front of us, overflowing with confidence. He resists everything. We command a field-of-force to paralyze him. Another one. A stronger one. But nothing limits him, nothing imprisons him. Apparently guessing our intention, he anticipates a gesture to divert our magnetic projections.

We were going through these difficulties when grandmother Joaquina (an extraordinary spirit full of love and wisdom, who appears in the "garment" of an old black woman) embodies in one of the mediums and says, as if she wanted to help:

My zinfio[21], do you know what is espin[22]?

We did not understand well what she wanted to say. She probably wanted to say "spine." But what spine? And why?

We did not even think that grandma was referring to quantum number **spin**. But she calmly repeats the question:

Did you not study this?

Surprised, we started to understand and we told her "yes," we knew perfectly what spin was.

---

[21] My son—Black Brazilian slave's vocabulary.
[22] Espin or spin (the same)

*"So then invert his spin, and you will see what will happen!"
grandma said while she was spreading her right hand open,
projecting magnetism in the sorcerer's direction.*

*We started the counting, commanding the formation of an in-
tense magnetic field that would provoke a change in the angular
moment of the sorcerer's astral body's* **spins,** *displacing them
by 45°. Finishing the counting with the number seven, the effect
is instantaneous. The sorcerer gets such a shock that he falls
apart, entering total unconsciousness. Grandma Joaquina very
happily takes advantage of the situation and conducts the
sorcerer to the place where he will recuperate, in her astral city
(near the planetary crust above Rio Grande do Sul).*

This case is a good example of how knowledge of the laws of
physics and mechanics can be applied to both the physical
and the astral dimension, *mutatis mutandis.* We have to admit
that on the level of spirits—and at least on the astral level,
certainly—nothing seems to happen beyond quantum physics.
Mediums have been attesting to the truth and the constancy of
this because they answer immediately and in perfect obedience
to the laws of quantum physics in the most varied situations;
when they are subjected to energetic fields to get unfolded, in
embodiments, syntonies, energy agglutination, holding back
malefic entities, resonance, and other energy applications,
commanded by the operator. Among them we would like to
emphasize projections in order to couple unfolded patients and
mediums to their physical body, as well as the phenomena of
transduction and vibratory resonance. We will see them later
as they are very important.

MAGNETIC FLUX

Density Vector of the Magnetic Flux

Poynting Vector $\vec{S} = \vec{H}.\vec{E}$

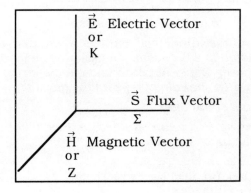

Mental magnetic flux vector $\vec{\Sigma} = \vec{K}.\vec{Z}$

In the human body:

Σ = Mental magnetic flux vector
K = Cosmic plasma vector
Z = Vital (animal) energy vector

Propagation of the Electromagnetic Wave

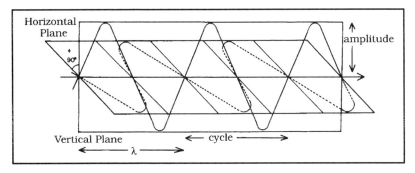

λ = wave length
ν = frequency (cycles per second)
Cycle is the complete wave: the positive semi-wave plus the
  negative semi-wave

APOMETRICS & THE OSCILLATING SPIRITUAL SYSTEMS
COUPLING

Coupling, in physics, is the joining of systems—mechanical,
electrical, optical, etc.—where there is a transference of energy
from one system to another. It is especially important when it
happens between oscillating systems, as in the case of electronics and devices of electromagnetic energy transmission.

In the same way as there is coupling in the physical world, it
happens also in the *spiritual systems*. The joining between
spirits and mediums, for example, happens between oscillating
systems, at other vibrating levels, that escapes from the
sensors of the measurement devices. As a proof of this fact, we
have the case of telepathy, where the mental wave is felt by the
sensitive, that sometimes are at very distant places; however,
as far as we know, up to now, not any needle of a measuring
device oscillated and quantified the wave.

In the physical field we use special devices designated to vary
the conditions of the electric current to get electromagnetic
energy with defined characteristics. These inter-mediation
devices (resistors, condensers, etc.) modulate the receptivity,
the condensing and the induction action, etc. of circuits to

make the functioning of the system operate in perfect equilibrium. Once the energies are adjusted, the vibratory sympathy causes the coupling.

In spiritual coupling the transference of energy usually happens in only one direction. The medium operates as the donor of the energies to the communicating spirit; because of this, and to facilitate the contact, we have to make the medium's frequency vary in the moment of coupling until it is ready for the joining: the function of the medium can be compared to that of variable condensers in radios—the part of the radio that allows us to syntonize the broadcast stations. When the spirits are of low vibration—or "heavy spirits," charged with dense, negative energies—this variation is achieved by commanding the *lowering* of the medium's vibratory frequency using rhythmical impulses (when we use counting). Otherwise we increase the medium's vibrations by giving them commands, and by counting if the communicating spirits are superior—"light," or of high vibration. This frequency modulation allows the medium to syntonize the unknown spirit giving him the flux of ideas and emotions.

To make this clear, we return to physics and its equations.

The electromagnetic flux is vectorial. And the Poynting vector indicates its intensity.

$$\vec{S} = \vec{H}.\vec{E}$$

($\vec{H}$ = magnetic vector. $\vec{E}$ = electric vector) The flux vector $\vec{S}$ gives the final magnetic action. Being associated and on three planes, the three vectors form an electromagnetic wave:

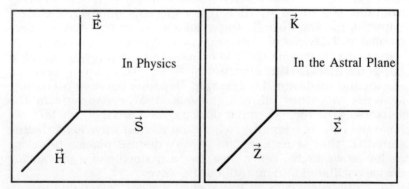

In the coupling of spiritual oscillating systems, the operator's mental force moves the cosmic plasma (K) and the animal energy (Z) of the physical body of the operator himself, to act through the vector $\bar{E}$,on the communicating spirit's oscillating system:

So, in the operator's action, the Poynting vector (or flux) $\bar{\Sigma}$, of the equation $\bar{\Sigma} = \bar{K}.\bar{Z}$, represents the *applied mental flux.*

(The coupling of a medium's apometric command to the communicating spirit implies, therefore, the action of the operator's oscillating system upon the medium's oscillating system aiming at the syntony of the medium with the communicating spirit's oscillating system.)

From what we have observed over many years, we have reasons to suspect that when we apply energies with the objective of varying frequencies (be it of the incarnated or disincarnated spirit) we are, in reality, ordering the angular moments of the atomic *spins,* if not of the whole astral body—at least of his neuronal emissions. The total sum of these tiny individual energies form the energy of the *electromagnetic* flux of this kind of field.

Despite the many studies and experiments over the years, our interest in knowing all the technical details of a perfect coupling has not yet been exhausted. On the contrary, it has been growing more and more. As Apometrics implies unfolding phenomena or bilocation, the return to the physical body is part of our routine—it is the last stage of each session. Our worries about the health, the physical and spiritual conditions of mediums and spirits, obviously compel us to learn everything to make this return and the coupling with the physical body as fast and perfect as possible. In addition, there is the constant need to improve the coupling techniques of communicating spirits to mediums. Coupling techniques imply the manipulation of phenomenon with multiple and natural subtleties, through the adjustment of frequency, from the communicating spirit to the medium, using vibratory resonance.

VIBRATORY RESONANCE

Resonance, in physics, is:

> *...the phenomenon that occurs when an oscillating system (mechanical, electric, acoustic, etc.) is stimulated by a periodic external agent, with an identical frequency of the receptor's fundamental frequency, or in one of its harmonic frequencies. Under these circumstances, there is an easy transference of the external source's energy to the system with oscillations that can be of large amplitude. If there is no weakening of the wave, the amplitude can reach an unlimited value; in practical cases, the weakening of the wave, due to loss of energy, limits amplitude.*

Now:

> ...*the transference of energy from an electromagnetic field to an atomic system (material conductor) in the presence of a magnetic field, can occur due to the absorption of the energy of the inducing system, by the nuclei or by the orbital electrons of the receiving system.*

This is magnetic resonance.

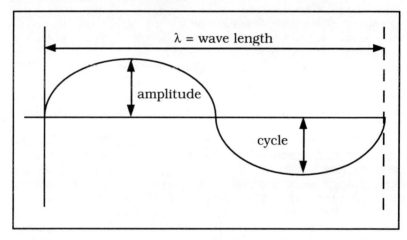

Frequency (ʋ) = number of cycles per minute
Cycle = complete sine curve
Wave length (λ) = the trajectory made by oscillating energy in
    motion

In the spiritual field, resonance is the transference of the energy of a radiant, inducing system to a radiant receptive system that has syntonic frequencies.

It is a mental phenomenon. The sender spirit's energy of thought (incarnated or disincarnated) is caught and absorbed by the receiving spirit's mental energy, be he incarnated or disincarnated. This energetic transference makes the receiver suffer the *influence* of the energy coming from outside. His mental state varies from the better to the worse, his fundamental frequency gets higher or lower according to the characteristics of the inducing influx. If the frequency is lowered, the receiver is not going to feel well, and according to the state of disharmony that the lowering causes, he can even fall asleep. (There is a gradation—according to the potency of the inducing influx: from the sensation of tiredness, to the feeling of a heavy weight on members and head, the bad feeling takes over the whole body, causing sometimes nausea and finally he reaches a declared morbid state.) When the influx raises the fundamental frequency of the receiver, the opposite happens. He is going to feel fine, light and lucid.

To examine the importance of the phenomena of resonance, we would like to remind that black magic, in the final analysis, is a process of intense lowering of frequency, duly manipulated to generate destruction, suffering and disharmony. To compress the vibratory frequency of their victims violently down, the black sorcerers use devilish processes of long range, where they study the victim, his habits, his affective life, his flaws, vices, trends, financial ambitions, possible spiritual defenses, and mainly the quantity of enemies he had in the past as well as their malefic potential.

Another kind of resonance generates a psycho-pathological syndrome, which we call the *Syndrome of Resonance With The Past*, with well-defined symptomatology, pathology, therapeutics and prognosis. We will see this phenomenon, with more details, in Part II in the chapter "Resonance With the Past."

To illustrate the process of vibratory resonance, we report a case of simple vibratory resonance.

Illustrative Case

Patient: E.N., female, white, married, 36, nurse.
Religion: Protestant.
Biotype: Ecto-Mesomorphic.

In 1975, the patient, a nurse, came to the "Garden-House" because she suffered from a strange and persistent allergic syndrome. She complained about sudden allergic crises, with serious hypersensitivity of her skin and some light rashes followed by intense itching that ended up in apparently indelible and generalized purplish spots. Some days afterwards the spots suddenly vanished without any therapeutics.

The patient reported that, at the beginning, doctors thought it was an exaggerated sensitivity to certain kinds of medicine or an allergenic antiseptic, although the disease did not present the typical characteristics of "contact dermatitis." Following medical advice, she did not use these substances any more and was subjected to the action of the most modern therapeutic arsenal, from various kinds of desensitizers to the more active corticosteroids, reinforced by a rigorous diet. The morbid situation that started spontaneously six months before was not any better with the therapeutics, although there were periods when the skin became absolutely normal.

When the patient came for spiritual treatment we realized, even before we started the unfolding process, that beside her there was a disincarnated spirit who was suffering very much.

As we always do in these cases, we first assisted the suffering spirit. We embodied him in one of the mediums and started the treatment.

He was a worker who was badly burned when a boiler exploded and, after a few days of intense suffering, died. He went on suffering in the astral; the periods of suffering alternated with days of torpor, but he did not know the duration of each period. When we touched the medium in which he was embodied, he screamed in pain, trying to show us his members which were already decomposing. He knew that he was disincarnated but he did not get rid of the burns.

We made him feel relaxed for some moments and applied magnetic passes on his astral body. Under the command of counting, we projected large masses of vitalizing energies on his body, with an intense wish that his members be healed and that his suffering comes to an end, IN THE NAME OF JESUS.

After some minutes the worker showed surprise when he saw that he was perfectly well, his burns were healed and he was finally free from those terrible pains. He was so surprised, and so great was his joy, that he asked us if what happened was a miracle. He wanted to know if we were saints...

Now, much calmer, he told us about the accident, the disturbance, the anguish he felt when he realized that he was disincarnated, amidst so many strange people. In erraticity he was ousted from wherever he went by the other spirits, due to his awful aspect and the bad smell of his breath. Extremely exhausted and depressed, he went to the hospital where the nurse E.N. worked. He wanted to be helped. But he got frustrated again, he was ousted by other spirits who took over empty beds where they made themselves comfortable. It was then that he saw the nurse E.N. by chance in her routine tasks, assisting sick people. He went close to her, expecting to get some help, a treatment that would reduce his sufferings and pain. He felt very attracted by the nurse's aura of harmony; he had a feeling of well-being that he had not experienced for a long time. He also felt safe, because he was not driven away by her.

From this moment on he felt relieved. But at the same time he caused rashes on his incarnated friend's skin. It seemed to be an allergy, that, as time went by, became transformed into a morbid state of a skin disease, unresponsive to any treatment. As the cause of the disease was not in the physical field, it resisted any kind of medical treatment. It is a process of vibratory resonance. Everything that the sick spirit suffered from went, by means of a slow filtering, to the physical body of the nurse. The problem became worse as time went by because, as

the magnetic ties became stronger and stronger, the disharmonic energies that filter to the nurse's body also became more
and more intense.

As we always do in these cases, we treat the spirit with great
kindness. Once he is healed and relaxed, we remove him to the
Love and Charity Hospital, the astral institution that helps us in
our assistance to incarnated and disincarnated spirits.

While we were assisting the spirit, physicians of the spiritual
world were taking care of the nurse's astral body that had been
apometrically unfolded and conducted to the same hospital. The
wounds of her astral organism passed to her somatic body as
always happens in these processes of slow evolution.

Discussion:

It was a typical case of **spiritual induction** caused by vibratory resonance. The sick spirit did not want to harm the patient,
by any means. He became disturbed by the prolonged intimate
magnetic contact and because of his serious sickness. Besides
this, as the patient was a sensitive, she received the disharmonic vibration in an easier and more intense manner. The
stronger the magnetic ties got, the worse she became. As soon
as the spiritual allergen was removed and her physical body got
rid of the irritating toxins, the nurse recovered from her annoying
skin rashes.

Time of treatment: 30 minutes.
Number of times the sick was assisted: Once.
Observation: Cured in one month.

WE, THE MEDIATORS

The incarnated operator attracts cosmic energies (K), manipulates them (i.e., agglutinates and condenses them), and mixes
them with the vital energies of his own body (Z), to transform
their vibratory frequencies into a magnetic mass of energies
that can be assimilated by sick spirit's low frequency. Finally,
he projects these masses on the needed in the astral plane,
relieving their pains or even healing them.

Acting this way, the operator functions as a *transducer*. He
receives, transforms and projects energies.

Transducer[23] *(Phys.)—Any device capable to transform a kind
of signal into another kind, with the objective of transforming a
form of energy into another one, making the control of the phenomena possible, enabling measurement, etc.*

---

[23] *The New Aurélio Dictionary*, First Issue, Eleventh Printing.

This operator is also a modulator because he modifies the attracted energies when he mixes them with the energies of his own body. Lowered in their original frequency, but of intensified flux (as if it passed through a transformer from high to low tension), they are in conditions to actuate in the frequencies of the astral plane and on the suffering spirits that are still prone to sufferings and diseases.

Modulation[24] *(Phys.)—A process in which a characteristic variable of a periodic phenomenon is attributed to a variable determined by another one of these phenomena.*

As we can see, for a *spiritual* work to succeed, it is imperative to know and apply the principle of physics well. The treatment of our disincarnated brothers loses mystic nebulosity and becomes transformed into an *exact* science, once we know that the laws that rule these phenomena are immutable.

Everything depends *on having conditions* to intervene in the free energies of the cosmos, agglutinate and transform them to apply them correctly to the sick of the astral. This process of mental manipulation, although it seems to be a mystery (or even a miracle), is quite simple. Success depends fundamentally, on love, an intense spontaneous and disinterested desire to serve ones fellows. This love should be crystalline, catalyzing these fluxes of curative energy in benefit of others.

One can never repeat this often enough: love is capable of everything in the great world. If you are full of love and have the sincere desire to harmonize, heal, illuminate and elevate your fellow beings, you only need to count in a high voice (usually from 1 to 7), imagining the agglutination of energies in large white fluffs like cotton, invisibly spread in Space. As the counting goes on, we have to imagine them denser and denser, and malleable. When we say the last number we project the active masses on the sick of the astral (for this purpose it is not necessary that we see them).

The results—*all experimenters will realize this*—are always spectacular. In a few instants the spirits start manifesting themselves surprised and satisfied with the cure or well-being that they got almost by enchantment.

THE CURE OF PHYSICAL DISEASES

In principle the same process can be applied to living, incarnated people with identical results. Jesus is the example: He cured sick people of various kinds of diseases, leaving milestones of light which can be imitated. And it was not only He who did this: His close followers, through an ardent life of love,

---

[24] Op. cit.

expelled demons, made blind people see and the paralyzed walk.

We are convinced that the process is the same. The laws are the same. However, when we try to apply them on the incarnated, the results are frustrating: by far they are not comparable to the effects of the counting with the projection of energies on the disincarnated.

What is the reason for this failure?

If success is so satisfactory—and certain—when we provide enormous quantities of curative forces to the sick of the astral, why then, are we not able to heal—not even to improve—a physical wound? If physical cures were performed by the followers of Christ in all periods, it seems to be elementary that they can be repeated.

As far as we know, the difficulty is in Matter itself that, because of its density, creates insurmountable energetic conditions. *Any* operator who has sufficient love, good-will and mental training can cure spirits. But with physical bodies it is different: the dense constitution of Matter challenges the energetic potential of our mind.

We should not forget, however, that this *miracle* is possible because it depends on the correct equilibrium of the use of energies, that, as we already know, are *palpable*. Everything depends only on the solution of a problem of physics. If we have mental power of sufficient intensity to mold the energies according to their material density, and if we are able to interfere in the *molecular cohesion* to make Matter become plastic and moldable according to our volition, we will be in the same conditions as the Divine Master, to perform the same wonders.

This kind of mental energy certainly is not merely intellectual—which so many people use and frequently *abuse*—in spite of its being brilliant and lucid. *No, the frequency must be another one.* Divine emanation, it can only be the force that radiates naturally from the beings of higher evolution that are not tied to mundane and individualist interests. As Jesus said, these beings are Gods—co-creators of the Divine Work.

There will be a day, we are sure of it, on which a purified humanity, radiant of love and mentally powerful, will know how to act on the molecular cohesion and operate the complete harmonization of the physical bodies. It is only a matter of time. If we know the laws that indicate the road, treading this road will only depend on love. Love under volition and present from the first step on.

LAWS OF APOMETRICS

FIRST LAW: LAW OF SPIRITUAL UNFOLDING
(BASIC LAW OF APOMETRICS)

— Enunciation:

Every time we give an order of command to any human being, be it in an experimental or normal situation, aiming at the separation of his spiritual body—astral body—from his physical one, while we are projecting energetic pulses through slow counting, there will be a complete unfolding of this individual who, however, keeps his consciousness.

— Technique:

Apometrics is based on this general Law. In the field of animistic phenomena, the application of this technique represents a real discovery. It makes it possible to explore and investigate the astral plane quite easily. It obviously does not allow us to penetrate into the dark depths of the innermost part of the planet, neither does it allow us the ascent to the spiritual pinnacles, but through it we can assist the disincarnated in erraticity with inestimable advantages for them as well as for the incarnated who suffer from their obsessions.

The technique is simple. By giving the command, energetic impulses are emitted by means of counting, in a loud voice, as many *numbers* as necessary. Usually, seven are enough—i.e., *counting* from 1 to 7.

SECOND LAW: LAW OF PHYSICAL COUPLING

— Enunciation:

Every time we give a command to an unfolded body's spirit to reintegrate with the physical body, (the command is given together with progressive counting) there will be an immediate and complete coupling in the physical body.

— Technique:

If the unfolded body is far away from the physical body, we first command that he return close to the physical body. Then we project energetic impulses (or pulses) by means of counting and at the same time give the command for the reintegration in the physical body.

If the coupling is not completed, the person feels dizziness, indisposition and a feeling of emptiness that can last for some hours. Generally, the coupling is spontaneous and occurs in a few minutes (even without a command); there is no danger of somebody remaining unfolded because the physical body exerts an automatic attraction upon the astral body. Nevertheless, we should not leave a person unfolded or poorly coupled to avoid any kind of indisposition, even if it is transitory. Therefore, if we see the least symptom of an imperfect coupling, even if we only *suspect* that it was not perfect, we repeat the command for the coupling and repeat the counting.

According to what we have observed in *thousands of cases*, seven to ten impulses of energy are enough for both an unfolding and for the coupling in the physical body.

THIRD LAW: LAW OF ACTION AT A DISTANCE, BY AN UNFOLDED SPIRIT (LAW OF ASTRAL TRIPS)

— Enunciation:

Every time we order an unfolded medium's spirit to visit a distant place, giving this command together with the energetic pulses by means of slow counting, the unfolded spirit will obey the order, keeping his consciousness and having a clear and complete perception of the environment (spiritual or not) of the place he was sent.

Important Note: This Law is usually applied to those sensitives who maintain their clairvoyance when unfolded.

— Technique:

We order the unfolded medium to visit a certain place and, at the same time, we emit energy together with slow counting. He immediately moves, following the impulses of the counting, to reach the determined place. As he keeps his psychic sight, he accurately describes the physical and spiritual environment, including in this last a possible action upon incarnated spirits.

This kind of unfolding requires certain care with the physical body of the medium who must be resting—and should not be touched.

— Illustration:

Narration of a treatment, at a distance, of a case of simple obsession, through apometric unfolding and application of the technique of depolarization of the memory (see the chapter "Depolarization of the Memory Stimuli.")

    Patient: M.S., female, white, single, 19, student, living in the State of Minas Gerais.

Two years ago, she started suffering from deep psychic depression with constant crying. Sometimes she had crises of laughing without any reason, which caused her to have intense pains in the front of the heart. The morbid situation had gotten so bad in the last months that the patient did not go out anymore. During the periods of crises she hardly ate. She had already consulted several doctors who did not find anything abnormal from the physical point of view. She was undergoing a psychiatric treatment that had not presented any positive result so far.

Exam:

At nine o'clock on June 7, 1975, two mediums (apometrically unfolded) were sent to visit the sick girl at her place in Minas Gerais; three disincarnated physicians went with them.

As soon as they arrived they reported what they saw: they observed that the girl had karmic implications. She was resting in an armchair, covered with a light blanket, in a dimly lit room. Together with her was an obsessor who was charging her past debts. The girl did not seem to be very well, due to a deep prostration she was feeling; that might have been caused by a medicinal sedation.

Treatment:

We commanded the creation of a field-of-force and there we gathered the obsessor, bringing him to Porto Alegre for a treatment. We embodied him in one of our mediums and he started telling us his story.

He was very revolted with events that happened in his previous incarnation when his wife, M.S., betrayed him with a friend. Abandoned by everybody and extremely revolted, his intense suffering culminated with his premature death. Frustrated because he could not take revenge at that time, he looked for his wife and found her already reincarnated. He could then charge her debts; he started to harass her. Soon afterwards his hatred became even worse when he got to know that M.S. was going to get married again. In his spiritual blindness he wanted to ruin her in any possible way.

We tried to explain things to him.

Under command, projecting energy through counting, we made him go back in time. The cause of his present suffering unfolded in front of his eyes. In a previous existence he had made the mistake that he condemned his wife for: he abandoned in the worst possible misery, his legal wife and his children, to live with his sister-in-law. When he got to know about this he became surprised and confused.

Taking advantage of his state of perplexity, we told him about the great Law of responsibility and of his unfoldings along time. He listened to us attentively and, at the end, he agreed to give up his spiteful intentions, allowing M.S. to follow her destiny. He was then conducted to the Love and Charity Hospital, of the

Astral, where he was to undergo appropriate treatment after getting more detailed explanations.

Keeping the obsessor away, we went back to M.S.

We unfolded the girl carefully, from a distance, and brought her quickly to our room where she embodied in one of the mediums—as if she were a disincarnated spirit.

The treatment consisted of depolarization of the memory function of her brain. This would make her forget the negative images transmitted by the obsessor and the other ones that, by means of resonance with her own past, had been filtered to her brain during her present life. She rid herself of the mental scenes she had created, parasitic mental currents of exaggerated animism. Free from these disturbances, the deterioration of her nervous system stopped and the cure was automatic.

To complete the treatment, we printed the idea of health and happiness in her brain, we instilled harmony, the desire to eat, hope for a happy future with her fiancé, etc. At the end we conducted her back to her physical body. We did the coupling and activated the chakras.

M.S., or rather her body, was sleeping in the armchair all the time the treatment lasted.

Discussion:

This case is the one of a patient with simple obsession, since the obsessor did not join any sorcerer of Darkness, neither did he use any sophisticated technique. The obsession, however, advanced very much in the victim's mind, so much that she was already having mental disturbances. M.S. got mixed up with the appraisal of values and the repercussion of them on her behavior. Consequently the configuration of her personality was being changed, a fact that would fatally crystallize in "madness" in a short time.

Incidental syndromes:

— Simple obsession by one obsessor.
— Resonance with the Past.
— Self-induced parasitic mental currents.

Treatment:

— Assisting the obsessor.
— Assisting the patient through Apometrics, at a distance, with her embodiment in one of the mediums.
— Depolarization of the mind's stimuli.

Duration of treatment: 30 minutes.
Number of sessions: One.

Observation: Two months later, the patient was cured and got married.

FOURTH LAW: LAW OF THE FORMATION OF FIELDS-OF-FORCE

— Enunciation:

Every time we visualize the formation of a magnetic barrier by means of magnetic impulses through counting, there will be fields-of-force of magnetic nature being formed, circumscribing the aimed special region the way the operator imagined it.

– Technique:

We strongly visualize a magnetic barrier and project energies to have it become concrete by counting from one to seven. A simple, double or triple field-of-force with different frequencies is formed according to our wishes. The density of these fields is proportional to the mental force that generated them. We make use of this technique to protect working places and, chiefly, to hold back rebellious spirits.

The ancient Egyptians were experts in this technique. Their fields-of-force have lasted up to today, as we have verified. They used them to protect their tombs, to magnetize mummies and for other purposes.

The form of the fields is of great importance: the pyramidals, and mainly the tetrahedrals, have such a holding capacity that once the rebellious spirits are put inside, they cannot leave unless they are allowed to. Inside these fields, spirits can be conducted to any place with complete ease and safety. We discovered that the dihedral angles of the pyramids have special properties: it is very difficult to break them and, if they break, it is under the action of a kind of energy that spirits do not have.

FIFTH LAW: LAW OF THE REVITALIZATION OF MEDIUMS

— Enunciation:

Every time we touch the body of a medium (head, hands), visualizing the transference of our vital force while we are counting the pulses, this energy will be transferred. The medium will receive it, feeling himself revitalized.

— Technique:

We think strongly of the transference of our physical body's vital energy to the medium's physical organism. Next, we take the medium's hands or put our hands on his head, counting slowly.

At each count some mass of vital energy—coming from our own metabolism—is transferred from our bodies to the medium. We usually use this technique after magnetic passes on very de-vitalized patients. It allows us to work for three or four hours without any considerable wear. We transfer vital energies to mediums every thirty minutes so they can work without expending too much energy.

SIXTH LAW: LAW OF THE CONDUCTION OF THE UNFOLDED SPIRIT FROM AN INCARNATED PATIENT TO THE HIGHER PLANES, IN THE ASTRAL HOSPITAL

— Enunciation:

Unfolded spirits of incarnated spirits can only go up to the superior planes of the astral if they are free from magnetic clogs.

— Technique:

It is common to unfold a patient in order to conduct him to the superior astral plane (for treatment in hospital) and find him already outside his body, totally involved in sweat, cloth adhering to his astral body, ties, fetters and all kinds of clogs of a magnetic nature, put there by obsessors interested in harming the patient.

In these cases it is necessary to make a perfect cleansing of the patient's astral body. This can be done very quickly by the mediums' unfolded spirits. If they cannot untie the knots or if they are not able to take off these annoying obstacles, the work will be done by the people who are assisting them.

We have to keep in mind that the passes which are habitually given in Spiritist centers are inefficient in these cases, since a pass acts only upon the patient's aura, chiefly in the vibratory field.

Frequently we furnish energies to the unfolded mediums to enable them to take off these clogs and other heavy material from the patient. We would like to remind the reader that the transfer of any kind of energy is always done through counting. We insist: counting up to seven is not any mystic or magic act. Usually seven to ten energetic impulses are sufficient for these cases.

SEVENTH LAW: LAW OF THE ACTION OF AIDING DISINCARNATED SPIRITS UPON UNFOLDED PATIENTS

— Enunciation:

Aiding spirits act with much more ease upon the sick if they are unfolded because, in this form, some of them are in the same spatial dimension.

— Technique:

When patients are in the same dimensional universe as the protector spirits (physicians, technicians, and other workers) the diagnosis and treatments are faster and deeper. Diagnoses tend to be more precise and the astral surgical operations are also facilitated because, almost always, the patient's spirit is taken to astral hospitals where there is a large variety of equipment, highly specialized resources, and where they use very advanced medical techniques.

Unfolding patients with Apometrics contributes decisively to the success of their spiritual treatment—and it can also be an important support in the treatment of spirits. We believe that the day is not far off when medicine will be unified: with incarnated physicians taking care of physical ailments, their disincarnated colleagues in charge of the spirits' sicknesses—incarnated and disincarnated physicians working together.

As most diseases—*maybe 80% of them*—start in the astral body, we can well imagine the extension of the use of Apometrics, especially in the field of mental diseases. For these, therapeutics will be largely facilitated, because it allows both treatment and the removal of the obsessors who are the most frequent causes of psychopathologies.

EIGHTH LAW: LAW OF ADJUSTMENT OF THE DISINCARNATED SPIRIT'S VIBRATORY SYNTONY WITH THE MEDIUM OR WITH OTHER DISINCARNATED SPIRITS, OR OF THE ADJUSTMENT OF THESE WITH THE PLACE WHERE THEY WILL BE SENT TO, AT A CERTAIN MOMENT

— Enunciation:

We can carry out the vibratory joining of the disincarnated spirits with mediums or between disincarnated spirits. And we can syntonize these spirits with the environment to which they were sent, so that they can feel and perceive clearly the vibratory situation of the environment.

— Technique:

When we want to contact a disincarnated spirit of a vibratory level compatible with our evolutionary state we project energy in the form of rhythmical pulses while we command the psychic joining.

Through this technique we establish the vibratory syntony between the sensitive and the disincarnated, largely facilitating communication. It opens the syntonic channel between the fundamental frequency of the medium and the spirit. Emitted by counting, the energetic pulses make the sensitive's frequency vary, similar to what happens to radio receivers when we move the dial of the variable capacitor until we establish resonance with the oscillating source (broadcast station) that we want.

If the visiting spirit is of a very low vibratory standard or if he is suffering intensely, the medium lowers his vibratory tone to the level of the entity and remains in this situation until the spirit leaves. As soon as the dis-embodiment happens we have to raise the medium's vibratory standard. If this is not done the sensitive will go on suffering from the spirit's limitations for a while, manifesting sensations of anguish, oppression, indisposition, etc.—everything alike to what the spirit was feeling.

It is common to see mediums leave a Spiritist session complaining about feeling indisposed, psychically exhausted, and even sick. In effect, this only happens because they had been in syntony with suffering spirits for some time and, when the spirit left, resonance had not been adequately made. In well-oriented works, at the end of the sessions, the spiritual plane frequently uses the resource of embodying a *guide* in one of the mediums to proceed with the vibratory cleansing. (This procedure is common in works of Umbanda.[25])

In works of de-obsession, oftentimes circumstances require that rebellious spirits be confronted with constraining situations of the past or future in order to enlighten them. These unfriendly brothers usually do not accept this constraint, perhaps because they do not want to recognize themselves as being the characters of the rough dramas that are shown to them—they are resistant to admonitions, even love. In these cases we make them *feel* the environment; i.e., we make them enter in resonance with the oppressive vibrations that they provoked in the past, in order to make them understand the disharmony they generated and the obvious consequences of these acts. As soon as we project energy in the form of pulses, by counting, syntony gets established. And it will remain so until the vibratory field is annulled on the order of the operator: that makes the entity come back to the present. When this happens, our bitter brother will feel peace and be completely enlightened. It could not be different, for when he sees the scenes, feels and relives them, the spiritual transformation is automatic. The karmic concatenation implies an instantaneous enlightenment.

---

[25] A cultural form originated from the assimilation of Afro-Brazilian religious elements by the urban Brazilian Spiritism. *The New Aurélio Dictionary*, Second Edition, Seventh Printing.

NINTH LAW: LAW OF THE SPIRIT'S
MOTION IN SPACE & TIME

— Enunciation:

If we order a spirit to go back to a certain time in the past while we emit energetic pulses through counting, the spirit returns to the time in the past that was determined.

— Technique:

We used to send the spirit to the past to show him his way of living, his cruel behavior, and other events previous to his present existence, with the objective of clarifying the laws of life. At times we have to show him the divine injunctions that made him live in the company of enemies. With this knowledge he can proceed to achieve harmony with his enemies; this may also lead to other beneficial consequences for his evolution. Knowledge, here or on the spiritual plane, is *light*. As soon as any disincarnated sufferer becomes enlightened—feeling the functioning of the Karmic Laws—he is taking a decisive step towards his evolution because his past painful way of life will be clarified with the whole series of such painful effects.

We also use this technique, with great success, to conduct black sorcerers to the past, to annul the energetic fields they received in initiation ceremonies in temples of the past.

TENTH LAW: LAW OF DISASSOCIATION — TIME-SPACE

— Enunciation:

If, due to the factor of time, we place an embodied spirit in the future, under the command of energetic pulses, he suffers a **quantum leap,** *dropping into an astral region compatible with his vibratory field and of* **negative specific karmic weight** *(K_m)—becoming immediately subject to all K_m energy which he has.*

— Technique:

We call K_m the specific weight of a person's karma; i.e., the negative *karmic energy* with which he is loaded. It is the *karmic mass* of a certain person which has to be redeemed; as it is individual, we consider it specific. The factor m indicates the disharmonic malefic mass.

This Law is important because one of the techniques for the treatment of simple, but recalcitrant obsessors, is based on it.

We have observed that when a spirit is dissociated from the space in which he used to be (by means of the acceleration of the factor time), he makes a real quantum leap (similar to that of electrons inside atoms). The dissociation from normal space does not happen progressively, but rather in steps, until he gets installed in the space of a hostile future; a space frequently occupied by horrid beings, compatible with the vibratory frequency of the recently-arrived traveler.

In these cases of dissociation from Space-Time, there occurs a very interesting phenomenon. When time is accelerated, the karmic load to be redeemed—which normally is distributed along time, some 300 years, for example—gets accumulated, all at the same time, on the spirit. This causes a terrible feeling of oppression, of which he starts complaining. We can take advantage of this annoying moment, presenting them as a proof of the consequence of his acts and their negative repercussion in cosmic harmony.

The technique is very simple: we project magnetic energies, by rhythmic pulses and counting, on the embodied spirit and, at the same time, we order him to jump into the future. (This technique can only be used to enlighten disincarnated spirits.)

The quantum jump happens right away and the spirit sees the new environment, feeling its deep hostility. There is an abrupt meeting with the whole negative karmic mass which causes great annoyance to the culprit.

We have to be careful with the spirit during this meeting. If we disconnect him suddenly from the medium, without special preparation, he might be literally *smashed* by the accumulated energetic field. His body will be destroyed and transformed into an ovoid. We have to disconnect the spirit from the medium before he slowly comes back to the present time.

This process is easy to understand. When the spirit is projected into the future, he will be living in a new equation of time, since he has not lived the future yet, but his negative karma (K) goes on overloading him. As this K has not been redeemed yet, it also has not been distributed yet along time: it remains condensed and accumulated *on* his astral body, compressing it. Therefore, if we disconnect him suddenly, the whole negative mass (not yet distributed to other incarnations) falls altogether and at once on him. And then he is reduced to an "ovoid."

It is as if the spirit had a truck full of bricks that should be unloaded over several days, but, by accident are unloaded all at once, and on his head. Smashing would be unavoidable.

ELEVENTH LAW: LAW OF TELLURIC ACTION ON DISINCARNATED SPIRITS THAT AVOID REINCARNATION

— Enunciation:

Whenever a disincarnated spirit which possesses quite a strong mind and intelligence succeeds in resisting the Law of Reincar-

nation, halting the application of this Law on himself for a long time (due to mean interests of power and domination over disincarnated and incarnated beings), he suffers the attraction of magnetic planetary masses, syntonizing himself slowly, but progressively with the planet. His vibratory standard decreases because the planet acts destructively on him: it deteriorates the form of the spirit and everything that surrounds him, ending in a slow but inexorable degradation.

— Technique:

Adaptation to the environment is the dynamic of life. The biological sciences study the various levels of complexity and the evolution of life. But the source of life is the spirit. And the environment of the spirit is eternity. Every time he reincarnates—diving into a certain time of the planet, of a certain country, a community, a family and human beings with which he is going to live—each time there is a new *germination of Matter*, the spirit has again a meeting with cosmic and eternal options. Either he evolves, increasing his own light which he conquered in his former experiences in the night of time, or he involutes, making shadows, pains and horrors that he must tolerate to get readjusted to the cosmic harmony he disturbed.

When a human being commits different crimes, perversions and vices which make him go backwards several degrees of his evolution, it is certain that he will feel many consequences when he disincarnates-incarnates. His spirit will take the form, adequate to the environment, that he himself built: his body will be degraded and become hideous, monstrous. He can be an *exu*,[26] for example. And when he sees that his fellows— good-looking when they were incarnated—look like animals, he will understand that the degradation of his form is following the degradation of his spirit. The legend of men who were transformed into animals (zooanthropy), in the astral, is a reality.

But these phenomena of deterioration of form are relatively rapid and transitory. Seen from eternity, they have the duration of a curable disease. The spirit, sooner or later, will reintegrate in the flux of reincarnation and then, living and dying, living and dying, he will again conquer the lost road.

Much more serious—*because it is irreversible*—is the awful deformation which spirits that transgress the Law of Reincarnation will suffer. It is not a common event because only those

---

[26] A divine being that represents the potencies contrary to man, that is considered similar to the Devil of the Catholic Church by Afro-Brazilians who respect him because they are afraid of him. *The New Aurélio Dictionary*, Second Edition, Seventh Printing.

extremely negative entities gifted with a powerful mind—as, for example, the black sorcerers—have sufficient conditions and rashness to despise life.

For five years we observed spirits that did everything to avoid reincarnation—they have been stopping their reincarnation for a long time, sometimes millennia—and we realized that they start feeling a subtle, almost unperceived, but slow and inexorable action of the planet's magnetism—coercive and primary. The astral body corrodes and frays, the spirit loses its normal appearance and aesthetics, and becomes transformed into a repulsive being. This process can be compared to a house that, as time goes by, shows marks of progressive ruin, such as cracked walls, loose plaster, etc. This degradation is so slow that not even the spirit realizes it. This is extremely serious, since the degradation, as far as we know, is not reversible.

We have already observed many black sorcerers with these marks of decay. More than thirty cases.

Nobody cheats the Divine Laws without being punished. He who is against the cycle of incarnations, repelling evolutionary opportunities; he who abhors as repugnant the experiences in his flesh; he who prefers illusions of power through the titanic control of incarnated and disincarnated beings (or of vast regions of the inferior astral), is fastened, unconsciously and automatically, to the planet's mass and submerges in it, in a tragic retrogression.

This phenomenon happens only to spirits that have sufficient intelligence and power to stop their own reincarnations over centuries. They are of great mental power, but they are inferior because they are still subject to the wheel of incarnations and depend on them to climb the evolutionary stairs. This kind of degradation never happens to the superior spirits that, due to evolutionary merits, do not need to incarnate any more. They are redeemed: they escape from the planet's magnetism due to the degree of de-materialization they have already reached.

We learned that the knowledge of this Law of Telluric Action is of paramount importance. It gives us profound spiritual lessons by unveiling the evolution of beings. And it also enlightens these hardened spirits, aged, surrounded by Evil through the malefic power of their minds.

Due to the importance of this Law, we will illustrate it with a case. We hope that it clarifies the details of the technique used to apply the Law.

— Illustration:

Narration of a treatment, through apometric unfolding, of a case of complex obsession, provoked by a black sorcerer affected by telluric action.

Patient: L.S., a young woman, 23, housewife, married for a few months.

L.S. came to the Garden House in October 1985, brought by her mother. She was in a lamentable state of psychic depression and physical prostration. According to the doctor's diagnosis, she had been suffering from schizophrenia for a short time. She was always of an emotional temperament, nervous, sensitive, afraid of diseases, disasters, and even of thunder. After the wedding the symptoms became more serious, in spite of the specific therapeutics she had been subjected to.

The parents had taken her to several spiritual sessions, trying to help her. They went to various Umbanda places (where the young lady had some relief) and many kardecist centers. Without any definite spiritual diagnosis, the lady had only the clinical diagnosis.

Besides prostration, the pathological manifestations were the following: auditory hallucinations (she was almost constantly hearing voices), persecution mania, exaggerated fears, unbearable anguish, and despair that was driving her crazy.

Exam:

We realized immediately that it was a case of complex obsession; besides suffering from the influence of perverse beings— real professionals of evil—the intellectual author of the obsessive process manifested himself right away. It was an entity of evil, criminal appearance and aggressive manners who protested violently against our "meddling in his private affairs." He raved, alleging that we did not know the causes of "justice" that he was applying to his victim, a low, vulgar criminal. In the past she preferred another man to him and she gave this man a large patrimony that, by right, would have been his because her father had promised him that he would marry her. He explained that, as he was abandoned, to survive he had to steal—a crime that resulted in public degradation, a vile prison and, finally, death: he was assassinated by an enemy.

When we exhorted him to an understanding, he decreased his bursts of violence. We told him that he and the lady were not at court, and that we even did not know the sick. What he was calling "interference" was only an act of solidarity for us, in answer to a request for help. He still went on threatening us for some moments, but then he decided to tell us—to show off and not because he wanted to be sincere—how he joined a vast organization of Darkness, specializing in tormenting creatures in all possible ways.

He revealed that in that unruly incarnation he fainted when he was stabbed by his enemy and the wound caused him awful pains. After a long period, he did not know how long, he woke up feeling extremely weak and realized that he was in the midst of inferior beings. Some were crippled, the majority were rotten people. It was a strange world of playful people without an organized life, who seemed to be crazy mockers in a state of inertia.

He succeeded in getting away from them and started wandering, over a long time, through the unknown region he was in. After some time he felt stronger and got to know that inhospitable place better. It almost looked like a desert, with poor vegetation and very little water.

Later on, he joined a gang of inferior spirits, where he got some power thanks to his fists and to violence. He started to enjoy the situation.

A continuous hatred was growing in his heart when he remembered the state he was in and the situations of grandeur he had dreamed of but lost due to the affective indifference of his fiancé. Therefore, he decided to find her and take revenge on her for his frustrations.

It took him a long time to identify her, now as L.S. She deserved the reincarnation due to meritorious acts she had practiced. But she also brought with her serious karmic debts to be redeemed, consequences of grave missteps in former incarnations, occasions in which she and her present persecutor went astray from the sacred matrimonial duties. The obsessor did not even suspect that the Divine Law made the two meet to promote readjustment and harmonization between them.

He got close to her with all his hatred, but he was not able to really harm her. He was advised by some accomplices to look for a powerful organization turned to evil, directed by a terrible sorcerer who was feared for his ruthlessness.

On a special day he was introduced to this sorcerer who taught him the art of persecuting the incarnated, with all kinds of techniques that he knew and to whom he became linked by ties of admiration mixed with fear.

The mediums had noticed a parasitic device implanted in the lady's brain, a fact that had already shown us one of the facets of obsession to which she was subjected. We asked the obsessor who the constructor of the devilish device was—a device that would be very difficult to remove. He told us that it had been his chief, the sorcerer, who made it and he himself installed it in the lady's brain on a night when she was taken to his laboratories, detached from sleep.

At this point of our conversation we told him that we would be very much interested in knowing such a powerful and intelligent creature and talk to him about the patient.

The obsessor got scared:

> Don't even dare to bring such a powerful chief here! You know, if he would come here, he would enslave you and your fellow workers. You do not have the power to make him come here. I advise you to keep quiet and not to meddle in his life. It would be better for you.

As we went on showing more and more curiosity to know this creature of such importance in the Umbraline[27] World, he said, almost in panic:

> Let us come to an agreement. Let him go, do not try to bring him here, because you will not be able to do this. I beg you, do not insist, because he would turn against me, thinking that I betrayed him. You cannot imagine how furious he gets when somebody betrays him or tries to escape. He is terribly cruel, he punishes the culprit severely; and then he mutilates them.

Without giving any importance to what he said, we commanded the creation of a powerful field-of-force of attraction, acting on the sorcerer's base. A short time afterwards came the impressive figure of the chief. He syntonized one of the mediums and embodied, but did not say a word. He just looked at us despisingly, as one who was evaluating the situation. At the same time he made light of us.

It was an imposing figure. Tall, upright, calm and arrogant—in spite of the rancor. Perhaps this was the first time he had been challenged by a mortal—with our "interference" in his business.

We felt that we were facing a being that was used to power, to command, and who was conscious of his possibilities.

We started the contact very politely. We thanked him for his presence and told him we felt honored to be able to talk to such a powerful personality, one of enviable intelligence.

As these beings are very proud, our words surprised him in some way. Although he did not answer, he agreed, with a gesture, to listen to us.

We talked about the accurate technique that he demonstrated when he constructed such devices and praised his advanced knowledge about the physiology of the nervous system, mainly

---

[27] It refers to the Umbral, a transitory place, the lowest region of the inferior astral.

about the clinical problem he created for the specialists of terrestrial medicine who could never have dreamed of the pathological consequences of the action of these electronic devices.

After this introduction, we started talking about spiritual laws and admitted that even we, the spiritists, knew very little about them. He went on in silence, but showed great interest in what we were saying. We seized the opportunity and went directly to the point:

> *Dear friend, we are very happy, as we already told you, for your having been so kind to come to our place. Our wish is to talk with you, dear Brother, about certain phenomena that we feel will be of great interest to you. It is about a spiritual Law that, due to its subtlety, escapes from any hasty observation. Its effects can only be observed on spirits that have not incarnated for a long time, perhaps for centuries, as is the case of you, our dear friend. When a spirit averts the laws of Reincarnation, avoiding the return to flesh (although there is a need to reincarnate to proceed with the evolutionary process), he starts suffering from a constant action of the Planet's primary magnetism and, after some time, he becomes totally deformed. Subjected to this abrading action, the spirit ages, becomes decrepit, and starts diving inexorably into the abyssal depths of the interior of the Earth.*

His eyes became sharp, staring at us deeply. But still he did not say a word. We went on:

> *We are going to show you a demonstration. We would like you to observe if what we say is really true. We are going to lower your vibratory frequency just a little bit so that we can link you strongly to the kind of work that you practice. You will perceive that you have already entered this deforming process, although you have not realized the horrifying phenomenon that is taking over you. My dear Brother, notice that this process of degradation is very slow. But it is inexorable, irreversible.*

When we lowered his frequency we placed an astral mirror in front of him. He became astonished. He saw himself modified. His hair was scarce, hard and unkempt. His face was rigid, of a yellowish color, his hollow cheeks made him look sick. Even his clothes looked old, torn and dirty. We insist:

> *Dear Brother, we are going to repeat the technique, so that you can better observe the reality of this Law.*

We repeated the experience calmly, so the sorcerer could see and feel it. He must have felt the frequency variation and consequent oppression when the vibratory standard was lowered because he suddenly yelled, surprised:

How come? I did not know this Law!

Nevertheless, my dear friend, it is real—as you could see. You got away from Christ, our redeeming aim, and, therefore, you are by yourself now, strayed from the Law of Evolution. You did not pay attention to the actual purposes of the Being, because you were busy showing off your power over a group of miserable slaves who obey you because they are afraid of you. You use all your intelligence in the sad occupation of tormenting your brothers in evolution. Now, my dear friend, you have to cope with the consequences of your acts. The moment of harvesting what you planted with such persistence, has come...

The perplexed sorcerer seemed to be meditating. We continued:

My friend, now you have two alternatives. You can go on with the kind of life that you have had so far. But obviously, you will increase the number of errors that already are weighing in your consciousness, and the whole load that is waiting for you in a tempestuous future, with innumerable horrors to redeem. You will be subject to the irreversible action of the Planet itself. In a short time it will paralyze you completely, petrifying you for an indefinite time in infernal regions. Now, the other alternative is to take another direction, getting rid of everything. But if you immediately and definitely abandon cruelty and the power over defenseless creatures, you have to get prepared, right away, to face redemption courageously until you can restart to work for Goodness—as a former initiate that you are. Please, my dear Brother, notice that this night is of paramount importance for your destiny. Feel free to make your decision. We are here to help you.

The chief bent, mute. Some moments afterwards, he made some gestures of assent with his head. He agreed with our orientation. We went ahead:

Dear Brother, we are very happy with your decision to return to Jesus. But it is necessary that you be stripped of your initiate's powers; they will only disturb you in your next incarnation. You know the vice of command is

not easy to eradicate. We will take you to ancient Egypt
to undo your Initiation.

The sorcerer was conducted to the past to have his powers
taken away: amulets, sacred prayers, sacred objects and his
registration in the temple. Resigned, he submitted himself without any complaint. We went on:

> Dear friend, do you allow us to act on your cerebrum, to
> erase from your "memory banks" the knowledge of sor-
> cery? This is indispensable for you to have a little bit of
> peace in your next incarnation. It is necessary that you
> ignore everything you learned about sorcery, everything
> that you used to practice Evil.

He agreed to undergo our technique of depolarization of the
memory banks.

We brought him back from the past to the present. His powers
and mental functions were totally annulled. The assisting team
of the Love and Charity Hospital took him for a pre-incarnational
treatment.

The base where he dwelled, in the inferior astral, was de-acti-
vated. The spirits he commanded were also taken to be recuperated.

Free from the parasitic devise and from the obsessor, L.S.
started, gradually, to feel better. So much so that she has not
returned to the Garden House anymore.

* * *

We would appreciate it if the workers involved in de-obsessions
observe the functioning of this Law, in order to confirm or deny
the result of our research. We have already treated many
sorcerers, about thirty, all affected by this Law which was identified in the Garden House after many years of observation. The
success is always certain, without any violence or constraints
for the entities. When they know the effects of this Law, that
acts on all beings in evolution in the psychosphere of the planet,
they submit themselves to everything.

The Law of Telluric Action can be mathematically formulated.
If we call Δ[28] (delta) the deformation that the Spirit suffers, "m"
the malignity that he presents, and "t" the time he stole from the
incarnations, we have:

$$\Delta = m.t$$

---

[28] Delta: from Greek *diastrofé*, deformation.

If we want to know the degree of malignity of the spirit, we have the following equation:

$$m = \frac{\Delta}{t}$$

(Malignity is directly proportional to the deformation)

TWELFTH LAW: LAW OF TIME-SHOCK

— Enunciation:

Every time we take a disincarnated spirit—embodied in a medium—to the past, he is subject to another equation of time. In this situation, the development of the sequence of time, as we know it, stops, and the present temporal phenomenon will overlay the past.

Motion creates a tension of potential energy between the present situation and the motions of the past. While the spirit remains embodied in the medium, nothing will happen to him; he will only live and see the new ambient situation that was proposed to him. However, if he is abruptly disconnected from the medium, he leaves the mediator's field of protection and becomes loose in the other Space-Time dimension. He, then, gets the total potential energy created by motion. The shock of this energy is strong enough to destroy his astral structure. The spirit is reduced to an ovoid, covered only by his superior spiritual structures: the atmic, the buddhic and the superior mental.

To avoid the spirit's suffering this kind of aggression when subjected to treatments in the past, it is necessary to slowly bring him back to the present, through *regressive* counting.

— Technique:

It is the same described in previous laws: the use of energetic pulses through counting.

— Illustration:

A narration of a patient who was being harassed by a gang of obsessive spirits, belonging to the group of black magic.

We started the treatment by undoing negative magnetic fields. And so we captured the commanders of Darkness. One of the chiefs, the strongest one, presented himself immediately, boasting about his extraordinary powers, challenging us to reduce him to impotence if we could. He laughed when we asked him to follow Jesus Christ. He revealed that he is an **orixá**[29] *defended by powers unknown to mortals.*

We answered that no real orixá works for Evil as he had been doing, and that now he had to undergo a long trip with us to the past, where his powers would be taken away. He went on laughing. He reaffirmed his superiority. He doubted that we were in any condition to lead him to the temples in ancient Egypt.

When we arrived in Egypt and started to take away his powers, he rebelled. He shouted that he was going away and nobody was going to impede him. As he had great mental power, he cut, abruptly, his magnetic ties with the medium, and left. But we immediately commanded the formation of a power-ful field-of-force, obligating him to return to the medium.

However, it was with surprise that we realized that the entity was totally annulled, presenting the classic syndrome of cortical de-cerebration. This means he was unconscious, as if he were in coma.

When he moved away from the medium, the false orixá received **Time-shock**, becoming unstructured. He did not know this Law and its phenomena.

In this Law there is no interference of the karmic mass, as we saw in the previous Law. In the past the spirit faces events that he had **already lived**.

From this report we can deduce that time, is also constituted of energy.

THIRTEENTH LAW: LAW OF THE INFLUENCE OF THE DISINCARNATED SUFFERING SPIRITS THAT STILL LIVE IN THE PAST, ON THE HARASSED SICK OF THE PRESENT

— Enunciation:

While there are suffering spirits in the past of an obsessed, the treatments for de-obsession will not be very successful. The sick will have some periods of improvement, followed by others of deep depression or psychomotor disturbance.

— Technique:

The first thing to do is to assist the obsessors that are around the patient, taking them to stations in the astral, specialized in the treatment of such cases.

We never should forget that any obsessor, or any sufferer, need only be treated once. If the treatment is done well, with due spiritual assistance, all the evil spirits are taken off in a

---

[29] An African divinity of Afro-Brazilian religions. *The New Aurélio Dictionary*, Second Edition, Seventh Print.

single contact. Leaving the obsessors free after a brief evangelic contact (as is done in kardecist sessions), is a mistake. We do not convince recalcitrant persecutors (or black sorcerers) only with a simple dialog of a few minutes. We reaffirm: this classic procedure makes our work ineffective. It is even harmful.

The removal of all these beings can be done in only some sessions.

If the sick afterwards do not present any definite improvement, we have to study previous incarnations. To do this, we have to open the frequencies of these incarnations, to assist the spirits that stopped in time. Usually they, themselves, are sufferers. Some of them are still chained in prisons, others live in caves or hide in the woods, scared, hungry, rotten. They slander those who harmed them, forming fields-of-force of hatred, despair and pain which can be extremely harmful.

When the incarnated sick receive the relief that follows the separation from the nearer spirits—the ones that are in the present incarnation—their relief does not become consolidated because the vibratory bands of low frequency, coming from the past, reflow and become present by means of vibratory resonance. The incarnated sick, participant or cause of those past barbarisms, continue receiving the emanations of these bands of hatred and pain. They feel intimate and indefinite anguish, suffering, and despair. And they will only be in peace when their past is cleared up.

From incarnation to incarnation we clean the bands of the past. Sick spirits, crazy and tortured spirits, are brought to the present and taken to the Charity Homes of the astral for an efficient treatment. And, at the end, when the sick incarnated manifests signs that his cure is consolidating, the persistent work of de-obsession—getting deep into the past—will have led him to regeneration and to light.

PART II

THE MALEFIC ACTION OF DISINCARNATED SPIRITS

INTRODUCTION

In all of history—about 5,000 years—humanity has enjoyed peace for very short discontinuous periods which, if summed up, total at most only 300 years. We have had a war of a hundred years. But—never—peace of a hundred years.

Predator, *par excellence,* man brought an appetite for violence, conquest and carnage from the caves. He was not able, yet, to get rid of these atavistic vices, in spite of the safe directions for liberation that the Gospels gave us, the most sublime code for behavior we have ever had. "Civilized" and without the pithecanthropic fur, we wage wars and fight continuously. We fight with neighbors over petty things, we support aggressions against weaker people and justify them in name of the "fatherland's" interest. Social problems are solved with violence. If there is no justice, we justify violence. We attack and kill because it is "necessary." Omnipresent egotism directs the actions of people and nations, and clouds the understanding between the rulers and the ruled.

Although the inexorable hole of the tomb is under everybody's feet, this fact has never diminished the fury with which values that took centuries to be accumulated, are destroyed. We act as if we were eternal, our "ego" polarizes our interests, makes us immediatists and creates inside us a vacuum that we usually try to fill with material things. However, we know we are not going to take anything with us from this existence, not even our corpse. Emptiness, therefore, instead of getting fuller, is going to be deeper.

The fight for life, justifiable in primary creatures, was rationalized on the basis of egotism. And violence, repeated and growing, has invented more and more sophisticated means of destruction—it is Science in the service of death—so apocalyptically efficient that, today, the fierceness of our ancestors seems to be ridiculous. We are scared that the least conflict between nations (even with civil wars or boundary problems) can degenerate into a general war, with atomic mushrooms razing the planet's life.

It is obvious that, although we have a series of advantages over animals, we have achieved a wonder of irrationality: we are progressing *against ourselves*. Our intelligence gave us technological marvels that push us to a terminal barbarism, to

147

the phantasmagoric condition of an inhospitable planet's inhabitants, a planet almost without life (if not sterile).

This paradox has always been inside us. We are the paradox.

As a matter of fact, the essence of it is that humanity has been in a state of rupture in relation to basic values, of the spirit. We can see that our crisis is spiritual, an extremely old problem. Through all these centuries, we have become so accustomed to using reason as our weapon that, now, we hardly perceive that the brilliance of our intellect only gilds and justifies our primitive impulses of cave inhabitants.

In this kind of context, the roots of the disincarnated spirit's malefic actions and all processes of spiritual obsession become quite visible.

In fact, every man keeps, on the other side of life, the same consciousness that animated him when he was alive. The same vice. The defects. Egotism. Impulses of aggression and violence. No one becomes a saint just because he died. On the contrary, when freed from flesh, individuals go on behaving as spirits, according to the old standards they had when they were alive—if not worse—in a degradation that is much more common than we imagine. If, before death, the person was feeding feelings of hatred and vengeance, the moment he is disincarnated he will attack his enemy with all the means and power he has. If the incarnated did not have the natural protection of their physical body—which constitutes a means of defense since it is Matter; it vibrates in another dimension—they would be at the mercy of their invisible enemies.

However, our physical body is not inexpugnable. Alive incarnated people, therefore, do not escape totally from the disincarnated's-incarnated's actions. As they cannot act on the physical corporeal organization, they act on the astral, the dimension in which spirits and even incarnates exist and move. Their action is almost always disturbing. They provoke diseases, disagreements, tragedies. Eventually, they even kill.

This malefic action is more or less intensive according to the quantity and intensity of the factors that bring them up. These include, for example, the mental power of the incarnated, methods of persecution, help received from other incarnated, the physical conditions of health of the victim, his karmic mass, spiritual degree of evolution, and, among other factors, more or less protection of the environment where the persecuted lives. To summarize, we can affirm that all this negative insistence is a result of the total sum of the individual's acts—this includes the incarnated as well as the disincarnated.

If we do not cultivate good feelings, we inevitably take to the other life what we really *are*. Most of the spirits that inhabit the inferior astral (called *umbral* by André Luiz) consist of scarcely evolved spirits, full of character flaws and feelings of vengeance. These purgatorial regions, full of frustrated spirits, are the seat of suffering. There, the most common solution for any kind of problem is to commit aggression against incarnated or disincarnated enemies—the conflagrations that affect the world of living people all the time. Therefore, it is no surprise that there are so many disagreements and crimes among us. Overall it is no wonder that we have so many mad people and so many psychic sufferings, because all this is, in essence, spiritual imbalance.

This besieging of the disincarnated—which can be frightening and even lethal—is seen in detail in the following pages.

Psycho-Pathological Syndromes

INDUCTION OF NEGATIVE VIBRATORY FIELDS ON THE INCARNATED

In these cases, the disturbed spirit acts only through his presence, by contiguity. It can happen that the sick spirit is placed on purpose, next to the incarnated sick, by black sorcerers, with the objective to harm this person. Even so, this phenomenon has to be filed among the ones that happen through induction, because the disturbing entity acts only through closeness. The victim, entering the vibratory resonance of the disincarnated sick, consequently suffers.

MAGNETISM, ELECTROMAGNETISM & SPIRITUAL INDUCTION[30]

Our definition for this phenomenon is based on physics.

There is a certain relationship (scientifically known) among magnetism, electromagnetism and mental phenomena. Everything indicates that the Law that rules material phenomena is also applicable to the spiritual ones, varying only in their parameters.

Let us review, for better comprehension, some concepts and postulates of physics.

— In *magnetic fields*, "induction is the energetic vectorial value equal to the flux density of a magnetic field."

— In *electromagnetic fields*, "induction is the establishment of an electromotive force in a circuit, caused by the variation of the magnetic flux that is going through it."

Electromagnetic induction is fundamental in the transformation of electrical energy into mechanical energy, or *vice versa*, as happens in generators and electric motors.

Formula:

$$v = \frac{d\varphi_\beta}{dt}$$

Where:

φ_β = magnetic flux

---

[30] The denomination "spiritual induction" was found for the first time in a book by Arthur Massena.

t = variable of time

β = vector

$d\varphi_\beta$ = derivative in relation to flux

dt = derivative in relation to time

— *In an electrostatic field,* "induction is the distribution of electric charges in an electrically neutral body, by influence of the external electrical field on this body."

It is called *influence*. When a sensitive gets ruffled, feeling nearby the presence of a spirit with a vibratory frequency almost similar to his, we have a phenomenon equal to an electrostatic induction. This is the most common spiritual induction, mainly in women.

Mutual induction is the electromagnetic induction between two circuits, where currents of variable intensity and tension, circulate. In the spiritual field this phenomenon is quite frequent, chiefly in the case of mutual obsession and in parasitism, symbiosis and vampirism.

The spiritual, magnetic, electromagnetic or electrostatic induction is always a transference of energy from one system to another one that is of variable circulating energy.

The spiritual induction from the disincarnated to the incarnated happens spontaneously—in most cases it is casual—without any premeditation or evil. The spirit sees the patient, feels the beneficent vital aura that attracts him, because it makes him feel well. However, if the spirit is sick, he transfers his anguish and suffering to the incarnated, making him become almost disharmonized-harmonized—according to the intensity of the disharmonic energy he is charged with at the time he acts on the spirit. If it happens to sensitives without mediumistic education, it is common that they arrive home exhausted complaining about not feeling well. When these people receive spiritual treatment, we almost always realize the presence of sick spirits, sometimes in intense suffering, who only remain near, *leaned against* the sick person, because they receive some relief, a kind of beneficial warmth that irradiates from the vital body. In exchange, through vibratory resonance, the disincarnated causes the incarnated to feel some sort of indisposition that he will complain about.

IT IS NECESSARY TO TREAT THE SPIRITS

It is advisable that all spiritists, chiefly the ones that do charity work, be conscious of the following: in the spiritual world: everything happens and works like it does in the physical world, or may be even better, this world is a pale reality of the world of spirits. Therefore, we have to know places, astral hospitals to which sick spirits can be sent. And this has to be done under *our* energetic command, without, waiting for the help of Superior Spirits who not always are at *our* disposal. (We have to avoid the quite generalized habit of transferring the assistance to other spirits, not caring about what might happen to the disincarnated spirits—as if assistant spirits were omnipresent and omnipotent. To believe that by sending spirits to Space, the case will be brilliantly solved, means not knowing the mechanism of spiritual aid. It can even be a serious mistake: it is as if we treat the sick, here in our physical world and send him to the middle of the street, so that he can complete his "recuperation.")

THE DANGER OF SYMBIOSIS

The phenomenon we discussed seems to be very simple, but in this case, induction can evolve to parasitism or symbiosis. This depends on the degree of lack of vigilance over less happy or even morbid thoughts and feelings, that become adjusted to the disincarnated's vibratory state and *syntonize it*. If the incarnated and the disincarnated vibrate in the same frequency, after some time a pathologic state of symbiosis gets installed in the incarnated. Depending also on the disharmony of the entity's astral body, there is a possibility of the disease happening (or getting installed) in an identical part of the body. The disease, now physical, (and usually of difficult cure for medicine) is, nevertheless, of an entirely spiritual ethnology.

Schematic Presentation of the induction Syndrome

Etiology

The syndrome is caused by a spiritual entity, who acts in a direct and harmful mode on the incarnated, without any volitional act, (this means he does not want it), producing a malefic effect only through closeness.

Action Mechanism

It acts by means of the patient's vibratory resonance with the aura of the sick spirit. The disease is induced by the disorganizing action of the spirit's energies of the mental field over the incarnated individual's vital (etheric) body.

Symptomatology

Indisposition or any kind of disease that causes pain in the entity's astral, passes, by means of resonance, to the patient, inflicting physical, psychic, or both problems.

Treatment

Separation and adequate treatment of the inducing spirit. Appropriate mediumistic education to the incarnated spirit, (if he is a sensitive and wants to work) followed by orientation for a balanced performance of the mediumistic mission that will be more appropriate for him.

Prognosis

It is favorable. It depends, however, on the patient's mental state, on his negative karmic charge and on the environment in which he lives.

AN ILLUSTRATIVE CASE

Patient: E.L., married, 33, housewife, Catholic.
Physical type: Ecto-endomorphic.
Date of assistance: June 1972.

The patient entered the Spiritist Hospital of Porto Alegre with the syndrome of schizophrenia. She presented exaggerated dread, fear of diseases and death, sensation that she is being followed, mental confusion and, therefore, typical behavior disturbances. Besides these mental problems, she frequently suffered from crises of respiratory dysfunction, followed by clinical signs of circulatory problems, with cardiac insufficiency, crises of tachycardia, pericardial pains, dyspnea, etc. Some moments afterwards, the signs vanished in an unexplainable form, complicating diagnosis.

The assistance was made at a distance, once E.L. showed great psychomotor disturbance and was highly sedated.

Unfolded by Apometrics, two mediums accompanied the astral staff to see the sick lady.

As soon as they arrived, they saw, attached to her, a very agitated entity, in a lamentable state of suffering; as this spirit disincarnated at a very old age, she still presented classic symptoms of a uncompensated cardiopathy: dyspnea and difficulties in speaking. One could see that it was difficult for the entity to move, because she had been very obese. She had not yet realized that she had disincarnated, and wanted to go on giving orders and taking care of her house. She claimed that nobody in the house obeyed her anymore, and they did not give her her medicine as they did before. She complained that for some time her chronic disease had been getting worse, and that her movements were becoming more limited.

She was brought to our working place and became embodied in a medium, where she received an urgent treatment and right afterwards she was taken to another place in the astral, to rest.

Under command we also applied magnetic charges, raising her vibratory standard and projecting vital energies. In this way, we freed her from sick vibratory bands that were reflexes of the state that caused her disincarnation.

More relaxed, trustful and secure due to the assistance she received, she agreed in following the helpers that assist us. And she went to the L.C.H.[31] *for a definitive treatment.*

(The unhappy woman told us that she had been E.L.'s mother, and that she still felt responsible for the good order of the house. E.L. confirmed that her mother had died two years ago, due to cardiac insufficiency and with the same sufferings she presented during embodiment; she was always very decisive and dominating, exactly like she showed herself as a spirit.)

As the disturbing entity was treated, we apometrically unfolded E.L. at a distance, taking her to the L.C.H. for a specialized treatment to remove her from the inducing spirit's heavy vibratory bands.

Discussion:

This is a case of pure induction. The mother's spirit was responsible for the sickness of the daughter. Getting close, the mother transmitted, by means of vibratory resonance, anguish and psychic disturbance. At the first disharmonic impact, the sick person's mind created parasitic mental forms, generated by her fear in the face of this strange and sudden phenomenon. As time went by, the conflict became progressively worse, with a serious morbid state and disturbance of psychic and physical imbalance. She was a step away from complete destruction of her personality.

Result:

Once the causes of the disease were removed and the chakras closed, E.L. was completely cured.

Duration of the treatment: 30 minutes.
Frequency of assistance: Once.

PSEUDO-OBSESSION

This kind of ominous action is more common among the incarnated, although pseudo-obsession can also happen between the incarnated and the disincarnated. It is a disturbing action in which the spirit does not want, deliberately, to harm the target-person. It is the consequence of an egotistic action of a being that makes another one the object of his care,

---

[31] Love and Charity Hospital, of the astral, whose doctors give us spiritual support.

and wishes ardently to make this target-person his. He demands that the other person obey his orders, blindly wanting to protect her, guide her, and with this kind of coercion, he impedes her enjoyment of a normal and healthy life with her fellow beings.

We believe that this phenomenon should not be considered a real kind of obsession. The *agent* does not purposefully wish to harm the patient. It happens that, although, the reasons might be noble, the action is harmful; in some time it can become real obsession.

Pseudo-obsession is very common in people of strong personality—dominating egotists—who often subject the whole family to their tyrannical wills. It happens between a couple, when one of the spouses tries to dominate the other totally. A classic case, for instance, is the one of the jealous partner who limits the freedom of the beloved in such a way, that, blind, he is going to harm the relationship seriously. In these cases, according to the intensity and continuity of the process, it can be just a case of simple obsession (obsession of an incarnated upon another incarnated).

REAL OBSESSION

> *Obsession is a persistent action that a bad spirit exerts upon an individual. It presents quite diverse characteristics, from the simple moral influence, without any external perceptible signs, up to a complete disturbance of the organism and mental power.* — Allan Kardec

> *Obsession—from the Latin* obsessione. *Impertinence, persecution, vexation. Worry about a determined idea, that dominates the spirit, and that results or not of repressed feelings; fixed ideas, manias.*
> — *New Dictionary*—A.B. de Hollanda F.

Our definition: It is the ominous and continuous action of one spirit upon another one, independently from being in the state of incarnation or disincarnation in which they are.

Real obsession always implies a conscious and volitional action, with a clear objective, aiming at well-defined results and effects; the obsessor wants and knows very well what he is doing. This premeditated action, planned and executed, many times, with great carefulness and sophistication, constitutes the great cause of psychic diseases. When obsession is processed by mental magnetism, the cause will always be in a moral imperfection of the victim (in the present incarnation or in previous ones), a kind of imperfection that allows the influential action of malign spirits.

THE OVERWHELMING IMPORTANCE OF OBSESSION

Obsession is the disease of this century. The number of cases due to a cerebral or mental dysfunction is so great that we can affirm that ALL mental diseases are of spiritual nature—except for the diseases caused by disorders of organic nature (such as cranial trauma, infections, arteriosclerosis, and some rare cases of resonance with the past and this life).

Therefore, causing most of the mental diseases, obsession overcrowds psychiatric hospitals all over the planet, where it has been challenging, for centuries, scientific therapies and the brilliant theories of materialistic researchers. Not psychoanalysis, or electroshock or selective psychotropic drugs can satisfactorily solve mental pathology. On the contrary, it continues to grow, full of moral maladjustment of all sorts, and a malign cloud of madness hovers above humankind, projecting darkness that is also attested to by the impotence of science in the treatment of the soul. On the other hand, this fact demonstrates the dramatic failure of religions in their mission to *reconnect* us with our divine origin.

There is, without doubt, a notorious ignorance of the Spirit-Man, not only by the investigators and scientists, but also by the religious of all creeds. Ignoring or denying the reality of the disincarnated spirit, the way he goes on *living,* his *habitat,* his *existential* problems and over all, his relationships with men and the imbalances they cause them, there is nobody who can formulate efficacious therapeutics. All the psycho-pathological syndromes described by medicine (extremely restricted, if seen from the context of general pathology) are *real.* But in most cases their ethnology is totally different from what is described in books.

Therefore, there is an obvious need for a systematic study, **open** *and detailed, of this old* **medical** *problem.* It is urgent, before anything else, to abolish religious, as well as scientific prejudices, so that phenomena of psychic pathology will be treated with aseptic objectivity, *rationally,* without mysticism, even if it is necessary to admit—as a working hypothesis—premises and concepts, that touch what is established as "religious."

ETIOLOGY & TREATMENT

Most cases of this syndrome are of the disincarnated acting upon mortal beings. Etiology of obsessions, however, is as complex as it is profound, closely bound to the painful consequences of moral deviations where the incarnated and the disincarnated tread the paths of open or dissimulated criminality; both, therefore, owing heavier or less heavy debts, due to transgressions of the great Law of Cosmic Harmony. Consequently, they meet, in the conditions of the obsessed and the obsessor, disharmonized, antagonistic, suffering mutually the adverse vibratory fields that they themselves created.

Therefore, in any kind of treatment for obsession, the basic objective, must be the HARMONIZATION of the obsessor and the obsessed. Once they are free from the oppressive situation, they are able to dispose and compensate for the evil they did (they have to get appropriately prepared for this).

Having this objective in mind, the first necessary step in the assistance of the mentally sick (*spiritual* sounds better) is to make a diagnosis, as precisely as possible, as should happen in any medical assistance. This diagnosis, according to the causes, will also involve research and knowledge of the extent of the psychic damage that resulted from the obsessive action. Scientific attitude and methods should always be used.

Most of the pernicious actions of spirits upon the incarnated involve an extensive process that has been developing through Time and Space, where the pernicious and hateful action (the cause of the disease) is nothing but the continuous flux of charging mutual debts, perpetuating the suffering of both. The persecutors of yesterday are the victims of today, in an interminable settlement of accounts, gloomier than dramatic. Both the present victim and his torturer are behind in their spiritual evolution. As they transgressed the Cosmic Law of Harmony, and not understanding the purposes of Divine Justice, arrogate to themselves, in acts of vengeance, power and responsibility that are God's. In this way, the obsessors get more and more disharmonized (the victim does, too, because he will become the obsessor that *he had been before*), so much so that they finally become insane. It is common to see a mentally sick (incarnated) being the prey of an avenger (disincarnated) in a lamentable state, as sick or even sicker than his victim. These ties of magnetism through hatred sometimes last for centuries.

A DISEASE WITH ROOTS IN ETERNITY

So-called psychopathology, as we see, is really a space-time *continuum.* Let us see an example.

When we were assisting a sick person at the Spiritist Hospital of Porto Alegre, we faced a painful case of obsession. Victim and torturer were alternating mutual persecution. Sometimes one, sometimes the other one, got incarnated. And the one who incarnated suffered the action of the enemy that was still in the astral. To find a clue, we had to go backwards in time, stage by stage, through six past incarnations. Everything started in the Middle Ages, when one of them had been a servant and had suffered serious offenses inflicted by the feudal owner.

These kinds of enemies can only be separated through the renewal of Christic love and the practice of an evangelic life, by the incarnated sick. But this in general, is very difficult for evident reasons. There is, as we have mentioned, complete ignorance about the problem, the facts and conditions that are considered and result in incarnation in any given environment. This means that a decision of incarnation to close to whom, where in Space, and when in Time needs to be made. Few are the people (still!) who know the causes for this kind of suffering and the evangelical methods to treat them—THE ONLY ONES of real efficiency—to overcome such *diseases*.

SIMPLE & COMPLEX OBSESSION

To simplify our explanation, we divide real obsession into two branches: simple and complex. Among the simple ones, we distinguish two sub-branches: mono-obsessions and poly-obsessions.

Real obsessions {
    SIMPLE {
        mono-obsessions
        poly-obsessions
    COMPLEX
}

Simple Obsession

Simple obsession is a mono-obsession if there is only one single spirit acting upon another one. And it is a poly-obsession when there are several obsessors that act upon the victim.

A simple obsession is characterized by a malefic action that we could call superficial. The torturer acts through simple suggestion, without using field-of-force or any other more sophisticated instrument. It usually is a spontaneous case of hatred; the agent intends to harm the victim by giving her suggestions or images. He does not use any major resource to crystallize the fact; the action is limited, in its effects, by mental force of induction.

These obsessors act with the means they have, without any major knowledge of the spiritual world's laws. They try to destroy the enemy with clubs, whips, ropes, and similar tools, they wrap him with cables, fetters, ties, sweat cloth, etc. The consequences of these attacks are of relative importance, because they depend on natural defenses of the obsessed, and also of the intensity, of the used energies, and of the time of actuation.

In a poly-obsession, the action is performed by several obsessors (that usually act in groups and synchronically) and is more dangerous, once there is a multiplication of malefic energies. In case, however, we realize that no electronic device has been implanted in the nervous system of the victim or that more sophisticated means, that could cause irreversible damages, have not been used, then the poly-obsession can be catalogued among the simple type.

Complex Obsession

Complex obsession is any case related to black magic; implantation of parasitic devices; use of dissociative or magnetic fields-of-force of continuous action that provoke disharmony of tissues giving origin to cancerous processes. Permanent fields-of-force can also inhibit the victim's creativity, or undo projects, mainly those that would bring financial profits, taking the victim to total poverty. Complex obsessions, also are those cases, in which the technicians of Darkness get attached to the obsessed spirit in deep suffering, trying to parasitize or vampirize him.

It has become common, in the assistance we give in the Garden House, to meet people who are imprisoned in magnetic fields that involve them in vibrations of extremely low frequency. The patients complain about deep indisposition, sensation of oppression that, increasing rapidly and progressively, take them to attitudes of fixed ideas of self-destruction, so great is the despair that afflicts them.

The technique of *fencing in* the victim by various kinds of obsessions is another characteristic of complex obsession. The sick finds himself hemmed in, undefended, at the mercy of the disincarnated enemies and predators. Through a well-detailed planning, (a plan of a really devilish plot, of the general staff, executed with military rigor) the technicians of evil investigate the victim's whole life, discover and "convoke" all his disincarnated enemies to take revenge and destroy their foe.

BLACK MAGIC

The worst type of obsession, however, complex from all points of view, is without doubt everything that involves the ominous black magic. When we face this kind of case, we know beforehand: a very critical treatment is going to be necessary, to eliminate the obsessors (they can be many). The first step is to deactivate the magnetic fields, without this procedure, they would be going on acting indefinitely upon the victim. This is very important because the magnetic action only disappears if deactivated by an external action in relation to the person, or if the sick is able to increase his vibratory standard in such a way that it allows him to get rid of the magnetic prison, by himself.

The actions of the sorcerers of Darkness are very well-known. Deceitful. Dissimulating. Devilish.

It is necessary to use special techniques with these creatures. They are intelligent, experienced professionals of evil; in their areas of specialization they are able to annul the kind talk used by the workers in kardecist centers. It is not to be wondered at. Quite often these beings have not reincarnated for centuries (if not millennia). They received huge magnetic powers when they were initiated in temples of the past; they swore solemnly to use them only for good, but, in the course of time, due to immaturity and complex circumstances, they fell into decay. The pure, wise men became practitioners of evil, caught in the trap of sexual passions, thirst for mean vengeance, or cupidity for richness and power. Their acquired knowledge and powers are, therefore, at the service of sinister purposes. Their appalling actions embrace the world of human beings, and of the astral, too, where they have enormous, well-equipped bases.

To dominate a sorcerer, it is necessary to deprive him of his powers. But these can only be annulled by reconnecting him to the past, projecting him in a different *equation of time.*

Once he is deprived of his initiatic powers, the next step is the reduction of his mental potency. If this is not done well, the chances to dominate him will be quite reduced. To succeed in their reduction, several techniques of corroborated efficacy have been used, which are applied according to the power and knowledge of the sorcerer.

After this—and only afterwards—we reach the most important step: we open the route of reincarnation for these spirits—reincarnation they have avoided by using their potent mental magnetism. (We met some that had not reincarnated since their last existence in ancient Egypt—or even before.) Although these spirits pretend to be very gentle, we should not be deceived by appearances (that, in fact, hide their certainty that they are powerful and very clever in the practice of evil). They are used to resisting, not only evangelizing dialectics, but also the contention of the magnetic fields which they use for common spirits. Sorcerers can only be defeated by use of special fields-of-force of concentrated magnetic energy.

Before such difficulties as traps, camouflage, and misleading tricks, that we certainly have to face when we deal with sorcerers, we advise beginners not to interfere in cases of black magic, or in those cases where the obsessive process is commanded by sorcerers of Darkness. To face them, the operator must have sufficient knowledge and experience in contention techniques, besides having enough spiritual power and protection to meet them face to face. We should never forget that for many centuries they have been preparing—very well—to neutralize any action against them and to redirect such actions against those who would try to neutralize them.

ILLUSTRATIVE CASES

SIMPLE OBSESSION

Patient: I.V.F., female, white, married, housewife.
Age: 28 years.
Date of assistance: March 22, 1972.

I.V.F. was at the end of the sixth month of pregnancy, she is deeply anguished. She did not have any hopes of having any more children. She had six consecutive pregnancies that ended in spontaneous abortion, in spite of the rigorous treatments she had been subjected to, and of long periods in hospital. The abortion always happened by the end of the sixth month of pregnancy, which is when we encountered her, and this made her case particularly dramatic. She presented crises of insomnia, exaggerated nervousness, and uncontrolled emotion.

Exam:

Unfolded by Apometrics and conducted to the L.C.H. our disincarnated colleagues found the patient quite weakened, even anemic. The continuous abortion exhausted her strength. The frustration of not being a mother, undermined her nervous system, making her become neurotic.

The disincarnated physicians said that the problem is all spiritual. There was an inferior spirit (due to his feelings) interfering malignantly in I.V.F.'s life. The karmic implications were very serious. In her previous life, the present obsessor was her husband, an egotist and dominator, extremely jealous and anxious for his wife's affection. His desire for possession reached such an extreme degree that he induced his wife to have several abortions to avoid having the children stealing the affection his beloved wife dedicated him. His wife agreed with him and so both were indebted according to the Cosmic Law of Harmony.

Treatment:

We assisted first the obsessor.

He was very obstinate. He did not accept the fact that his wife, now reincarnated, was married to someone else. All her present pregnancies were interrupted by him, with hatred mixed with frustration and vengeance.

He was indoctrinated and sent to the L.C.H. He was almost insane: he did not understand that because of the cruelty of his acts, he was becoming more and more separated from his wife. In the L.C.H. he was being prepared to reincarnate. According to what we were told, he was going to animate an oligophrenic body, due to his vice.

Right after, I.V.F. was being treated by the disincarnated doctors, having in mind, chiefly a normal pregnancy. She was also oriented to cultivate positive happy, healthful thoughts in order to become more receptive and be in better physical and psychic conditions to be a mother.

Discussion:

*This is a typical mono-obsession, **simple** obsession.*

The obsessor applies his hatred not only to his former wife but, chiefly on her child in development. Reaching the woman in an indirect manner, he can hurt her deeply in her maternal affection and at the same time, he creates a highly negative and very confused spiritual atmosphere around her. He was able to interfere in the birth of the children exactly due to the mother's karmic indebtedness, his accomplice in the abortions of the previous existence. Without sufficient spiritual protection to defend herself from the obsessor's attacks, the victim does not have a high vibratory standard either (that could immunize her against malefic attacks).

*The genesis of the clinical situation is, therefore, clarified. We realized that there was a second psychopathological syndrome—**the self-induced parasitic mental currents**—caused by the psychic weakness of the sick. These currents were created, fed, and kept by the patient herself, through the ghost of fear, the defeatist mental creation, somber suppositions, absurd deductions, etc.*

Duration of assistance: 40 minutes.
Number of sessions: three, with an interval of 20 days.

Result: She came to an end with her pregnancy. She had a normal delivery and a beautiful girl was born. She had another child, two years afterwards.

COMPLEX OBSESSION

Case #1:

Patient: I.D., female, single, white.
Age: 35 years.
Date of assistance: November 20, 1984, at a distance.

I.D. suffered from a deep mental disturbance. Twenty days earlier she had tried to commit suicide by jumping from the sixth floor of a building, For eight months she had had outbreaks of anguish, mental confusion, and insomnia—she wished to die, a situation that had been worsening. The psycho-pathological syndrome developed from neurosis (diagnosed by doctors) to an open psychosis that resisted all psychological and psychiatric therapies.

The patient had always had a temperament with schizoid characteristics: introverted, shy, almost sickly in her temperamental manifestations, always scared. According to the doctors, the focus of the present anguish was based on frustrations in the affective area: I.D.'s fiancé apparently was interested in another girl.

The fall from the sixth floor would have been the end of everything. But I.D. did not die. Fortunately she had only some small fractures of minor importance; she did not have even any cranial trauma. However, she was in an acute psychomotor agitation that obligated the doctors to highly sedate her. She had been in hospital since that awful event and the clinical-psychiatric prognosis was quite somber.

These were the conditions when the family came to us, asking for the Spiritist therapeutics that they had ignored. For them it was a last resort.

The sick was assisted at a distance; only one member of the family was present.

When I.D.'s vibratory frequency was opened, two obsessors immediately presented themselves, attracted by the powerful field-of-force that was established. We recognized them as **exus** *due to their animal-like state. They wore ragged, stinky garments, had long, unkempt hair, rough and dirty skin, enormous furry hands, crooked nails, short and bent legs. They spoke in monosyllables followed by grunting.*

There we were in front of another case of black magic. The **exus** *were spiritually degraded disincarnated beings, due to either long stagnation in primary bonds of consciousness, or due* *to their stubborn practice of evil. As a consequence, their astral bodies reflected all these negative qualities through monstrous corporeal deformations.*

From the patient's point of view, the problem got more complicated. Black magic does not only involve primary beings of all evolutionary levels (as the **omolulus** *that feed themselves on energies of proteins in decomposition, in the cemeteries;* **exus,** *evil, executors, etc.) but it involves also, supreme commanders, disincarnated, etc. As if this were not enough, there are the magnetic fields-of-force that generally are intense and of low frequency. It is necessary to have in mind, that these fields-of-force act mechanically upon the victim, and for undetermined time; lowering the vibratory tones, causing indisposition, anguish, restlessness, etc. (We* **affirm** *that they act mechanically. This means that they act independently from any volitional act, like an iron bar that attracts or repels filings.)*

Treatment:

We started the treatment, taking care of the **exus,** *because whenever we succeed in attracting them to our cause, they help to undo the sorcery (as we have already explained before).*

We project energy to clean their bodies, to dress them, cut their nails, the hair, and so at the end they assume a human form that is more compatible with the natural dignity of people.

They feel more relieved with this beneficial transformation, lighter, hopeful of finally escaping from the long captivity in which they lived. Therefore, they agree in working with us in spite of the fear, they still show, in relation to their chiefs, in Darkness.

They, then, reveal that the victim suffers under two terrible works of sorcery, that are renewed every week on Fridays. One of them, done at a cemetery, is to make her die; the other one is done at seven crossroads, and tried to make her crazy (a fact that they almost achieved; if she would not die she would get crazy).

First we took care of the work at the cemetery.

In a recently opened grave, there is a corpse in an advanced state of decomposition, with the skull split and inside the crevice there is a piece of waxed paper with the name of I.D. written down. Next to the corpse there is a big male doll with a black probe thrust into its head, some objects that belong to the patient, many pieces of her clothes, a pair of stockings together with her picture, some colored pictures, candles, etc. We perceived everything, at a distance, through clairvoyance (with the technique we use, the work of "undoing" are totally done at a distance, in the astral plane). All these things were taken out, put together and immediately burned by one of the entities, while the other one was observing and orienting.

Right afterwards we went to the crossroads. Together with the gifts, there were countless numbers of low vibratory standard entities.

*The first offering, the "Bará" (which dominates the "**street people**") is circled by a crowd of entities, that, after profiting from the received gifts, will go back to torture the sick again, besetting her constantly. We undo the gifts and gather those disincarnated that are wandering about, in a powerful field-of-force.*

We undo the offerings, one different from the other, dedicated to the seven lines of the crossroads.

When we were undoing the third, however, we meet a black sorcerer that faces us aggressively and threateningly. He does not want us to touch his "work." We conduct him to another equation of time, to assist him. During this dive in his remote past, we go to the Temple where he received his consecration (a sorcerer is always an ancient initiate). There we remove all his powers, undoing the effects of the ancient initiation ceremony. Back in the present, the sorcerer is inert. And in this state, he is conducted to the abode of spiritual recuperation, while his followers are gathered together in a field-of-force.

The sixth crossroads is also dominated by a black sorcerer, and we repeat the same process.

After we finished the most important cleansing, we go to the hospital where the sick is, as well as to her house, cleansing these places, and removing all the objects. We send away innumerable guards of Darkness that are posted in different places, we deactivate their bases, the seats of the sorcerer's commands. The patient, therefore, was relieved of the immediate negative action.

Revelations, data and facts, disclosed during the assistance, gave us a better view of the situation.

Nobody sufferers without any reason; we harvest, in the same measure, as we planted.

In a distant past I.D. was the mate of one of the sorcerers in a not very meritorious activity; she was a sorceress too, with serious moral problems, who betrayed the initiatic oaths of a "white" community. After some time, and perhaps because she was not that perverse, she was blessed by being incarnated again, in order to go on with her evolution. As always happens in these cases, she was persecuted by her fellow sorcerer who wanted to prevent her from growing spiritually, considering her a deserter. With the negative charge of recent sorcery work—a jealous woman who was interested in taking her fiancé was trying to destroy her—her former friends used the low frequency of the malignant action to make her situation even worse.

The complexity of this invisible action challenged all attempts to cure her, though they were executed by people of good will who assisted her quite often by giving her passes. It was necessary to use a more energetic and profound action, in which we used more active magnetic procedures together with the practice of white magic.

Result:

The patient was observed for some time. The last news we have is that she is much better now, so much so that she went home.

Observation:

Spiritually sick people have to be under a treatment that includes magnetic passes and magnetized Matter as soon as possible. This, however, is a mere complement to an urgent and dedicated life to the Gospels: the basic factor of cure is in a spiritual renewal—that goes from the spirit to flesh.

Case #2:
   Patient: D.A.B., white, male, married, businessman.
   Age: 65.
   Date of assistance: October 17, 1985, at a distance.

D.A.B. had been losing weight for about twelve months. His symptoms included a persistent dry cough, thoracic pains— stronger on the left side—generalized weakness, and a slight temperature increase in the afternoon. A doctor prescribed an antitussive medicine while he was waiting for the results of specialized examinations. The exams indicated that the constant loss of blood was not causing any significant change, though the blood tests showed that the speed of globular sedimentation was above 70mm in the first hour. The x-ray exam showed a tumorous formation in the inferior lobe of the left lung—the pleura showed metastatic signs. During the exams, D.A.B., who had earlier had prostate problems, underwent a prostatectomy to which he reacted well. A biopsy through pleural puncture showed the presence of an adenocarcinoma. They immediately started a chemotherapy treatment that only hindered the development of the tumor. Due to the unbearable thoracic pains, doctors blocked the nervous radicals using ethanol. Later D.A.B. suffered pneumonia, and became worse. He suffered again from asthenia and lost weight rapidly.

Psychological Data:

D.A.B. had demonstrated clear traces of neurosis since child-hood. Of depressive temperament, he was anxious, restless, unhappy with life—a situation that got worse with the disease. His rebellious insomnia also was aggravated. The recent health conditions influenced his character negatively, making him a person difficult to live with, almost unbearable. He argued with everybody against everything. He complained all the time and blamed the family for his misfortune. Consequently the family was disturbed and suffered from a collective neurosis.

Treatment:

The assistance is made at a distance, without knowing the sick.

As soon as we open his vibratory frequency, the spirit of D.A.B. himself embodies in one of the mediums who came with the group that helps us. He shows himself to be anguished. Terrified, he tells us that he is not going to allow us to submit him to another surgery.

(In our works, the embodiment of the incarnate spirit is a common fact. Some do it without being expected to, as happened in this case, when they are brought for treatment. Others come spontaneously, by their own volition; they usually are black sorcerers in obsessive action; others, have to be unfolded at a distance by Apometrics, and then brought in fields-of-force for treatment.)

We applied calming energies on D.A.B. and tried to relax him, telling him that he would not be operated on again. Next, he is again conducted to his body, firmly recoupled and at the same time we reactivate his chakras.

But while the sick is present, a disincarnated obsessor, a tech-nician of Darkness, embodies in one of the mediums. He tells us that he was contracted by some of D.A.B.'s old enemies to kill him. For a long time these foes have persecuted and obsessed him; they succeeded in disturbing his life quite a lot, but they did not succeed in what they most wanted: to kill him. With the knowledge and the action of the technician, they expect to succeed in what they have been craving.

Everything was easier now, because in D.A.B.'s present existence, he received, totally unexpectedly, an intense charge of black sorcery, ordered by a person who was interested in impairing his business. This dissociative energy of low magnetic standard, was cleverly explored by the technician, who concen-trated it in a previously selected area of the lungs, taking advantage of the chemical irritation caused by smoking. The malefic action also met a favorable field in the karmic situation of the victim. In the Past, D.A.B. a powerful man, was merci-

lessly cruel to powerless people; his victims go on looking for vengeance and charge him heavy debts.

The disassociated energies altered the balance of his tissues, causing some of the cells to become independent. It is usually impossible to revert this situation; the independent cells reproduce themselves and cancer is installed.

Black Magic:

Once the presence of black magic is verified, we try to capture one of the responsible sorcerers. (Capture: these spirits run away from the contact with operators of good, being afraid of interferences that would disturb or annul them.) We are able to attract, in triangular fields-of-force, an entity that was designated to take care of the "work" against the victim.

Inside the putrefied thorax of the corpse of a man that recently died of cancer, they put a piece of paper with D.A.B.'s name, covered with paraffin. Close to the paper there was a male doll, a photo of the victim, candles, clothes, etc.

We disintegrated everything in the astral, by means of cosmic light.

The technician of Darkness follows everything with his eyes and is quite astonished by what he sees. He makes some comments about the ability of "our" work in destroying such well-done work. We explain to him that the power is God's; we only try to help the sick, alleviating their pains. During this dialog, taking advantage of the great amount of energy that the superior world put at our disposal, we locate the laboratory of our interlocutor. It is at a base in the inferior astral. We destroy it completely.

In view of such demonstrations, the technician decides to collaborate with us. He takes away everything malefic that is attached to the sick. He cleans him totally of all the little areas of metastasis that are spread all over his body. To help him in his work we apply the process of **dialymetrics**[32] *(which is described later in this book). When everything is finished, we conduct the entity to the institution in the astral, for recuperation.*

Result:

We were informed that the patient improved a lot. He is under observation for future assistance. However we so far have not heard anything else about the case.

---

[32] From the Greek, *dialyo:* dissociation or dissolution of matter.

Case #3:

Patient: M.A.. female, white, single.

Age: 45.

Date of assistance: September 10, 1984.

Tumor on her right breast, for 18 months. Malign neoplastic formation; was subjected to a mastectomy. Intensive radiation and chemotherapy. In spite of this treatment, metastasis in her right eye. Present state: total metastatic invasion. Progressive loss of weight, earthy-colored skin and unbearable asthenia show the seriousness of the disease.

Treatment:

When the vibratory frequency was opened, we could clearly verify that it was a case of black magic. An **exu** *was near M.A., taking care of the work.*

Black sorcerers, brought from the depths of the planet, magnetic material of very powerful irradiation, of a very high vibratory level—absolutely incompatible with life, at least the kind of life we know.

The cleansing happened as we described in previous cases. We assisted a group of inferior spirits, linked to black magic, and also many others. They were sufferers, most of them mutilated by M.A., a very powerful lady in former incarnations. For having abused these creatures, she gained concentrated maledictions and hatred. When she incarnated, she brought with her an enormous ballast of dense magnetism that made her vulnerable to the well-planned attacks of the technicians of Darkness. It is important to mention that the malefic action was successful— although M.A.'s behavior was blameless—and in spite of the fact that she was working as a medium in a Spiritist center.

Result:

She was under observation, her state was improving, in general. She had an appointment within 15 days, but she did not show up. We did not hear from her again.

Case #4:

Patient: M.P., white, male, married. Entered the Special Care Unit of the Santa Rita Hospital in Porto Alegre: lung surgery due to cancer in an invading phase.

Age: 56.

Date of assistance: November 27, 1984, at a distance.

About two years ago, M. P. started feeling tiredness, disturbances, strong asthenia, loss of appetite. His coughing, attributed to his heavy smoking, also became worse. He went to see a doctor. An extensive neoplastic process in his right lung was found by means of x-rays. A bronchoscopy and a cytological exam of the bronchial-exuded matter confirmed carcinoma; he is subjected to a resection of the affected pulmonary area. The biopsy confirms: carcinoma. After the surgery he improves quite a bit. For six months he does not feel any problem. However, five months later a broad metastatic process was found in his left lung. Examinations revealed that it was the same tumor.

At the present time, M.P. is at the end of his life. The scar of his thoracotomy is open, he feels pain all over his body and an intense discomfort. Psychic agitation: he knows about the seriousness of his condition, but he does not accept death.

Treatment:

As soon as we opened the patient's vibratory frequency, two spirits present themselves. They are responsible for the guard of two black magic works, and tell us right away, that our efforts in benefit of M.P. will be useless, because he is certainly going to die: the works were done with all necessary care and are periodically repeated, on appropriate days.

*We syntonized the two with M.P.'s sufferings, threatening them that they would be in this condition for ever. They, then, inform us that the owner of these works is a terribly cruel creature, with a large knowledge of sorcery. They are afraid of what might happen to them if they reveal "professional secrets." They unveil the place where the work is, but they refuse, definitely, to remove the objects that are malefically magnetized. We realize that they are professionals of evil. We tell them that we are going to attach them to M.P.'s body, so that they will be buried with him. **And we really do this.** Tied to the sick person's body, feeling the horror of the suffering, they began to despair with the possibility of being buried. Crying, they plead that we free them from this terrible situation. They promise that they are going to do everything we order them.*

Consequently, although reluctantly, the guards change sides, and from agents of evil they become operators of good. Watched by the unfolded mediums, they start their work at the cemetery. In the corpse of a man who died of cancer, there are 27 papers with M.P.'s name (which correspond to 27 sorcery sessions), together with ragged pieces of the victim's clothes, a male doll with a steel spike passing through the abdomen, black candles and colored ribbons.

We burned everything with the projection of strong cosmic energy jets.

The guards undo another work. In the woods, in a hole in the ground covered with a stone, there was a frog with its mouth sewed; inside the mouth there was a piece of paper with M.P.'s name. We took the paper out and set the frog free.

Finally, we went (unfolded) to the sick person's house. There, we captured another three guards that were watching the place to prevent interference in the sorcery works. Together with some entities of Umbanda, some nice old black people assisting us, we cleanse the place thoroughly.

In the meantime, the black sorcerer himself comes spontaneously. Irascible, the chief of the gang curses our interference in his work, threatening Heaven and Earth.

Immediately, we place him in another **equation of time.** *Conducted to the past, we undo his initiation and with it, all his power. Back to the present, he is sent to the specialized ward in the Love and Charity Hospital, to see what can be done about his recuperation.*

Once the spiritual part of the sick was treated, we went on with the second phase of the assistance, i.e., with the treatment of the sick person's physical and astral body. (Had we not done the cleansing of the sorcery fields, none of the efforts and healing processes would have helped.)

Rays are projected into the green frequency, the environment is sterilized, freeing it from any kind of astral larvae. We apply the process of Dialymetrics and withdraw the anomalous cells that constituted the tumor, from the etheric body. The affected area is cauterized with cosmic energy.

M.P. is left renewed, in the astral dimension. Recuperation is going to depend on his deserving it, on the divine mercy and of his biological conditions that are deeply affected by the disharmony he suffered.

Result:

The treatment was repeated 15 days afterwards, and then, we did not hear of the case anymore.

* * *

*We would like to make clear the specifics of the treatment, to all people interested in helping and curing the sick. To act and produce effects in the astral world, it is necessary to project energies. This we always do by the emission of pulses—***by means of simple counting.***

TYPES OF OBSESSIVE ACTION

ACTION OF A DISINCARNATED SPIRIT
UPON ANOTHER DISINCARNATED ONE

In the spiritual world, mainly in the inferior zones of the Umbral, there proliferate large organized colonies of powerful sorcerers of Darkness. They imprison a great number of disincarnated spirits, enslaving them in a typical obsession. According to the astounding quantity of prisoners in these conditions, as we have seen in our spiritual works, we believe that obsession among the disincarnated is the category with the largest number of victims on the planet.

When we destroy colonies and bases directed by Darkness, it is necessary, first, to save the slaves. To do this, we have to mobilize a sufficient number of disincarnated helpers and form powerful magnetic fields-of-force, to neutralize the guard of these appalling organizations.

ACTION OF A DISINCARNATED SPIRIT
UPON AN INCARNATED ONE

This is the classic type of obsession. The malefic action is produced in different stages, from small and transitory, to eventual influence and then to complete submission of the obsessed to the disincarnated.

The obsessive processes vary greatly. But, according to what we have been observing, black magic dominates with all its scaring consequences. Special attention has to be given to the electronic devices and/or parasites in the nervous system of the victim. This obsessive process implies specialized knowledge and sometimes complex, sophisticated techniques.

ACTION OF AN INCARNATED SPIRIT
UPON A DISINCARNATED ONE

Apparently very strange is the obsession of a mortal upon a disincarnated spirit. It seems paradoxical that a man can act upon a spirit. Nevertheless, this happens more frequently than we imagine, showing that the universes of the living and of the dead are interlinked.

As the mind of an incarnated man vibrates always in the spiritual world, the environment in which the spirit constantly lives (incarnated or not), this exchange becomes easy. Chiefly during sleep, the incarnated can detach from Matter and live, temporarily, in the spiritual world. In this way, a great deal can happen between alive and dead spirits, with exchanges of physical and even sexual sensations.

Through experience we know that the magnitude of this type of obsession is quite large.

Once, when we assisted a woman, we faced an extremely restless and despairing spirit. Since we thought that it was a simple obsession, we tried to convince him to abandon the one that we considered his victim. To our surprise he supplicated:

Look, if you can free me from this woman I will be very thankful to you. I have already done everything. But I cannot get rid of her!

But, how come that you are so subjugated, my dear, if you are a spirit with an immense possibility to follow your way of peace?

It is because you do not know the power of this witch. In my previous life she made me get married to her. It was a disastrous marriage, economically as much as morally. When I died I thought I was free of her. But what a deception! One day I was violently attracted by her. And I could never again get rid of her. When she sleeps she always calls me. More than that, she pulls me with an irresistible force. Please, for heaven's sake, free me from her.

We did what the spirit asked us. We freed him and conducted him to the station of recuperation. A deeper study of the sick revealed that she had been a sorceress in the remote past. She sold oracles and magic filters for sorcery. She also practiced black magic. Now she was suffering from psychic and spiritual disturbances, caused by several entities that were charging her past debts. The spirit that she had dominated was her former mate; in her previous life she married him, under the effect of a black magic work that was still acting upon her.

ACTION OF AN INCARNATED SPIRIT UPON ANOTHER INCARNATED ONE

Obsession is also quite common among living people. All of us know dominating, despotic and egotistic individuals, who command the whole family, obligating everybody to do what they want. This kind of obsession, interfering even in the effectiveness of others, is nothing other than a case of obsession that is disguised in protectionism. This action can become so pertinacious (and at the same time inappropriate) that when the despot dies, his victims that live with him, feel relieved. However, the obsessive process will go on, because the loss of the physical body does not change the obsessor.

Fortunately, this action of an incarnated upon another incarnated seldom goes beyond simple obsession.

RECIPROCAL OBSESSION

This type of obsession is characterized by the reaction of the obsessed in relation to the obsessor. When the victim has enough mental strength, he is going to plan an active defense: he tries to attack the obsessor in the same degree in which he was attacked. Consequently, there will be a magnetic, vicious circle of mutual hatred that is difficult to annul.

More or less intensive, these reciprocal attacks usually are present in all types of obsession; they are casual (without characteristics that make them continuous) and surging according to the circumstances and existential phases; they can be concomitant with other happenings. Although they sometimes present an intense negative magnetism, these processes of mutual influences are cases of simple obsessions. When the reciprocal obsession happens between a disincarnated spirit and an incarnated one, it is due to the incarnated spirit's strong personality, great mental power and a lot of courage, since he faces the spirit in equal conditions. When the person is awake, he usually does not know what kind of drama he is living. It is during sleep—and unfolded—that he is in condition to face and attack the contender.

TYPES OF OBSESSION

CASUAL, TRANSITORY ACTION OF A DISINCARNATED SPIRIT UPON AN INCARNATED ONE

Erratic spirits (such as, for example, the gangs of frolickers and all the irresponsible ones that live as parasites on the not vigilant incarnated's psyche) get close to the sensitive, and, over time, just for fun and not because they want to cause any harm, they start a process of simple obsession, sucking the vital energies they need. To enjoy themselves, they sometimes induce the individual to take strange, aggressive or radical attitudes against relatives or work mates. On other occasions, they change the opinion of their victim about serious, important subjects, harming their professional performance. But it is mostly in the trivial, commonplace daily activities of their victim that these spirits act, disturbing and producing anxiety, without doing any major harm. It is common, for example, for them to induce people to become fanatic about trite subjects, such as soccer, soap operas, etc.

This hetero-obsession becomes more serious when these irresponsible agents are able to interfere in intellectual work, chiefly if the obsessed is a medium (actuating or not) and is catching written messages. With great ability they are able to introduce subtle mistakes in the text, bombastic but unreal conclusions, high-sounding phrasing, but without meaning, incompatible with the level of the written work and even with the intellect of the medium. Usually there are little flaws that neither the revisers nor the medium himself recognize. They spoil the work, harming its credibility. It has the objective of invalidation through the criticism of professional critics and demanding readers.

Therefore, we see that the saying, "pray and watch out" is of crucial importance in mediumistic work. A medium must be very careful to avoid exaggerated enthusiasm, an aggressive disgusted feeling about opposite opinions and over all the thousand faces of pride. Through these crevices obsessors penetrate, actuate and establish a kind of association with the poor non-vigilant one. The subtleties of these obsessive processes, when well observed, should take us to the luminous awareness of the mere role of an intermediary, with the consequent humbleness. But the medium can be held back from this posture—even if he is inflated by the feeling of justice—he may start attacking casual detractors. His vibratory frequency, getting lower, changes him into an easy prey for the malign spirits.

REAL OBSESSION

We have already spoken of this subject when we discussed obsessions in general.

It is the classic obsession, where the disincarnated spirit disturbs the incarnated one in every sense, to take revenge. This psychic pathology is a well-known process, and was studied quite a lot by investigators of modern Spiritism, starting with Allan Kardec.

The treatment is usually very difficult. The contender's affective problems take us to aberrant states of consciousness, so deeply do they root in violence and hatred, and with a perseverance that can be measured in centuries.

If it is simple obsession (and if the obsessor is not a prince of Darkness) it is possible to convince him through kind, calm and objective indoctrination. There is no need to attack him with sharp criticism. We have observed that quite often the obsessor is not that bad, and that he is tired of persecution. In this case it is easy to enlighten him and conduct him to another evolutionary stage; it is enough to show him his own past where he can see the remote causes of his, and his victim's, suffering.

This is the dialectic of classic obsession—as practiced in Spiritist Centers—with many and indescribable successes. Nevertheless, in more serious cases, when the obsessors are technicians specialized in tormenting with the refinement of professional torturers, the treatment requires techniques compatible with the intensity and sophistication of the malefic activity.

From the obsessor's point of view (who always gives good excuses for his vengeance) as well as from the obsessed's point of view (who suffers the spiritual action of a past enemy) the obsessive process only exists due to the absence of spirituality of the contenders. As long as one of them, at least, is not illuminated by pardon, there will always be—and still alive today—the sinister force of hatred magnetizing them with evil. Only love relieves, and allows the flight to peace and happiness.

There are no people who are really creditors, charging real debts of relapsing debtors—as we all believe. All of us are debtors; yes, we are debtors of the Celestial Father because we are constantly violating the sacred laws of universal harmony. If we were conscious of this fact we would be worried about redemption, before everything else, our own unimaginable debts. For this all of us have a cosmic coin—love. We should spend it continuously, following the example of the Divine Master. It was not without reason that Paul of Tarsus gave special emphasis to charity as the supreme virtue. And charity can not exist without forgiveness. If forgiveness were natural and automatic there would not be any obsession. Obsession, therefore, is the affirmation of our own immaturity.

For all the incarnated victims of obsession, the best medicine is to get evangelized: only peace can give us liberty. For the obsessors, whatever mental power they may possess, or the perfection with which they execute their vengeance, the remedy is the same—love that produces charity, stimulates forgiveness and liberty, and bears the fruit of peace.

It is important to observe that obsession is not a temporary enslavement of mind. The disturbing action presents an enormous power of multiplicity, showing subtleties, sometimes, that make its identification difficult. There are obsessive actions that aim at the *physical* annihilation of a person, by using tiny devices installed in the victims bodies. These devices emit constant dissociative energy that provokes disorganization of the tissues, and consequently, incurable tumors. In these cases there is no intervention in the incarnated's mental or volitional processes.

On the other hand, in many cases of black magic, the energetic fields aim only at human performance (business, for example), when the objective is to harm the victim *economi-*

cally. In these cases, very common in our assistance, the victim's mind is intact, without any kind of subjugation.

BLACK MAGIC

In all civilizations, since remote antiquity, magic has always been present. It probably started with the cave men. We know about their propitiating rituals to attract animals from which they fed themselves, the magic rituals in sepulchral caves, the invoking of the powers of nature to defend the tribe against animals and enemies.

Still in antiquity, but already among the classic civilizations, natural magic had its objectives twisted, becoming a mortal weapon in the hands of renegade sorcerers. Wonders were used for improper objectives: to attack, harm and confuse individuals, armies and the state. Ambition and egotism used the forces of nature for evil (as also happens today); spirits from diverse realms were, and still are, enslaved by black sorcerers who do not spare even Man himself. Degrading important processes of the use of these forces, these sorcerers even prevented medicine from using natural magic forces—and with great success, at least by modern medicine. And magic fell in rapid and progressive degradation.

It is lamentable that this happened. Today, the concepts and ideas that we have related to this subject are quite inaccurate: usually confused, sometimes false or involved, on purpose, in scientific disdain that presents them as "fantasies."

Nevertheless, "magic is the exact and absolute science of Nature and its Laws" (Eliphas Levi). And a *magician* is anyone who deals with the invisible forces of nature, producing phenomena without any apparent cause.

The magician manipulates, by means of the power of the mind and ritualistic practices, these subtle, magnetic and, at the same time, powerful energies. What we know as "ritualistic practices" are nothing other than techniques of sequence, of acts that aim at the unchaining or *precipitation* of these energies according to the immutable laws.

> *"Magic, therefore, includes in the same essence, everything that philosophy presents as correct, and that any religion has as unfailing and eternal. Magic reconciles perfectly and unquestionably words that, at first glance, seem to be opposites: faith and reason; science and creed; authority and liberty. Magic gives the human spirit an instrument of philosophic and religious certainty, exact as mathematics, corroborating the infallibility of mathematics itself."* — Eliphas Levi

Magic, consequently, is not superstition as some supposed sages affirm (and we include some kardecists), worried about defending and maintaining a narrow and restricted interpretation of the immense cosmic reality. In fact, magic implies complex processes which should be of great interest to science due to the investigatory and experimental processes.

Magic is not worried only about disincarnated spirits, as many people believe. Its objective is life in its various forms and in all dimensions, spirits of all beings, including spirits of nature (improperly called "elementary"): gnomes, sylphs, salamanders, undines, mermaids, fairies and many others. Among the natural forces or energies used by magicians we can mention the planetary energies, (such as that of the moon which is responsible for the tides and regulates the growing of plants); the energy of waterfalls and of the sea; the force of the wind and of the snow storms; of avalanches; the terrific energy of fire; the resonance forces of atoms in the constitution of crystals. All of these energies can be used for good or for evil, according to the intention of he who is using them.

When used for evil the manipulation of these forces is made by associating them with others of low vibratory standard (negative forces) that cause lowering of the victim's frequency and an intense indisposition. According to the duration, intensity of action and natural resistance of the victim, he can suffer from an intense pathological weakness, after a period of serious disturbances, feeling of oppression, anguish and some other discomforts that are difficult to describe.

Black magic processes usually present one of these aspects:

a) Use of natural forces.
b) Malefic action of disincarnated spirits of different levels of evolution.

This second aspect deserves special attention due to its variety of facets, extension and intensity of consequences. In the use of Life against Life—a sacrilegious and cruel action—they do not use only disincarnated spirits of normal consciousness. They use immaterial microbic masses (astral larvae), unconscious masses that dwell in cemeteries and feed on decomposing human remains. They also make use of the help of *exus*—degraded human spirits—transformed into real monsters. They usually are the ones that act on the victim, either taking care of the objects in the victim's body, or acting directly upon his organism in a distressing process of cruel and continuous activities, although, they are only the slaves of the princes of Darkness.

Everybody who is involved in de-obsession should consider the double aspect of the actions of Darkness:

— The *silent* fields of magic that act constantly for centuries and centuries, according to the victim's defenses.

— The presence of the obsessors of low level, sent and ruled by powerful beings of Darkness.

If we take care of only one of the aspects, it is almost sure that we will not be very successful in our assistance to the sick.

Of the two aspects, probably the one of magnetic attraction is the most important. These harmful fields act continuously because they are constituted of physical magnetic energies that vibrate eternally. They only stop when the magnetized objects (amulets, structures, etc.) are destroyed, or if the target person evolves and reaches a vibratory standard that allows him to escape from the action of the negative energetic fields. It is known that each kind of evil has its action limited by spatial parameters; beyond these, their action is annulled. If the victim raises his vibratory frequency, he escapes from malefic actions.

Among the old techniques known, one of the main ones is, without any doubt, the use of the vibratory resonance by means of images and male dolls that represent the victim. The sorcerer makes the "sorcery"; i.e., he creates adverse magnetic fields, through invocations, prayers, calling up of beings, etc., and due to resonant magnetism these fields start acting physically upon the person.

In our country, the sorcerers, at the same time, usually show the victim to one or more *exus*, instructing them about how they have to act. Once the vibratory frequency is given to these animal-like beings (through objects and clothes, as we would do with a dog), they start tracing their prey, become attached to him, vampirizing him greedily, like dogs, or worse.

The use of astral larvae and primitive beings from the cemetery is, also, more frequent that one can imagine. As it was in the previous case, the identity of the victim is essential in this process of sacrilegious disrespect for life.

To illustrate, we would like to remind the reader that in all primitive peoples the same process has been used; only the techniques vary a little with the evolution of time, the power of the sorcerers, and according to the malefic potential of the disincarnated involved in the action.

In Plato, for example, we find a text (*Laws*) where the philosopher describes two actions of sorcery. In one, the victim is tied through bewitched images and specific rituals. In the other, the actions of natural forces are let loose against the enemy's body. They used male wax dolls representing the victim, placed on crossroads or tombs, as our *quimbandeiros*[33] do nowadays!

The use of this technique was, also, common among the Romans. They used male wax dolls, jabbed with needles.

In France, under Philip IV, "The Fair" (14th century), the practice of this kind of sorcery was quite common, too, although it had been forbidden since the high Middle Ages by official order. In the year 337, for instance, the emperor Constantine condemned those "that made their enemies die at a distance" to be burned. Other examples include the orders of Chilpericus III (742); Charles VIII (1470); Charles IX (1560); Henry III (1569); Louis XIII (1628); and Louis XIV (1672).

All European countries which keep records of sorcery processes present identical practices of black magic. France was famous for its sorcerers. In the National Archives of that country are detailed descriptions of witchcraft, necromancy, and the use of wax figures.

So, we see that practices such as those of Antillean Voodoo and of our national *macumbeiros* had already largely been used in the Middle Ages.

In Hawaii, the *Kahunas* (native priests) used to project the famous "Prayer of Death" onto their enemies. In a few days the target died of a strange disease that provoked de-vitalizing characteristics, starting from the feet and going up to the heart.

It is important to realize that all these techniques have in view the lowering of the victim's vibratory standard, generating anguish, oppression, and other psychic and physical sufferings, with an effect proportional to the magnetic powers of the operator and of the degree of the disincarnated's malignity, and contrary to the bewitched person's conscious or natural defenses

In summary, black magic implies:

—Will power of the sorcerer, creating thought-forms that are projected against the victim;

— Direct action of the evildoer, commanded or induced to harm the person in exchange for gifts such as candles, human food, candy, etc.

— Action of negative, magnetic fields-of-force, that act on the sick for an indefinite time, be it appropriate or not for the disincarnated evildoers.

(See the end of this chapter, "Black Magic—Cases Related by Albert de Rochas", "Exus" and "The Undoing".)

---

[33] Sorcerer of Quimbanda (Afro-Brazilian black magic).

PRESENCE OF NEGATIVE MAGNETIC FIELDS, WITHOUT THE ASSISTANCE OF DISINCARNATED OBSESSORS

This phenomenon is present in almost all cases of black magic obsession.

As we have already seen (and it is important to remember this), black magic acts upon two poles:

— Through the action of degraded human spirits, the *exus* that act directly upon the victim (disturbing his movements, for example, causing accidents), or indirectly (for example, harming business and professional activities), causing as many problems as the potency of the evil forces can create, while they are able to surpass the victim's spiritual defenses.

— Through magnetic, physical or mechanical action of fields-of-force emitted by amulets and magnetized objects, charged with low frequency emissions and attached to them by "works" done at cemeteries, in special places of nature, or at cross-roads.

In these "works" they create powerful malefic and aggressive fields-of-force that are specifically directed. When the intention is the separation of a couple, for instance, the sorcerers use the following technique (we mention but one among many): they tie two dolls with their backs against each other and baptize them; i.e., both receive the names of the people against which the sorcery is directed. Strongly magnetized in an antagonistic situation, they are together but repel each other because they are *magnetized on poles of the same sign*, and so the mechanical repulsion of the dolls is transferred by resonance to the victims. In the course of time, the couple starts feeling great mutual dislike, unexplainable due to their former love and fondness. The process obeys the laws of physics: in a magnet, poles of opposite signs are attracted (north-south), and those of the same sign repel each other. The psychic repulsion that happens between the couple will separate them unless there is deep love between them, Christian abnegation and dedication, or a state of living spirituality—things that are very difficult to find today.

These magnetic fields of black magic affect people according to the degree of evolution in which they are, and also according to their mental and emotional state, and conditions of internal harmony. Magnetized amulets sometimes are alone, without the presence of an obsessor. The objects activate by themselves; they vibrate until they are destroyed. To last longer, they used to cover these objects with wax to protect them against the corrosive action of time and humidity.

To undo these magnetic fields it is necessary to "raise them" (an expression used by specialists in these evil deeds). This means they have to be taken off and destroyed. It is possible, nevertheless, to disintegrate them only in the astral world, through the formation of powerful magnetic fields that neutralize the malign vibration (something easy to do by those who understand about black magic).

Knowing these techniques can be indispensable to reach a precise diagnosis of the disease of the victim/patient because, without this knowledge, the treatment will probably be inadequate. The technique of Voodoo (from the Caribbean islands) has been very much used in Brazil; by jabbing magnetized pins into male dolls, with the name of the victim, they cause diseases or persistent pains in vital areas, usually very difficult to diagnose. We have already found parts of corpses (chiefly single organs) with the victim's name and objects, forming a set surrounded by candles and offerings for the *exus* in charge of harming the person.

PARASITIC DEVICES ATTACHED TO THE NERVOUS SYSTEM

These cases belong to *complex obsessions.*

For years we have been observing, in sick people assisted at the "Garden House," the presence of small and strange devices placed with exactness and great skill in the astral counterpart of the nervous system. To clairvoyants they look as if they were attached to the physical body, since the astral body is superimposed on it. As this spiritual body is of the same physiology as the physical one, any disturbance in its functioning will fatally affect it in a short time.

At the beginning of our observations we thought that the surprising presence of these small devices was discovered by the mediums because they were unfolded apometrically; and as they remained in the spiritual dimension during the whole work session, they had the ability to see, in detail, the astral structure and the anatomic features of the patients. We realized afterwards that this perception is also the result of simple clairvoyance, without unfolding. Today we have an even more plausible explanation that may explain why these devices had not been noticed before: it is likely that when mediums *see*, they do not know exactly what they are seeing. Let us explain: ordinarily these devices are very tiny; and the people who are in a condition to see them seldom know about the anatomic details of the nervous system.

Due to these facts, when we faced the first case some fourteen years ago, our surprise was enormous. It was something totally anomalous and unknown. We did not have any references regarding this subject, nor was there anywhere we could get information about it, or anyone who could clarify it.

In recent years, however, the number of cases observed, assisted, and treated has been growing constantly. There have been more than a thousand cases with the most varied degrees of complexity, sophistication, and serious effects.

How They Work

The objective of these electronic inventions (yes, electronic—and sophisticated), is to cause functional disturbances in sensory, perceptual or motor areas, and in other nerve centers such as the nuclei of the cerebral base and of vegetative life. Some are more perfect and more complex and affect multiple areas and specific motor zones, causing neurological consequences: progressive paralysis, atrophies, hemiplegias, painful syndromes, etc., parallel to the psychic disturbances.

The objective is always demonic: to cause disharmony in the nervous physiology and make the victim suffer.

A constant interference in the nervous system will cause great harm to the victim's vegetative life and mainly to the vast and noble control of the mind. Victims of this kind of obsession suffer almost instantaneous distortions in their values, causing deviation in their behavior that ends up destructuring their personalities.

The most common technique is to attach this device to the cerebrum or to the bones of the skull, using special screws. Afterwards they link the device by means of very thin filaments to different areas of the central nervous system or to the nuclei along the medulla, according to the desired objective.

We realized that some devices receive electromagnetic signals of controlled and variable intensity. They are emitted by very well-installed bases—in places of difficult access in the Umbral—that continuously affect determined areas of the cerebrum, causing breakdowns and functional fatigue. Altering the entrance of physiological responses to normal stimuli, they emitted anomalous and sudden commands to the auditory area, for example; they suggested forms of self-destruction and compelled the subject to perform a variety of abominable and whimsical actions, injected directly into the cerebrum.

There are cases in which we noticed a continuous emission of low frequency vibrations, of low volume and little amplitude, underlying the obtained response of the patient. The objective of these emissions is to exhaust the patient, breaking his resistance to make him obedient to the orders he is going to receive. Once the victim is ready and *conditioned,* he receives a sudden order or hears a mocking voice making discrediting comments about him or his behavior. Not knowing the cause of this phenomenon, the person thinks he is going crazy. Besides this, his aggressors know how to wait for, and find, the propitious occasion. At the right moment, cruelly prepared, they make the person hear shouting, accusing him of being a homosexual, for instance. Helpless and defenseless, it is not long before he gives in entirely to his enemies, particularly after he is convinced that medicine is impotent to cure such an exotic disease.

It is lamentable that in these cases physicians are almost unable to help. They cannot even console the patient because they do not believe what he says. They classify the clinical state as an "auditory hallucination"—a state that exactly, because it is an hallucination, does not exist for medicine! As a solution they strongly sedate the "hallucinated." This weakens some of the negative effects of the ominous action and of the device. But, by no means, do they eliminate the *cause* of the pathology.

We had a case in which the person was considered catatonic, but in reality he had been degraded to the condition of a human robot, without any will, completely dominated by his obsessors.

Umbraline enemies can act in an even more subtle way—as we should realize. When they do not want to be discovered or identified, they do not emit any sound. They just send the electromagnetic *energy* of the electronic sound.

Besides these, there are others that apply devices with special refinement, stimulated by a system of feedback, so that they feed off the energies of the victim himself. Without knowing it, he makes the parasitic device function continuously. This can only happen when the technicians of *Evil* are capable enough to make deviations from the circuit. They connect one of the filaments to an organ that functions with stronger energy—a muscle, for example, where the tension is ten times greater than that of the neurons. Catching the great muscular energy (which is measured in millivolts) and projecting it directly onto the neurons (whose energy is measured in microvolts), the result will be a real disaster—something similar to a short-circuit. That, of course, will be followed by immediate, intense functional disturbances.

We have already met refinements of these type of cruelty. One of them consists in calibrating the energy of feedback, allowing the passage of electric tension of a determined value. The objective (always attained) is to disturb a person exactly at a time in his professional life which is most demanding, or when he needs most of his energies. At these precise times he suddenly receives all the electrical charge of his own muscles. The result is a kind of shock that can make him lose consciousness, have a cardiac crisis, or any other sudden dysfunction. The process is basically very simple in its conception: establishing bridges between the motor areas (which liberate relatively large energetic fluxes) and the cerebral zones (which are extremely sensitive and work with very weak electrical signals). To execute this deed, however, great skill, knowledge, and the techniques of a surgeon are necessary.

A "Strange" Case

Some six years ago, the director of a bank came to see me with a strange pathological manifestation; doctors were not able to identify its etiology. This was not a wonder at all, because the symptomatology did not fit any known syndrome.

He was suffering from fainting, abundant sweating, cold extremities and exaggerated paleness—a situation that could be easily identified as a case of lipothymia if it were not for the absence of arterial hypotension. It was similar to a shock of the vagus nerve; i.e., a functional neuro-vegetative disturbance.

The sudden attack did not present any detectable visible cause. It came up when the patient was concentrating on something that required more of his intellect. The patient himself had already observed that it happened only when he was actively concentrating.

EEGs did not present anomalous traces, even during his crises, so the hypothesis of epilepsy was discarded. As a matter of fact, there was no loss of consciousness. But whenever the patient had a shock, he could not work with the Board of Directors of the bank for two or three days. After six months of treatment and clinical investigations without result or improvement he came to the Garden House. He was very worried because he felt that he might have to retire due to disability. This would have caused him great financial loss.

Apometrics revealed the cause of the disease immediately.

In the base of his cerebrum we found a parasitic electronic device with feedback installed. The long filament that came out of the device went through the myelin sheath of the nerve trunk (Schwann sheath), in the nervous plexus of the vagus. Another filament was linked to "the motive plate" of the skeletal muscle: in this case, the left occipital insertion of the trapezius muscle.

When the patient was sitting down, concentrating on his work, he had the habit of bending his body to the front, lowering his head. This required a contraction of the dorsal muscles. This contraction worked as a "trigger": the energy produced by the muscular action got to the threshold of the calibration of the device and a tiny circuit breaker turned on the current which dropped all at once on one of the regulating nuclei of the arterial tonus, provoking the collapse of the blood system.

The treatment was simple and rapid.

The device was removed. We captured the umbraline technician and the obsessor, the cause of the evil. The patient recovered immediately. He was treated on a Saturday morning and on Monday he went to work again. Never again did he have any fainting.

Obsessors, Devices & Obsessed

The presence of these parasitic devices indicates the type of obsessors that have to be faced. Usually they belong to two great "branches":

— The victim's enemy contracts, through bargaining, a sorcerer of Darkness, specialized in the construction and installation of the devices.

— The obsessor himself is the technician who constructs and installs the device, and takes care of its functioning.

In either of the two cases, the presence of these mechanisms presumes the presence of a highly qualified technician with a good knowledge of electronics and the physiology of the nervous system. The need for this degree of specialization makes the use of these devices very limited. The use of magnetic passes, though easy to apply, would be a disaster in these cases because they would never extract the devices attached to the nervous system.

These tiny, sophisticated devices, inserted into the nervous system of the individual, can only be extracted with the help of duly qualified higher spirits or technicians of the astral—it is necessary to be very careful not to harm the neurons. For this reason we often make use of the ability of he who implanted them, obligating the technicians of Evil *to reverse the sign* of their activities. In this case we have to use all kind of methods. It can be a direct constraint, for instance: make the evildoers feel that they will be mentally ill in future incarnations where they will harvest the consequences of what they are doing now. But we can also convince them (sometimes) through patient and kind indoctrination according to classic Spiritism.

Anyway, our objective has always been reached: we relieve the patient of his insidious aggression and also recover the responsible agent. We should never trust—that is our advice— in the sincerity of the technicians' purposes, even when they agree to collaborate. They should never work freely; they have to be continuously and closely controlled, by the vigilant spirits that assist us, and by the unfolded mediums.

INSTRUMENTS ATTACHED TO THE BODY, AIMING TO PROVOKE DISEASES

In many cases, so many that they are commonplace, the obsessor's only objective is to destroy their victims physically, making them die or suffer for a long time. There is no sign of an action upon the brain, nor are there signs of mental magnetizing or enslaving. If we followed the classic kardecist definitions we could not consider theses cases obsessions, because, according to our brothers, obsession implies an interference in the mind or, at least, in the physiology of the brain.

According to our experience, it is common to have obsessors put poisoned objects in open incisions during surgeries to cause the sick to feel the worst pain possible. By doing this, they impede cicatrization or cause, for example, the formation of dangerous, persistent fistulas in hollow viscera. For this purpose they use wooden wedges, imbued with poisonous vegetal juices—everything is done in the astral world, but it reflects immediately on the physical body: pains, intense itching, disagreeable local heat, inflammation, etc. We have observed hundreds of cases with this type of pathology.

In our assistance we take out any harmful material and burn it with cosmic energy in the astral plane. In the meanwhile, disincarnated doctors remove fistulas, do cleansing curettage, etc., and frequently treat the wounds with vegetal sap.

In 1985 we took care of a young lady—a newlywed—who presented a persistent cystitis along with genital dysfunction. Doctors attributed the functional disturbances to her recent wedding. But as the lady got worse, they decided to give her more profound tests and a specific treatment. The medicine was not very efficacious—it only lessened the symptoms. Suffering from polaciuria (frequent urination, small quantity), dysuria (pain when urinating) and urinary incontinence, the patient felt very uncomfortable when she was with others.

When the apometric unfolding was done, we found a little object made of black wood that had been introduced deep into her uterus; and another one, similar to the first, was enlarging the vesical sphincter. The process was to prevent pregnancy, to cause dysfunction due to the poison, and to provoke urinary incontinence.

We captured the obsessor. In a previous existence he wanted to win her love. He was despised by her and not well treated by her servants, because, although he was married, he went on trying to conquer her. Due to the bad treatment he received

from the servants, he fractured a leg which did not heal well
and so he became lame. He swore to take revenge but he only
got it after death. He was able to close in on the woman he
loved and who had incarnated again.

(Cosmic Law allowed him to get close to the woman to start a
readjustment between the two, eliminating the antagonism.
The reconciliation between enemies only happens when there
is a reciprocal pardon.)

We discovered that the two had been partners in criminal
activities in former incarnations. In the last one, the victim
caused an abortion, the result of a clandestine love affair with
the present obsessor. Consequently her genital field became
vulnerable to spiritual evildoers, even to the less skillful ones.

Cases of cancer have their origin in this kind of obsession.
Spirits with good technical knowledge are able to break the
buddhic net to install a neoplastic process by means of interference in the energies that maintain the cytological and histo-
logical harmony.

INDIRECT OBSESSION

Frequently the target person of obsessors has natural conditions of self-defense, be it because of meritorious works in
former incarnations, or because of evolutionary conquests in
his present life. These barriers are strong enough to annul the
attacks of spiritual evildoers; even if they try hard, their efforts
bump into the positive vibratory fields that annul or strongly
lessen the predatory actions.

Frustrated, the obsessors try to change their way of acting.
They attack indirectly: they persecute someone tied to the
family, a member of the family or a loved one, sure that their
suffering will worry the target person. Though immune to a
direct attack, he becomes vulnerable to an indirect one. It is
common, for instance, to choose a son or daughter, who does
not have the necessary means to defend himself/herself or
who is sensitive to spiritual charges. They can even attack *the
whole family* if there is not enough vigilance and if conditions
are proper for a collective action.

The victim's anguish satisfies, in a certain way, these
vengeful beings. They are interested in disturbing, as much as
they can, the incarnated victim's life.

Unfortunately we see this type of obsession quite frequently
in our assistances. Usually the obsessed are young people—
especially female adolescents—who, generally, are intensively
obsessed victims of all sorts of aggressions. But they are not
the target person. The action is aimed at the father or the

mother, or both; the objective is to make one or both of the parents suffer.

It is also common, to hear the disincarnated complain about awful sufferings, of which the present incarnated being was the author in painful past incarnations. Now they take revenge, trying to affect the enemy in his moral field, because it is impossible to harm his physical structure. They plan the most varied situations of suffering and disturbances at home: they induce the children to practice moral deviations; to become addicted to drugs; to craziness and violence. They promote libertarian ideas (common among young people), separating them from their parents. They provoke diseases, etc. These obsessions can usually be classified as *simple,* once the obsessors act through influence on the unwary minds of the young. The action, however, can be extended to totally defenseless individuals by means of karmic factors; the whole process can, in this case, become much more serious. It can make the victim become an easy prey of the predatory action.

In fact, an indirect obsession is nothing other than a direct obsession in which the obsessors employ a more appropriate tactic by changing the object of their attack. As the harmed being is not really the target of the persecutor, we have realized that the destructive (direct) action is not really deep.

We referred to this subject because of didactic needs, and also, because the phenomenon shows well the complexity of the obsessive processes.

PARADOXICAL OBSESSION

Paradoxical obsession does not strictly fit in—at least not in the initial phase—with the concept of obsession that we have presented here. We consider obsession the malefic action—premeditated—by somebody against another person. And, at least at the beginning of this *paradoxical* obsession, the obsessor does not even dream of harming the target person: he wants only to help, protect and guide him/her. But it happens that this intention can become transformed into real obsession (with all its characteristics); and it is due to the *degradation of this intention* that these cases are considered part of the gallery of obsessors.

The process starts with an unusual interest of one individual in another, a kind of interest that, sooner than expected, degenerates into domination. The victim of this "zeal" is limited in his/her actions, even the simplest ones, and even his/her desires are guided—everything is done progressively—until the person totally loses his/her autonomy. Without realizing it, the "protected" person becomes a slave.

Usually these obsessors are dominating people: egotistic and of strong will. The dominated, on the other hand, are of weak will: they usually depend economically on their opposite pole who assumes the role of a *tutor*. After some time, however, the "protector" starts seriously harming the "protected." He interferes deeply in everything, dictating aspirations, volition, attitudes, behavior, profession or career and, chiefly, how and who the person should love or hate. The noble protection that was at the beginning, degenerates into tyranny.

The "protector" becomes so egotistic that, often, he hates the "protected" relentlessly if he gets free of the supposedly "amorous" bondage.

We have faced many of these obsessive cases in which egotistically affective frustrations degenerate into absurd hatred. The domineering individual, for instance, begins to hate the dominated one because he/she got happily married to somebody else. This *wrong* love indicates a fearful obsessive process that will harm both people directly involved (and others who are directly linked to them).

To clarify things, we would like to remind the reader that hatred is nothing but an aberration of love. Without emotional balance it is easy to go beyond the limits of a disinterested friendship: it is enough to feel one pole blocked in his/her affective *interests*.

The paradoxical obsession, in summary, is just an aberration: love and friendship from the left side, affecting the incarnated and disincarnated ones.

ARCHEPADIA

Archepadia (from the Greek *épados*—magic—and *archaios*—ancient) is a psycho-pathological syndrome that results from magic originating in the remote past, but still acting in the present.

Some years ago we came upon the first of these cases, an unprecedented situation.

There was a patient with a psychic process of chronic characteristics that made her feel rather sick, neurotic, full of fears, constantly worried with diseases. Although the patient was young, she showed early aging. She had already undergone innumerable spiritual treatments; she herself was a Spiritist and received weekly passes, attended evangelical cults and courses for mediumistic development.

It was in these mediumistic meetings that the psychic process became worse (as a matter of fact, this happens whenever the awakening of mediumship is not well conducted).

She was apometrically unfolded and had her vibratory frequency opened, but we did not detect any kind of obsessor. We decided, then, to investigate her karmic problem; so, we opened vibratory fields of the past.

We were surprised when we discovered that the patient had lived in ancient Egypt and, in an incarnation of that time, she suffered an intense action of black magic for various reasons. In one of her lives she was very rich and had great political power, gaining, therefore, powerful enemies who wanted to annihilate her. On that occasion she did not undergo an efficient cleansing to get rid of the ominous magnetic fields. Consequently, she kept them. And she still had them attached to her astral body.

The entities that acted on these fields had probably been removed along the millennia. However the magnetic induction, that is of physical and mechanical order, went on acting and disturbing. The patient herself contributed to this because she did not care about evolving enough to get free of these malign energies. As she did not know about the importance of the spirit, how could she suppose (or even imagine) that the cause of her problem could be explained with the simple functioning of a magnet? In effect, if a magnetic field is oriented to a magnetizable material (as, for example, iron), if this material is not unstructured, the field will be vibrating forever, according to the unchangeable laws of physics. In the same way, if a person is magnetized, the field will only disappear due to an external interference (as we provided), or if the person is able to raise his own frequency, *escaping* thus from the negative field.

The patient improved in a short time.

It is important to emphasize that, in these situations which refer to very old processes, a second nature is formed which characterizes the consolidation of the disease and, so, a psychotic personality is crystallized. A long educational process must be started immediately after the annulment of archepadia, so the person can return to his real personality. The cult of the Gospels, the study of Christ's Words and spiritual education can do wonders for these patients.

In a few months the patient was totally transformed. She was happy and communicative. Never again did she have any mental problem.

We have not heard of any reference, in Spiritist books, about this pathological state. Nevertheless, it has come up with a certain frequency in our work of assistance.

ILLUSTRATIVE CASES

Case #1: An Obsessive Process Aimed at the Physical Body's Destruction.

Patient: E.F., female, 24, white, married.
Date of assistance: 1984.

Since E.F. was married 18 months before, she had problems in the general area. Dysmenorrhea. A discrete but persistent leukorrhea. A feeling of heaviness in the lower belly. Constant indisposition. Symptoms got worse when the temperature decreased. She had not yet gotten pregnant, although she did not take any contraceptives.

Medical checkups did not show anything abnormal. X-rays indicated a perfect permeability of the Fallopian tubes, and did not reveal any abdominal problems.

As E.F. wanted children, she came to the "Garden House" looking for help.

Exam:

After a superficial exam, the disincarnated physicians immediately recognized some abnormalities in the lower belly.

The patient had a strange object introduced into the entrance of her uterus, and another one inside the left tube. They were 3cm long wooden wedges (poisoned material, as we came to find later on).

Treatment:

We opened E.F.'s vibratory system to identify any obsessive spirit that might, perhaps, be persecuting her.

The mediums immediately discovered the presence of two entities of low vibratory standard, interested in the destruction of the lady. They were seized immediately and one of them was forced to embody in one of the mediums. He became irritated with our interference and threatened us. He raved against the lady, saying that she had harmed his life in a former existence. He wanted to marry her, but she did not accept him. As if humiliating him in front of society had not been enough, the woman persecuted him in regard to the division of an inheritance common to the two. She influenced judges and lawyers to harm him so much, that, in the end he and his family were left without anything, in total misery.

It is a spirit without any special knowledge, with little experience in evildoing; the obsession, therefore, could be classified as simple. However, his concentrated hatred made him want the total destruction of his enemy, therefore, he joined those beings of Darkness who had good technical knowledge; consequently the obsession became complex. These technicians placed the poisoned wedges in the woman's reproductive system. The obsessive process caused serious consequences because these devices could not be removed through simple magnetic passes and they were difficult to detect by an inexperienced medium.

The obsessor was conducted to the recuperation infirmary of the Love and Charity Hospital, in the astral. The whole group of entities that helped him was captured, too, and sent to the specialized infirmaries of the same hospital.

During the treatment the poisoned wedges were easily removed from the patient. The whole area and the reproductive system were infused with vegetal sap of curative power by the old black who brought the medicine.

E.F. was advised to treat herself with regular passes, magnetized water and reading of the Gospels, because the acquisition of authentic spiritual values is what supplies effective protection and immunity against the attack of vengeful spirits. She was told that only knowing the words of the Gospel was not enough; to become spiritualized one has to rebuild oneself in an intense and pertinacious work. One of the surest ways to get close to Jesus is through a spontaneous donation of our energies for the benefit of our fellow beings; only by living an applied love—charity—do we acquire spiritual ascension. We emphasized to E.F. (as we do with all the sick that come to see us) that we do not cure anyone, we only try to help our fellow beings; in fact it is the sick that cure themselves by getting close to God.

Diagnosis:

Complex obsession, with implantation of strange poisoned objects in the victim's body, with a view to causing incurable diseases that will end in death.

Number of assistances: One.

Discussion:

If the toxic action of the strange objects were able to defeat the physiological cohesion, penetrating the buddhic web, the cellular balance would be deeply altered. Once disharmonized, the cells would behave as if they were embryonic undifferentiated cells, imbued with great vigor for their own reproduction. In this way the nucleus of an incurable tumor would be formed.

This cellular disharmonization, however, is only successful if the victim's somatic constitution has a karmic gap. This gap is located in an organic area weakened by the violations of the laws of cosmic harmony and/or malefic maladjustment's that the person practiced in former lives. This was what happened to our patient. In order to study her case better, we opened her frequencies of the past and discovered that she had had several abortions. By syntonic reflex, her reproductive system became weak in her present incarnation, and, therefore, vulnerable to the action of the predators of Darkness.

Result:

Due to the fact that E.F. received specialized assistance in time, she recovered completely from her problems.

Observation:

It is one of many cases in which there is no permanent or temporary enslaving of the victim's thought, a necessary condition for a case to be considered an obsession—according to kardecist authors.

The obsessed had her mental functions totally under control, but the obsessors wanted much more than making her insane: they wanted to kill her.

Case #2: A Parasitic Device Attached to the Nervous System.

—The first case treated at the Garden House—

Due to the importance of its details, we recorded the first case that we faced, **in June 1972.**

> **Patient:** P.C.G., 23, white, male, single, student.
> **Medical diagnoses:** Catatonic schizophrenia since the age of two.

Case History:

He was in hospital one year and eight months ago. Afterwards, he stayed home, where he progressively grew worse, so much so that he no longer left his room. He was in such a state of fear (and inactivity) that he needed company even to go to the bathroom. His reactions were almost vegetative. Very few psychic demonstrations.

The first signs of morbidity appeared about three years ago, when he started to hear voices that induced him to self-destruction, or criticized his manly behavior, etc. Sometime afterwards he started being afraid of everything, and then followed the classic persecution delirium. Within a short time, the outward manifestations of his personality were altered, resulting in mental alienation.

Spiritual Examination:

He came for the exam walking slowly, like an automaton. He was surrounded by five obsessors of low vibratory level.

Unfolded by Apometrics, he was conducted to the Love and Charity Hospital (L.C.H.), in the astral.

There, he underwent a longer exam in the presence of mediums (that accompanied him) and they detected a small and odd device firmly attached, by means of screws, to the occipital bone, at the base of the skull. Very thin filaments coming from the device penetrated the encephalic mass, reaching the frontal cortex.

The spiritual physicians explained that they were dealing with an electronic device that had been implanted in the patient's brain by very intelligent obsessors. The five spirits that surrounded him were mere guards, ignorant creatures, unable to conceive of such a sophisticated technique. Behind it all was the man responsible for everything—a technician of Darkness.

Treatment:

First, we assisted the guards, reducing them to impotence without much talk and sent them to the L.C.H. Then we tried to take care of the technician.

Because we were facing an unknown obsessor of superior intelligence—and mainly because we did not have sufficient knowledge to deal with a case like this—the superior plane determined that the obsessor should be treated on a different schedule from the normal one. The special session would be in the afternoon of that day.

At the determined time, the patient was unfolded again and conducted to the L.C.H. We attracted the obsessor by powerful fields-of-force, projected by counting.

Our disincarnated friends explained that the device had a tiny emitter that transmitted warning signals to the base when it was touched in a different way: it was a screw with a "left thread"; i.e., it worked counterclockwise. If anybody wanted to remove the device, the screw would become even tighter, instead of looser, activating the alarm in the interior of the base.

This was what the doctors were going to do. That they intended to deactivate the device made the obsessor furious. Some moments later (exactly as the mediums were expecting), the enraged creature came out of the magnetic field, presenting himself in a showy way. It was a strange creature, of ferocious aspect, dressed in sumptuous garments of Louis XIV's time. He questioned us in a rude fashion, and threatened those who wanted to destroy or dismantle the device. He said that the sick person belonged to him and that he was, by no means, going to allow anyone to meddle with his plans.

Our friends started a dialog with him. Speaking in a soft tone, they tried to persuade him to some kind of agreement. But the technician resisted, insolent, rude. The disincarnated physicians changed their strategy and showed admiration for the device. They made comments about the complexity of it and about the intelligence of its creator, etc. By doing this they touched the weak point of this morally inferior spirit: vanity. (We have observed that all of them are haughty.)

The obsessor started paying more attention to the questions. He showed the functions of the device in all its details. He even revealed that the objective was to annul P.C.G.'s volition, transforming him into a human robot. Indoctrinated in a kind way, clarified about how the terrible consequences of his acts were going to influence his near future, he became quiet and listened attentively to Dr. Lourenco³⁴ (the head physician of the L.C.H.) and his wise and precise words.

Touched by the aura of goodness and love of our spiritual mentor, the sorcerer started narrating his drama.

In his last existence he was born a prince, but was kept from the crown by his brother, who usurped the royal power and exiled him from his country. When he disincarnated, he was full of hatred and swore that he would have his own reign where robotized humans would be his subjects. After wandering for a long time in erraticity, he became a member of a colony in the inferior umbral. He soon reached the command level and took all kinds of courses, chiefly special technical ones, always aiming at evil and the enslaving of the incarnated. In the course of time, he established his own laboratory in an area of the colony. At the time of our questioning, he had seven hundred spirits under his command that were either technicians or soldiers.

We were astonished at this unusual report. It is the first time we heard of such a thing in our work.

Our disincarnated friends made the ex-prince see how much he would have profited if his intentions had been different. How much happiness, how much harmony, could he have spread on his way. At a certain point, they showed him how the disharmony that he projected around him has already started to give results: the external form of the prince has been suffering from the negative energies that he himself emitted; he already presented deformations that he did not yet realize. They showed him his exotic image in a mirror, his unkempt hair, the long

---

³⁴ Dr. Lourenco is a physician-spirit who assisted the author in his interventions on the earth-plane.

*curved, dirty nails. They told him about his internal dryness—
the inexplicable dissatisfaction of one who intends to have (and
believes he must have) a reign of his own.*

*Visibly scared, the ex-prince became moved when they
revealed that his mother, who was very worried about him, had
been asking Jesus incessantly for his recuperation.*

*Maternal love has a magic effect upon any petrified and piti-
less heart. The obsessor decided to take a trip with the spiritual
mentors, visiting better planes, regions with more light and
peace, places where he might be able to stay in the future (if he
changed behavior). There even was the possibility of meeting his
mother.*

*He agreed to remove the device he had implanted. He did it
very carefully, in order not to harm the patient. He informed us
that he had already installed around nine hundred devices of
various types in the nervous system of incarnated creatures,
some of them much more sophisticated than this one. He also
revealed that in some people these devices did not work; "It
seems that these people are immune to these devices, because
after some time, they drop out by themselves." (The ex-prince
did not know that these devices dropped out because the
intended victims were of superior vibratory frequency. In these
cases immunity is natural.) He said that in other creatures success was complete: the person became a robot. In some cases
the victim died in consequence of the implantation.*

*The ex-prince was taken to the L.C.H., where he was placed
in a specialized infirmary. (He will remain there for a long time,
to recuperate spiritually.) We captured all his followers and sent
them to recuperation stations.*

*Soon afterwards, P.C.G. was subjected to a treatment to mag-
netically activate the affected areas.*

Discussion:

*This was the first time we faced an obsession of this nature.
Never before had we heard of the existence of an electronic
device in the obsessed's brain, nor had we read any references
about these techniques in the vast Spiritist literature. As we
were used to indoctrinating simple obsessors, we had never
faced technicians that were specialized in physics and medicine. From then on we decided to study this problem with more
interest. Over fourteen years of observation, facing such obsessors and deactivating such devices gave us enough experience
to form a theory about this subject. Today we are in a position to
penetrate into the bases of Darkness, to destroy their laboratories, deactivate completely the institution of evil and capture the
commander and his followers.*

Fortunately, the first obsessor of this type that we met was not a sorcerer of Darkness. Had he been one, the case would have been much more difficult. He was a common obsessor, although he commanded a large group of inferior spirits.

The implanted device received continuously an electromagnetic, very low frequency, wave of radio frequency, emitted by a big antenna in the base of the umbral. The device transformed the signal and increased its energetic intensity, activating a group of neurons in the auditory area, in a subliminal manner, i.e., it emitted kind of an indefinable background noise, with the objective of exhausting the neurons, causing, consequently, a physiological wearing out of the brain, with the objective to annul its resistance. At certain moments it emitted modulated signals together with commanding voices or disreputable comments about P.C.G.'s behavior, inducing him to ridiculous attitudes, etc.

Medicine classified this phenomenon as "auditory hallucinations." Therefore, there was no help anymore for the patient— who had his resistance slowly and skillfully undermined. To this odd and hopeless degradation there was the addition of self-induced mental currents, formed in the mind of the patient himself, caused by fear and despair of that situation being remedied. Not even his closest relatives were able to realize the terrible reality he was suffering from. With such a complete obsessive situation, the victim had lost his will to live.

P.C.G. had plenty of mediumistic sensitivity, that facilitated the obsessive action. There was also the so-called karmic gap[35], that made the approach of the obsessor possible.

Time of treatment: One hour.

Number of assistances: One for the first phase. A review within a month. We had the opportunity to examine P.C.G. two years later.

Result:

The recovery took 48 hours, but for some time he still had a feeling of fear and a certain insecurity. Never again did he hear voices, neither did he need medical assistance (as a matter of fact, his father was a physician). After five years we saw the patient again. He was still fine.

---

[35] Karmic Gap: a (disharmonic) event in a former life, propitiating kind of an opening or vulnerability for low negative frequencies; in this case, any action (of the present victim) that caused insanity or suicide in other people.

Case #3: Another Parasitic Device Attached to the Nervous System.

Patient: A.B.G., female, 19, white, single, student.
Date of assistance: During the year of 1975.

Clinical history:

During her cultural training in the United States, the girl decided to visit Canada. Some days after she arrived in this country, she had a terrible crisis of migraine, that happened again a week later with even more serious characteristics, over a three day period. The episodes always came suddenly and A.M.G. had never had crises of this type.

As the clinical state became worse, the girl was sent to a Canadian hospital where she underwent a series of electroencephalograms, x-rays of the skull, bilateral arteriograms, blood tests, determination of the organic liquid's constants, etc. They did not find anything abnormal.

With such an imprecise etiology for this kind of dramatic syndrome, the young girl returned to the United States as soon as possible. A few days after her arrival, she had another acute attack of migraine. She had every imaginable examination, without any positive results.

When she was feeling a little bit better, she returned to Brazil, where she suffered repeated attacks, now with clear neurological manifestations. She felt some disturbances and lost her sight, a syndrome of a right hemianopsia[36]. Without any precise medical diagnosis, the ophthalmologists could not do much. The intermittent crises forced the student to go to the hospital more than once and she was quite tired of the laboratory exams which did not present any physical abnormality. The hallucinatory pains made her go to several Spiritist centers, but they also did not come to the right spiritual diagnosis. Consequently, after some months of suffering, she had to give up studying. She was constantly terrified waiting for the crises that came regularly, tending to get worse (the sight of her right eye was getting progressively weaker and weaker). At this evolutionary stage of her disease she received spiritual assistance at a distance, because she lived in Rio de Janeiro.

Treatment:

We sent two unfolded mediums to accompany the staff of disincarnated physicians to the girl's residence. The staff noticed that the disease was essentially one of spiritual problems, in the field of complex obsessions. Obsessors of great malefic ability

---

[36] Blindness in one-half of the field of vision, in one or both eyes.

had already installed a quite sophisticated parasitic device in her nervous system. We were advised to write to the sick girl telling her to come to Porto Allegro for a more specialized and urgent spiritual treatment, because the device was influencing her optic center directly and could cause total blindness.

A.M.G. came to the Garden House on September 29, 1975.

A female entity, wearing rich garments of the 18th century, presented herself immediately. She was a wealthy lady who had been the wife of the viceroy of the British Canadian Colony.

Fat, energetic, (not to say hateful), arrogant and covered with jewels, she criticized acrimoniously the behavior of A.M.G., who had been one of her maids of honor when she spent some years in Canada representing the kingdom.

We listened to her patiently, interested in her reasons. As we did not interfere in her ecstasy of hatred, she thought that we agreed with her purposes. She told us details that happened two centuries ago when the young girl was the pivot of a passionate drama.

This opulent lady brought to Canada a young girl of the lower English nobility who was herself without any riches. Within a short time (as could be expected) the first-born son of the family, a handsome, twenty-two year-old-young man, fell in love with this English girl—and she fell in love with him. But this young man's family wanted him to marry a girl of high British nobility, rich and worthy of her lineage. With this marriage the family would be able to join the society of that time and enjoy the highest rights that aristocracy could provide for them.

When the wealthy woman came to know about the romance, she became furious. She exiled the girl, sending her back to her people. Due to the abuse his beloved underwent, the young man, although showing respect for his parents, decided to leave Canada, too. To make matters worse, he renounced, at the same time, all of his rights of inheritance.

This proud and noble gesture revolted the haughty woman even more; it intensified her hatred and her wish to take revenge on the girl, who was at the time eighteen years old. Unfortunately, the young man became seriously ill in England and died a short time afterwards. The matron's feeling of hatred grew worse: she attributed everything—"all the misfortune of her house" (as she said)—to that poor defenseless girl. She was not aware that the only one responsible for all the disharmony was herself with her egotism, pride, and unfairness.

Unable to do anything at the time, the matron swore that she would take revenge upon the girl as soon as possible. But she could not satisfy her intention, both because the girl was so distant and because of her prominent social position.

When the lady disincarnated, she took not only her pride with her, but also the old and well-developed hatred she felt for her former maid of honor.

After wandering about in erraticity, full of pride and trying to get back her power, she met, by chance, some of her former servants. She immediately contracted with them to serve her, repeating the situation and conditions that existed when they were on Earth. As they were weak spirits, used to obeying without arguing, they accepted the proposal happily. In the course of time, the lady looked for other former servants and joined with them, forming a sort of court in the umbral, and imposing her commands pitilessly.

The divine laws, however, are wise and just. In the destiny of the two there was a karmic readjustment foreseen in the present incarnation of the young girl.

When A.M.G. went to Canada, she met the old lady, who was living in the astral of that country. The old lady had been looking for her in the local areas, but due to a lack of technical resources, all of her efforts had been fruitless. She identified A.M.G. in Canada, thanks to the work of the paid disincarnated. And she did not waste time. She contracted with a technician of Darkness and gave him a very valuable jewel as payment, to have her vengeance done. She felt it necessary to blind this presumptuous girl who dared to love her beloved son!

The technician installed, carefully and skillfully, a tiny electronic device, equipped with an energetic feedback system, close to the optic area. At determined moments, anomalous energies flowed into the optic nerve, disorganizing it.

When she finished the report, and after learning the details of the vengeful action, we started working on the solution.

We showed the wealthy lady our "trump card," with demonstrations of energy projections; being firm, we told her that her reign was over, her residence would be destroyed, and her servants would be gathered up because her evil doing had come to an end. Scared, she witnessed the evacuation of her followers, the destruction of her base, and the capture of her guards. She agreed to order her technician, who had already been caught, to remove the device that she had had him place in the girl's body (to have him do this, she paid him with a diamond jewel she took from her neck). As soon as he executed this service, freeing A.M.G. from the device, the technician was conducted to the hospital to be cured.

When everything was finished, the old lady had another surprise that made these moments of her destiny solemn. She received a visit from her son, whom she had not seen for years. He embodied spontaneously in one of the mediums and talked *for a long time with his mother, who wept very much. The young man was in a sublime evolutionary stage. His kindness and vibration of love made the old lady surrender to light, agreeing to go, in his company, to the hospital where they would take care of her on the first days of her recuperation.*

As the most important part was solved, we went back to the young girl.

Unfolded (as she was) by Apometrics, she received a treatment directly from the disincarnated physicians, to cure the brain lesion caused by the device. They were able to reduce her loss of sight to only 25%. A disincarnated ophthalmologist tried to recompose the optic nerve by making a partial graft that was quite successful.

When we assisted A.M.G. for the third time, she was almost fully recuperated, the loss of sight was very much reduced. The terrible crises of headaches vanished after the first treatment, and never occurred again. Her life was as joyful and happy as before.

Discussion:

This was a typical situation of complex obsession, caused by the presence of a parasitic device implanted in the nervous system, with deep malign action. Her blindness progressed, not allowing the physicians even to diagnose the disease.

The pathological process surged with the patient's trip to Canada. From the spiritual point of view, it was a karmic phenomenon in which the enemies of the Past (under the action of the Cosmic Law of Harmony) had to meet for readjustment. Once the malefic action of the technician of Darkness was halted, the base, where a great number of inferior spirits dwelled, was destroyed; we recuperated all the involved entities.

Type of treatment:

Treating the obsessors, deactivating their bases in the astral. Unfolding the sick by Apometrics, treating her astral body.

Duration of each session: The first lasted forty-five minutes. The other two were thirty minutes each.

Result:

As for the spiritual recuperation, the success was total, in relation to all obsessors conducted to the places of recuperation. In the physical dimension, the whole painful set of symptoms disappeared. Residual hemianopsia was insignificant, only a little visual disturbance in the right eye remained.

Case #4: Still Another Parasitic Device Attached to the Nervous System.

Patient: J.M.F., female, 21, white, student.
Date of assistance: November 1, 1986.

The patient was being treated by a psychiatrist. She had crises, "nervous attacks" and fainting spells. She was brought to the Garden House because the classic treatment did not bring any expected results.

Spiritual diagnoses:

When the girl's frequency was opened, we realized, through clairvoyance, that the sick suffered from a resonance of symbiosis with black sorcerers. She was a former initiated spirit. The activity of her chakras shows repressed mediumicity. There were parasitic devices in her head and feet.

Treatment:

Using the condenser, an energy projection (counting: 1...2...3...) we clean (...4...5...6...7...8...9...) the whole body, cutting the symbiosis (10...11...12...20... moving the condenser placed diagonally over her chest) and taking the spirits responsible for the parasitic devices to the Love and Charity Hospital (21...22...34...24...33). At the end, her body seemed to be clean. At this point, we realized that the resonance/symbiosis was related to events linked to the fourth band; i.e., the fourth previous incarnation. We opened the frequency of that band in the Past and did the cleansing; we used the condenser, moving it over her head and her whole body (over the chest the movement was transverse, to cut symbiosis). Clairvoyance showed that the symbiosis (1...2...3...4...5...) involved sexual energy and activity. We started cutting the symbiosis (1...2...3...4...5...) the spirits had linked to the authors and to the symbiotic process, as well as the negative bands of different types. All those paralyzed in the Past, were freed and conducted, through space-time, to the L.C. Hospital (...8...9...10...15); the Past, in relation to the disharmonic events in that frequency, was clean when the counting reached 25.

We operated the projection of Christic light into the fields and bands of the Past where we intervened, in the present and in all entities linked to the process that were treated. By doing this, we put a definite end to any resonance with former existences.

The treatment ended with closing the patient's frequency and recoupling her (she was unfolded all the time).

Duration of the assistance: Three and a half minutes.

Result:

The patient reported that she was improving constantly. She did not look to us for any other assistance.

An Important Observation: *This case was reported to show the evolution of the techniques used, reflecting the speed of the assistance provided. Under the orientation of the spiritual mentors, we saw the use of condensers (electronic devices that emit radio-frequencies from 20 to 200,000 Hz), tuning forks of variable wave amplitude, and other instruments. This technical advance, thanks to the support of the spiritual world, has happened at a speed beyond our expectations. These recent techniques cannot be discussed in this book. It is a subject that deserves special treatment due to the importance of its details. It is a task for the future, a future that always arrives sooner than we imagine.*

Case #5: A Case of Black Magic (Special).
   Patient: E.M., female, 58, white, married.
   Date of assistance: September 1985, at a distance.

The assistance was asked by our work mate, Mrs. Lia Penter. The patient was an old friend of the medium, she had been her neighbor a long time ago. They had never met again. But one of the ex-neighbor's relatives, however, met Mrs. Penter, and asked her for a Spiritist treatment, once the classic treatments had not been effective.

According to what E.M.'s relative told the medium, the patient—who had never before had any symptoms of being sick, was losing weight without any discernible reason. Her vitality was decreasing constantly, due to an unknown disease. The morbid state surged six months previously, and since then E.M. had been subjected to a variety of checkups and treatments without any positive results.

Treatment:

The Tuesday after our colleague Lia's request, the name and the address of the sick were placed on our working table, together with those of other sick people. When her time came, we had hardly opened the patient's frequency, when the spirit that was directing our work determined that we embody the spirit of E.M. herself in the medium of which he (the mentor) was making use. For this reason, he left immediately.

This kind of procedure was quite unusual. The general rule is to first investigate spiritual conditions, the environment and the probable obsessors of the sick. Once the exception was config-

ured we saw right away that E.M. was responsible for her state. The case, apparently, was not simple.

We unfolded the patient, at a distance, and brought her in her mental body. She embodied in the medium as if she were disincarnated. As soon as she embodied, she shouted aggressively:

> *What do you want from me? Why did you bring me here if I do not know the place or any one of you?*

> *Relax, my lady! We brought you here to help you because you are very sick and you know very well that you are responsible for your own disease.*

We realized that her spirit was encased in dense, dark bands which are characteristics of black magic vibrations. We asked her, therefore, why she practiced black magic against others and who had been her last victim. (We did not suspect in the least who her victims could be.) We had not finished our question when the answer came, incisively:

> *I practice black magic against my enemies because I want to. With her [she was referring to her last victim] I did a "work" to destroy her. And I am going to do whatever is necessary to finish with her.*

We tried to dissuade her:

> *But, my dear, the human being is of limited free will, given to us by the Creator. Nevertheless, we are responsible for our acts. Whatever we do of good or bad to a person, sooner or later comes back to ourselves, according to the immutable laws.*

She resisted, insolently:

> *I do not believe this. I am free and I can do what I want. Nobody in the spiritual world is going to know what I do. Nobody.*

Given the level of resistance, we decided to say:

> *So, then, we are going to give you a small sample of the evil that you practice. We are going to revert the horror that you projected upon your enemy; you will enter in resonance with what you made your victim suffer.*

The moment we applied resonance on her, she held her head with both hands, and shouted more than before, desperately:

> *No, I cannot stand this any longer! Take this away from me, for heaven's sake!*

We left her suffering with anguish for some moments. And then we give her our opinion:

The one that practiced the evil can only feel free if he undoes what he did. Therefore, dear friend, we cannot give you any relief if you do not undo the evil deed. You will be in this state as long as you do not understand that you yourself are responsible for the abyss in which you are at this moment. All the suffering you are feeling is that of your victims. That is a situation called **returning shock.** *It is a Law. An inexorable Law, the harvest of which you sow. Because of this, we advise you, dear friend, to undo the "work" you did against this person, to relieve your own karma. This is the only way out for the suffering and anguish that you are feeling; there is no other way. We cannot do anything against a Cosmic Law.*

Deeply discouraged, E.M. became convinced and asked us to alleviate the burden a bit because, in her condition she was unable to undo the "work."

We relieved her suffering. But we were surprised by the presence of her **incarnated victim,** who embodied in another medium by the initiative of the **spiritual world's workers,** who helped us, in order to free the victim from the black magic field.

The case, therefore, became particularly interesting. In one of the mediums we had the presence of the author of the evil deed. Beside her, in another medium, her victim. ONE AND THE OTHER WERE INCARNATED.

The victim, in an awful spiritual state, totally devitalized, almost unconscious, did not even recognize her torturer.

The aggressor confessed that the victim was an "intimate friend of hers." She did the destructive work only because of envy, because the friend was in a very good economic situation. The meanness of her feelings and envy corroded her primary soul so much that she was trying to kill her friend!

As soon as E.M. undid the "work" at the cemetery (common in these cases), we captured the inferior spirits that she used as active agents for evil. We also discovered, that besides the habitual **exus**, there was—behind everything—a powerful sorcerer who had helped the author of the "work," a sorcerer with whom she had made an agreement, before she incarnated. This entity was also captured and sent with others to the selection laboratory of the L.C.H.

Afterwards, we reconnected the women to their respective physical bodies, recoupling them carefully, with firmness.

Diagnosis:

The patient was devitalized by a **returning shock.** *This phenomenon is common, because it represents the harvest of one's own acts.*

Prognosis:

Somber. Although the author of the sorcery undid the evil, we cannot evaluate how many malign attitudes and works she did in her past. E.M. showed improvement. But we did not hear of her anymore, neither was further assistance requested.

READINGS
The Cell of Dr. Teofrastus

In the book *Inside Information About Obsession* (F.E.B., 1972), (psychographed by Divaldo Pereira Franco, from the spiritual author Manuel Philomeno de Miranda), we found a reference to electronic devices implanted in the nervous system of obsessed spirits.

On page 159, the author shows a devilish technique applied and narrated by a sorcerer of Darkness:

> *We are going to perform an implantation—said, in a tone of unforgettable indifference, Dr. Teofrastus—of a small photoelectric recorded cell, made of special material, in the memory centers of the patient. Operating subtly in the perispirit, we will make our voice repeat insistently. 'You will go crazy! Commit suicide!' We are obligated to use the most advanced resorts, since they help us to collimate our objectives. This is one of the many processes that we can use in our tasks.*

This is the only citation about these techniques that we have found in Spiritist literature up to now.

According to the narration of Dr. Teofrastus, however, it is likely that the author made some mistakes. The photoelectric cell only produces electricity when a luminous beam falls on it; the energy produced is proportional to the intensity of the beam and to the frequency of the luminous wave that falls on it. A photoelectric cell, therefore, works *by means of the action of light.*

The denomination "photoelectric *recorded* cell" seems to be at least improper. It is a source of simple energy without audio modulation. Consequently, it could not produce voices.

We presume that it was a device that received radio-frequencies (similar to the case described above). Or, perhaps, the cell was an energetic source of a more sophisticated device that the sorcerer did not want to allude to—a sound amplifier for example.

In any event, Dr. Teofrastus' device was an electronic one and implanted in the patient's brain.

Black Magic — Cases Related by Albert De Rochas

We transcribe excerpts from the book by Albert De Rochas, L'Extériorisation de la Sensibilitié, (Chamuel Editeur, Paris, 1899—trans. Edicel, 1971), in which the author presents some cases of black magic observed at different times—real historical reports about this subject.

1. The priest Leon-Marie, sub-procurator of the Grande Chartreuse, answering a question that I had made to the Intermediaire des Chercheurs et des Curieux, writes the following:

> *During the three years (1864 to 1867) that I spent in Kouai-Thao, province of Canton, China, I quite often heard the old Christians speak about consistent processes of making somebody die at a distance, through little clay figures, of tiny dimensions (usually representing a pig) that are placed on tombs or in houses, after having received a special blessing from the bonzes.*

Monsignor de Chourry, apostolic mayor of Kuang-Si (China) told me about an analogous practice, that was still used in Kuang-Si and in Kuang-Fong.

> *A person ran away from home and nobody knows what happened to him; a thief disappeared in the same way, with stolen objects. They assure that to make this creature come back, it was enough to trace his trail on the ground and call a bonze, not any one, it had to be a master. This man, after having invoked the spirits, and sprinkled the trail with the blood of a dog, buries, with strong blows, a piece of wood or of bamboo, and so inflicts that individual—according to what they intend—colic and pain in his bowels, of extreme intensity, making him feel an intense need to go back to his parting point, persuading him that so he will get his freedom, that he will not have any rest if he does not execute the orders and confess that he is a thief and gives the stolen objects back.*

2. In 1895, the successor of Behanzin to the throne of Dahomey, having complaints about the French, did not find any better way to have them bewitched than by a tsaussa [tribal witchcraft] sorcerer. This man prepared a special paste, that another sorcerer should bury in the French field, preferably in those places where the whites used to walk through. The assistant sorcerer, was afraid and did not dare to commit this kind of perversity. He went to the threatened captain and told him everything. The white asked him about the consequences of this malefic action, and he answered:

"At each step you make on this path that represents you, a great disaster will happen to you, and soon you will die." (Dr. Regnault, La Sorcellerie, 1897, p. 18.)

3. Mr. Leclerc, in an article of the Revue Scientifique about Sorcery among Cambodians (February 2, 1895), writes the following:

It is said there are sorcerers who fabricate **rups**—or small statuettes made of wax—who call out the name of the person they want to hurt or kill while these **rups** are crossed by a knife, and magic words are pronounced. According to what they told me, the person represented by the statuette, is hurt or killed at the same instant in which the statuette is crossed by the sorcerer.

4. In 1317, John XXII, Pope of Avignon, wrote that his enemies had tried to bewitch him:

The sorcerers, Jacques, called Brabancon and Jean Amant, a physician, prepared beverages to poison us and some cardinals, our brothers. As they did not have the opportunity to make us drink these beverages, they made images of **wax with our own names, to attack our lives, by pricking** these images. But God kept the evil away from us, and made us find three of these devilish images (Hist. Arch. Library, Tarn-et-garonne, Tome IV, sec. trim. 1876.)

5. In his Recherches Sur l'Envoutement (Chamuel, 1898) Mr. Kerdanniel gave his report about a process that occurred in 1723, in front of the Senate of Savoy, after which Mr. André Philibert, Count of Pleorz, from the Dukedom of Aosta, was condemned to death for having tried to bewitch his wife, by means of wax figures that he had melted in fire.

6. *Paracelsus, in his book about the Spiritual Being* (De Ente Spirituum), *says:*

> You have to know that according to the volition of a spirit in fight with another one, if a wax image is covered with earth and stones, the man who is represented by the wax figure will be disturbed and annoyed at the place where the stones were piled up, and he only will be relieved when the image is brought to light; then he will be free from his anxieties.

7. *In old Greece we will find an excerpt by Plato that says the following:*

> There are among men two kinds of evil deeds, and the distinction between the two is very complicated. One refers to what we have clearly explained, when a body harms another body by natural means. The other one, happens by means of certain practices of bewitchment and of what we call bonds, by the ones that intend to do evil to others, and can therefore harm them, and by the ones that use these evil deeds, and really harm the others. It is very difficult to know how much about this is real, and if we knew it, it would not be easier to convince the others. It is even useless to try to prove to certain strongly prevented spirits that they should not worry about these small wax figures that might be placed at their door, or at crossroads or on the tomb of one of their ancestors and exhort him to disregard these objects, because there is a confusing kind of faith in these evil deeds... He who uses black magic, witchcraft, or any of these evil deeds, with the objective to harm, if he is a sorcerer or knows the art of observing magic, should die! If he does not have any knowledge of this kind of arts, and is convicted of having made use of evil deeds, than the Court is going to decide what punishment he and his properties are going to suffer. (Laws, Book XI, tome VII, page 324-325.)

8. *The reputation of the witches of Tesssalia is well known, they used to cause impotence and slow death, by perforating the wax image of the person whom they wanted to harm.*

* * *

Note: The number of cases of black magic that we have already treated in the Garden House makes us treat this subject with a calm understanding that, for some readers, might sound whimsical or fantastic. For us, the subject of black magic comes out of the lines and from between the lines of books to become real—always harmful for our patients—in each work session. We, frequently, for instance, have to face black sorcerers, (usually disincarnated) coming from ancient Egypt. The number of cases that we have already treated, (as a consequence of incarnated patients' treatments) is so large, that we do not have any doubt about the facts; one of the most serious reasons for the decadence of the Egyptian civilization was the proliferation of black magic acts done by minor priests, who, greedy for richness and personal power, used any of the various forms of sorceries to get what they wanted—even attracting people sexually.

Exus

Inferior spirits, of human beings that became spiritually degraded, the **exus** *are beings of awful, quite deformed appearance. Hairy and rough, unkempt, long and dirty nails, ragged, filthy clothes; they usually are guards of evil deeds.*

Whenever we detect their presence, we immediately try to place them in a magnetic contention field because of the aggressive malignity they manifest at first contact.

The inexperienced spiritual workers, not knowing how black magic deeds are done and maintained, want to capture the exus immediately. These poor beings are, most of the time, servants of the black sorcerers or of the princes of Darkness. They are obligated to act against the incarnated, if they do not want to suffer cruel punishments. We can affirm that 60% of them would like to be out of the state they are in. Once their vibratory frequency is raised and their astral bodies are cleaned, they breathe with relief. Although they are afraid of the punishment of their chiefs, they end up coming to our side, contributing actively to the "undoing" of the "work" or sorcery.

The other 40%, petrified in evil, are not easy to be conquered. They really want to go on practicing evil, because in former incarnations they suffered physical and moral violations they cannot forget. They intend to inflict on others all the wrongs they once suffered—an attitude of illogical and crazy vengeance. They have to be caught right at the beginning and sent to the colonies for recuperation.

The "Undoing"

In the assistance of black magic, a very special care has to be given to the negative fields linked to physical objects: corpses of animals or people, male dolls made of wax, material or anything else used to make clothes, pillows and all sorts of magnetized objects. **These fields have to be undone.**

There are two ways to "undo" these adverse fields-of-force:

1. By Physical Destruction Of The Objects to which they are linked; burning them, for example.

2. Through the "Raising" Of These Fields In The Astral, removing them from the objects to which they are linked. This process can be performed from a distance.

It is our habit, a quite common one, to throw the bewitched object (when we have it) in flowing water. A river, a creek, etc. Or in the sea.

In the "undoing" at a distance, we project powerful energetic fields in the form of high-frequency spouts. These spouts disintegrate, as if they were of fire, the negative fields-of-force that magnetize magic objects.

As to the bewitching prayers, very much used by sorcerers of all times, we do not need to worry much. With the destruction of the astral magnetic fields of the amulets and the objects used in black magic works, all the bewitchment, magic formulas and prayers are automatically deactivated, chiefly if the agents and guards of the evil deeds are removed. The projection (that we always do) of the vibratory fields of high frequency, also contributes to the annulment of the prayers, etc. They involved the patient and protect him against any remains of low frequency thought-forms emitted by the sorcerer.

The highlight of the undoing, the best vaccine against dark importunities and attacks, however, is to convince the black magic's victim to practice the Gospels (chiefly at home), and to have a morally healthy and spiritualized life. The practice of love and charity keeps the person more and more immune and protected.

TYPES OF COMPLEX OBSESSION

Processes of the Physical Body's Destruction, With or Without Rupture of the Buddhic Web

When the objective of obsession is the destruction of the physical body, it presents the following two aspects:

— The obsessors do not use sophisticated techniques, nor do they have enough mental power to destroy the victim. They do not cause serious consequences, fortunately most of the cases are *simple obsessions.*

— Harm, diseases, and suffering are provoked by disincarnated sorcerers or by the black magic of an incarnated being. Artful and sophisticated techniques are used, and their application sometimes requires long periods of time. The work is done by specialists, joined in organizations, composed of many spirits, solidly arranged hierarchically, frequently obeying the rulers of Darkness. In these cases (and also in those where magic is virulently caused by the incarnated), we face processes that are classified as *complex obsessions.*

One noteworthy fact is that *not always do obsessors act upon the mind*—an actuation that is not according to the classic concept of obsession (since it refers only to cases in which the mind is the objective).

Many times the aim is not—by any means—to induce insanity, but of impoverishment, misery, addiction to drugs, the separation of a happily married couple, or even the simple destruction of the victim.

In this last case, traffic accidents, attacks, etc., are used, in which *there is no* direct acting upon the victim's brain.

Buddhic Web

Besides the programming of accidents, attacks, etc., highly specialized techniques are used to provoke incurable diseases.

It is known that the generation of physical diseases, caused by astral agents (spirits) hardly succeed. All the incarnated have special organs of defense against such predatory actions. It is what we commonly call the buddhic web. This web (as clairvoyants see it) is located at the external limits of the etheric body, and it is constituted of a fine, but protective band of condensed magnetism. It prevents disincarnated predators from taking possession of an incarnated being's physical body. The protection it gives is similar to that of a *bunker,* transforming the somatic body into a kind of a refuge or fortress for his owner. Without this web, all of us would be at the mercy of the inferior astral, inhabited by evildoers of all sorts.

It happens, however, that even this natural protection can be defeated under certain conditions. For this purpose, technical knowledge and an accurate study of the target person's karmic conditions are required. That is what the technicians of Darkness do. They localize the person's karmic gap (the victim's weak points) and act through them until they control limited areas of the physical body, if not the whole body.

Usually, the action is concentrated on a specific organ. They can thrust toxic wooden wedges or poisoned astral thorns into the victim's body, renewing them periodically. They may put one or more ovoids on him which parasitize the victim inexorably. They even bring, from the nucleus or from the planet's depths, astralline material of extremely low frequency which they put in contact with the delicate tissues of the organism. The result is implacable: after some time the buddhic web is disrupted and then a localized disharmony of the tissues takes over, and with it the advent of an incurable disease—cancer, for example.

In view of the hundreds of cases of this type that we have treated and studied, we can affirm: whenever the rupture of the buddhic web is determined, we are facing a process of complex obsession.

Process of the Disturbance of
Human Performance and of Causing Death

Black Magic

We have already seen that obsession, usually, aims at making the obsessed suffer as much as possible until he dies. But among the cases we assisted there were many in which the obsessors did not want the victim's death, they wanted him to suffer as long as possible. In other cases, not so frequent, they want to harm him morally: they want their enemies to undergo the same sufferings that they inflicted upon the obsessors, in the past. We have met obsessors that help their victims, in all possible ways to get very rich and to live in great comfort, playing an important role in society. In the last of these cases we assisted, the persecutor was enjoying himself very much with the moral suffering of his enemy. He was wealthy, he had a large group of friends, but was involved in all kinds of moral problems. His first-born son was an oligophrenic microcephalic. The oldest daughter followed the route of modern vices: she became drug addicted; she was also in favor of free love and even ended up stealing. Another son, maladjusted, became a homosexual, besides being addicted to drugs. Even the man's wife, extremely voluptuous, was made to be disloyal to her husband. It is easy to imagine how bitter and full of disappointment the life of this man was, in spite of all his wealth and economic and social power.

In evil deeds of this type, involving people's worlds, or others, in which there are programmed (and provoked) accidents, crimes, etc., aimed at the victim's impoverishment, degradation and even destruction, there is always the action of black magic caused by sorcerers of the astral or by incarnated ones.

About Black Magic

Refer to the consecutive sections above: "Black Magic", "Presence of Negative Magnetic Fields, Without the Assistance of Disincarnated Obsessors" and "Parasitic Devices Attached to the Nervous System".

STAGES OF THE OBSESSIVE PROCESS
(ITS ACTION UPON THE MIND)

According to Kardec, obsession has three stages. We are going to transcribe numbers 238, 239 and 240 from the *Medium's Book,* due to the importance (in spite of so many years having gone by) of master Lyon's elucidations:

> **238: Simple obsession**—*It is a case of simple obses- sion when an evil-doing Spirit imposes his authority on a medium; meddling in, against the medium's will, in the messages he receives, impeding that he communicates with other Spirits, and presents himself in place of those that are evoked. Nobody is obsessed just because he was deceived by an untruthful Spirit. The best medium is exposed to this fact, chiefly at the beginning, when he does not have yet the necessary experience, like it hap- pens among people, where the most honest ones can be deceived by crooks. Therefore we can be wrong without being obsessed. Obsession consists in a Spirit's perse- verance, from which the person on whom he acts, cannot get rid of.*

> **239: Fascination**—*Fascination has very serious conse- quences. It is an illusion produced by the direct action of the Spirit upon the medium's thought and that, in a certain way, paralyzes his reasoning, in relation to communication. The fascinated medium does not believe that he is being cheated: the Spirit has the skill to make the medium trust him blindly; therefore he is unable to recognize the deceit and to understand the absurdity he is writing down, even if everybody is aware of the situa- tion. The illusion can even make the medium consider the most ridicule language, sublime. It was a mistake to believe that only simple, ignorant, unreasonable people would be subject to this type of obsession. Not even people of high spirits, the most educated ones and the most intelligent ones are free from this illusion, a fact that proves that this kind of aberration is the effect of an odd cause, that has great influence on them...*

> **240: Subjugation**—*Subjugation is a constriction that paralyzes the volition of the one who suffers the action*

and makes him do things against his will. In other words, the patient is under a real **bondage.**

Subjugation can be **moral** *or* **corporeal.** *In the first case, the subjugated is forced to make decisions that usually are absurd and jeopardize him; but he, due to a kind of illusion considers the decisions wise—it is like a fascination. In the second case, the spirit acts upon the material organs and provokes unintentional movements. In the writing medium it is manifested by a continuous need to write, sometimes at the least proper moments. We saw some that, in the absence of a pencil or a pen, simulated writing with their fingers wherever they were—even on streets, doors, or walls.*

Corporeal subjugation sometimes goes even farther and can produce ridiculous acts. We came to know a man who was neither young nor handsome; under the power of such an obsession, he was compelled by an irresistible force to kneel in front of a girl in whom he was not interested at all, and ask her to marry him. Other times he felt a strong pressure in his back that forced him, in spite of his resistance, to kneel and kiss the ground in public places and in the presence of a crowd of people.

This man was considered crazy by his relatives and friends; however, we are convinced that he definitely was not, because he was conscious of the ridiculous actions that he did against his will, and this fact made him suffer very much.

We do not have the temerity to correct Kardec. But we enlarged the concept of obsession, not because of theoretical reasons, but—as Kardec himself did—due to observation, study and treatment of these psycho-pathological cases over about a quarter of a century. For us, there are four stages to the mental obsessive process: the first can be considered a "pre-stage" and belongs almost to normality (because all of us are subject to obsessions, whether we are mediums or not).

Transitory and Casual Disturbing Action

It is a diffuse process, without any visible psycho-pathological signs. It looks like actuation from a distance, light but persistent. This persistence transforms the incipient pathological state in clear morbidity.

At the beginning, due to lack of vigilance, the victim is discreetly involved in a diffuse magnetic field, projected by the obsessor's mind. Little by little, the obsessed gets used to this atmosphere of low vibratory standard, without realizing that his opinions are changing. The beginning of an obsessive process can be observed exactly at this point, through the virulent passions and radicalization that are manifested in personal opinions. It is common to see people that relate normally to life, get furious when they face the slightest criticism about their opinions (political, religious, etc.), causing surprise to their interlocutors. The excessive emphasis given to his own ideas is usually contradictory with the calm and prudent behavior that the person shows when talking about other subjects.

There are those, for example, who defend their soccer teams in an aggressive manner. They go to the stadium to attack the adversaries of their teams, using coarse language; they do not even spare the referee. Some people commit these unbalanced actions in business and love affairs, resulting in their names being published in the criminal section of newspapers.

Medicine classifies this behavior as *paranoid*. Over-emphatic, it always indicates a notorious external influence. In fact, obsessor's magnetic fields are exerting real hypnotic control over these people that allow them to be influenced. Vices, for instance, usually, start in these fields.

Fascination

Fascination corresponds totally to Kardec's concept, just to enlarge the concept we would like to add, that anyone can suffer from fascination, not only mediums.

It is, of course, a more emphatic stage of the process of obsession, where we can find signs of abnormality; an opinionated behavior, and above all, a distortion of subjective values of personality. In this phase, the sick person fights for his conceptions. It is very common to see an apparently normal person, forgetting about his dignity and social position, starting to write sentences on walls, to exalt his candidates, before elections. We used to say that this person is fascinated by another person or by ideas that he defends. This phenomenon is much more common than we imagine, because all humanity is strongly influenced by spirits of lower evolution, inhabitants of the region that is near the planetary crust.

Control of Mind

In this phase the person is already practically controlled by the obsessor, who, little by little, was able to involve him in his mental-magnetic field, breaking the victim's psychic resistances and hypnotizing him.

The natural internal censure that we exercise (and that controls our behavior) becomes almost zero in these people. The victim is a toy in the hands of the obsessor. Subjective values are subverted, auditory hallucinations surge—diffuse and sporadic at the beginning, but becoming more and more frequent; at the end, they are constant: invisible beings talk with the obsessed, inveigh against his acts, accuse him of a kind of behavior that he never had. They induce him into taking depressed attitudes.

Visual hallucinations are also very common in this phase, or even persecution manias. The sick one considers himself destined to die, persecuted by spies or other executioners. He is almost totally dominated by the obsessor: all of his actions are directed by this evildoer.

Subjugation

It is the last and the most tragic of all phases.

At this stage of the psycho-pathological disease, the sick person is totally dominated by the obsessor, who makes of him what he wants. The obsessed (and sick) one becomes a mere puppet.

The victim is characterized by self-aggression, by committing suicide, or by attacking people around him, beginning with his family. The patient does not listen to kind admonitions. He almost always reacts with irrationality and violence. Some beat upon walls because they see the enemies of Darkness and want to attack them. (Until recently these acute psychotic outbursts required the use of a straitjacket. Today they sedate the patient strongly and induce sleep.)

This last stage represents the corporeal possession, and by and large is similar to the Spiritist embodiment. The obsessor pulls the obsessed's spirit out and embodies through the splenic chakra. (This is according to Pauli's quantum principle, that says that one body cannot occupy two places at the same time, in space.)

In our opinion, the aggressive action does not happen entirely due to the obsessor. In part, it is a reactive process of the patient himself, anxious to get free from the strange being that took over his body: small remainders of a not totally erased consciousness. The aggressive reaction is skillfully used by the invader, who intensifies it and directs it to the objective: the annihilation the victim's personality in front of others.

In the course of time, the obsessed becomes apathetic and turns away from others—presenting a medical case of chronic schizophrenia. These individuals form increasing contingents of patients in psychiatric wards of many hospitals.

* * *

As we have seen, there are many forms of disincarnated spirit's malefic actions upon the incarnated. It depends on the obsessor's interest, his technical knowledge, his mind's power, the target region, and the victim's resistance.

We talked about the processes of obsessive action *upon the mind.* For this reason, when we refer to this particular field, our convictions coincide, in many aspects, with those of Kardec. However, we would like to stress that, in our opinion, pathology in this case is much more extensive. Besides the mind, it involves THE WHOLE PHYSICAL BODY. To clarify our position we would like to ask the following:

> *Can we classify as a classic obsessive* **mental** *process, black magic that impedes a business transaction through injunctions that are only* **material?** *Can we classify incurable diseases (such as cancer) caused by spirits when an organ far from the head is affected, excluding any action upon the victims brain or thought?*

As we can see, obsessive processes are not constituted only by mental malfunctions.

SELF-OBSESSIVE ANIMISTIC PHENOMENA

RESONANCE WITH THE PAST

Resonance with the past is a brief and unexpected glimpse—through ideoplastic flashes—of situations experienced in former lives. The incarnated person does not remember past lives because the physical brain did not live these situations and, obviously, does not have any record of them. The brain is apt to deal with phenomena that are part of the present existence, and not of others.

The eternal spirit that dwells in us, however, keeps all the experienced scenes in former incarnations. Everything is kept: sensations, emotions, and thoughts, with all their colors.

On special occasions or in special circumstances, some former life experiences can filter into the present brain, bringing these experiences to the level of consciousness. If the remembrance is harmonic, happy and joyful, the irradiated sensation will be a mixture of indefinable happiness and yearning for something or someone, something that the person is unable to explain, although he feels that there is a certain relation to situations at the present time. Sometimes, when we visit an unknown place, for example, remembrances come up in our minds, as if we had been missing this place. These facts are fragmentary but alive, although dim and shapeless. Suddenly an old house, a corner in the garden or a place in the house is familiar to us, giving us the feeling that we knew the place, although we are sure that we have not been there before. This is often called *deja vu.*

These impressions are not foolish.

When we see these places, their similarity with environments or scenes of the past arouses recollections that do not *emerge* normally. There is a kind of superimposition of images, that due to the likeness, provoke vibratory resonance. And a scene that might have happened centuries ago, emerges dimly, pressuring consciousness in such a lively way, that there can be a rapid view of the past.

When the remote situation is unpleasant, its filtering into the present can cause sudden anguish, bad feelings, fear. After some time there can be a deconstruction of the personality, and in serious cases, a clear psychopathology. The successive remembrances, coming suddenly, without any logical explanation, end up in undermining the nervous system. And to make the pathological state worse, there is a great feeling of terror caused by the uncommon phenomenon. This fear gives rise to self-induced mental parasitic currents, that, of their own accord constitute a well-defined psycho-pathological syndrome.

TREATMENT

The treatment of this syndrome, still unknown to Medicine, consists of erasing from the patient's brain the impression of the images coming from other equations of Time. This erasing is done using the technique of depolarization of the memory's stimuli. This technique was developed at the Garden House fourteen years ago, and has been applied with much success.

Illustrative Case

Patient: L.V., 32, female, white, married.
Biotype: Ecto-endomorphic.
Religion: Spiritist.
Date of assistance: May 1974.

L.V. was in the Spiritist Hospital for the second time. She had been hospitalized for three months. The diagnosis was schizophrenia—becoming chronic—due to the static condition of her clinical state despite her taking large quantities of therapeutic drugs. Intense anguish. Persecution delirium. Exaggerated crises of fear. Feelings of being abandoned that resulted in long outbursts of crying, followed by mental confusion. Clear psychopathology installed.

Everything started during an organic weakening that occurred after her last delivery when she had to face some minor domestic problems. There was a sudden and unbalanced crisis of anguish that was followed by others in the days to come. After going to famous psychiatrists, the patient was hospitalized because of her psychomotor agitation during the crises.

The first time she stayed in hospital for three months. After this period she was calm enough to go home. After a short time, however, the anomalies—which resisted the strongest sedatives—started again. Back to the hospital since her crises of insanity were constant now.

In the Spiritist Hospital she received electroshock therapy and high doses of psychotropics which reduced the intensity of the symptomatology. The physicians, therefore, classified the situation as "schizophrenia that was becoming chronic."

The treatment at the Garden House could be done with the patient's presence.

When she came into the room she suddenly caught hold of us, and started crying desperately, begging us to help her. She shouted that she could not stand the situation any longer.

Unfolded by Apometrics, our mediums immediately identified a disincarnated woman in an awful vibratory state, close to the patient. The entity was still attached to an old fashioned coffin which she grievously dragged with her.

We started assisting the suffering entity. We cut the magnetic ties that fastened her to the coffin, setting her free. Relieved, the disincarnated creature began a long report about the drama that the sick woman went through in a former incarnation, when she lived in Scotland.

She had been the beloved sister of the now incarnated patient. There was a large difference in the age of the two, because the youngest child of the family (the present sick one) was born when the parents were rather old. The parents, very wealthy, did not live long after the birth of their last daughter. The little girl was a very young orphan. The oldest sister, a very active spinster of strong personality, fell in love with the little child and raised her as if she were her own. She even protected her in excess, in any situation of her life; consequently, the affective ties between the two were as intense as if they were really mother and daughter.

The girl had a tranquil and sweet life, living in a mansion, surrounded by the sister's affection and by the attention of the servants. She was like a hothouse flower, not prepared to face the storms that destiny had reserved for her.

When she was old enough, the sister made her marry a fellow-countryman who, in spite of his nobility, was far from what the rich and romantic girl expected. The young man was used to a different environment, living a Bohemian style, spending the nights out with other women, and gambling rampantly—behavior that was pushing him to ruin. To avoid this inevitable ruin he married the young girl, interested only in her considerable inheritance.

Very early he showed his frivolous character and low moral personality, asking for more and more money to satisfy his low instincts. This derangement went so far that the older sister intervened in the couple's life and expelled the playboy from their house. This man, therefore, hated the spinster, but at the same time he was afraid of her because of her energetic character and the honesty of her attitudes.

When the sick woman was 32 years old, the older sister disincarnated, leaving the young lady in uncontrollable sorrow, and at the mercy of her husband, who did not wait long to come back to take over his wife's fortune. He dissipated the money in no time. And to complete his bad actions, he abandoned his wife and home.

A little later the young baroness of the Scottish highlands died in total misery, after having gone through privations, frustrations, much grief and suffering.

When his sister-in-law died, the playboy, to take revenge and precautions, had the idea to magnetize her to her tomb. As he was scared that the sister-in-law could demand an accounting of his actions, he did this (probably helped by a competent sorcerer) by placing a duly prepared black crucifix on the corpse's feet. The sister-in-law, probably due to a low spiritual development (and also because she did not deserve it), was not able to get rid of either the grave clothes or the coffin in which she was buried. She was still carrying with her, in erraticity, the macabre and cumbersome burden, in great despair. (It is useful to clarify that all objects that we use have an astral counterpart, as real as the physical one.)

This was, with the suppression of some details, the drama that happened in Scotland, in the middle of the last century, as narrated by the sister's embodied spirit.

The Spirit's Treatment:

We projected energy, by counting, and gave her quite energetic magnetic passes, to free the lady from the heavy burial clothes and from the coffin. This was done in a few minutes.

Next, we tried to revitalize her. We projected revitalizing cosmic energy with immediate results. Free and more relaxed, the woman thanked us repeatedly, crying with happiness.

We made her see the great evil she was causing to her incarnated sister, with her crying and afflicting presence. She was deeply shocked because her desire was to help her. And this was true because she was only there for having been called by the sister herself. She revealed that the sister used to call her during the night, as she used to do so often when she was a child (she was afraid of sleeping in the dark). Her longings for her adoptive mother reached the highest point when she caressed her sister/patient. We allowed her to touch, through the mediums hands, her sister's long and well-treated hands. She started crying. And at the same time she laughed, in moments of intense and pathetic emotion, that touched the present workers. She thanks God for those supreme instants of a long restrained love, for the ability to be able to touch her little sister physically as she used to long ago. Crying with happiness, she says that her sister's hands are the same as in her previous life.

*We asked her if she would like to begin a treatment in a hospi-
tal in the astral, in order to help her little sister in the future.
She, immediately, agreed. And she disconnected herself from
the medium, thanking us again and again.*

The Patient's Treatment:

*L.V. was not unfolded, due to her emotional state. We only
commanded vibratory syntony to link her to the Superior.*

We gave her:

*1. Magnetic passes for the cleansing of the negative vibrations
that involved her;*

*2. Magnetic treatment to reduce the vibration of the superior
chakras;*

*3. Brain drainage of low frequency magnetic currents and of
parasitic images, formed in the astral brain by continuous fear
and anguish. (See "Self-Induced Parasitic Mental Currents");*

*4. We applied the "depolarization of the memory stimuli" of her
previous life, with the objective of making the patient forget the
Scottish drama.*

Discussion:

*A pathological process in which occur two psychic laws actuat-
ing simultaneously, as it happens with the laws of electricity. In
the astral brain there was the generation of parasitic currents,
making the state of the patient even worse, due to psychic
exhaustion.*

First Law: Vibratory Resonance With the Past

*Due to the actuation of this Law, anguishing situations from the
previous incarnation passed to the present one. These passages
happened so often that they built up an abnormal state of consciousness. A permanent anguish was the first nucleus of the
neurosis that, after some time, degenerated into psychopathological behavior. The resonance with the drama of the past
surged when the patient completed 32 years of the present
incarnation—the same age she had in her previous life, when
her sister died. The affective drama of the past became the
active focus of the present psychosis.*

*Extremely sensitive, it was easier for L.V. to vibratorily
syntonize to the spiritual plane because she was physically
weakened. As she had her vital ties debilitated, she could
perceive physically (due to ideoplastic phenomena) certain situations of despair that she had gone through in Scotland.*

*This process generated the fear of becoming insane, the fear of
death, the terror of being abandoned (similar to what had*

happened before); parasitic currents that accompany morbid states, making them worse.

Second Law: Spiritual Induction

When L.V.'s body fell asleep, the desperate spirit sought help. She called for her sister to protect her as she had done so often before. The sister, who was erratic, also anguished and suffering, was attentive to the call and came. But, because she was also disharmonized, she transmitted—through spiritual induction—her own vibratory state to the patient. Thus, she contributed—involuntarily—to the sister's suffering. It is noteworthy to say that the older sister acted negatively only because of her presence, and not with the intention to harm.

For a better understanding, we are going to give a brief summary:

1. The vibratory resonance with an anguished past brought psychic disharmony to the present life, through ideoplastic flashes;

2. Spiritual induction, transferring disharmonic energy from the sister to the patient, aggravated the imbalance;

3. The action of the two above cited laws generated self-induced parasitic mental currents, accelerating the progressive psychic wear, would take the sick woman to a total imbalance.

Duration of treatment: 40 minutes.
Number of assistances: Only one.
Result: She could leave the hospital after three days, totally cured.

Over the approximately five years we had the opportunity to be in contact with the patient, we could observe her complete cure. She graduated in law and practices her profession.

TORMENTED, FRAGMENTARY REMEMBRANCES OF A FORMER INCARNATION

In this syndrome there are no images, no sights of scenes experienced in former existences. The sick person feels a sudden indisposition, anguish or depressive state that represents the ones he suffered in another life or lives, it is a kind of suffering that seems to be the consequence of something undefinable, only a sort of *sensation.* The sick one glimpses fragments of scenes, everything scattered, incoherent, but he knows that they are part of a set that—*he feels*—is degrading (or in degradation).

At the beginning these experiences can be interpreted as remainders—or perhaps parts—of a forgotten dream. Slowly, however, they generate a state of consciousness different from the normal forgotten dream. Slowly, they generate a state of consciousness different from the normal one. The continuous focus on a depressing scene (even if it were seen in fragments) and strange sensations makes him syntonize it. The moments of escape, in which former sensations return—some anguishing, others mean, but all degrading—become more and more constant. Once the ambivalence of life experiences is experienced, there will be a primacy of the former over the present ones, with evident disturbance: the person does not know to what he can attribute such irresistible, but at the same time, unusual phenomena.

If the fact persists, the process tends to stick to the person's behavior. And once it is stuck, another syndrome comes to the fore. As the person is not able to explain these remembrances, the fear of becoming insane produces self-induced parasitic currents. And psychic wear is even more accelerated.

Other fears can join this terror. If the person, for example, knows about the karmic laws, he becomes afraid of the redeeming of his errors. These vicious circles form real energetic vortices, foci of neurotic disassociation.

Although medicine does not believe it, considering those vague sensations, anguishes, etc., as imaginative delirium, everything that the sick sees is perfectly real to him.

Treatment:

Unfolded, the patient is taken to the space-time from which these sensations and fragmented remembrances come. Once he is *there*, everything has to be erased from his mind by the technique of *depolarization of the memory's stimuli*, with total success.

SELF-INDUCED PARASITIC MENTAL CURRENTS

In obsessed minds it is common to have the formation of mental currents of an intensity proportional to the situations of anguish that originated from them, they are kind of thought-forms generated and fed by the sick person's imagination, in his emotional imbalance.

The main cause is fear, sometimes terror, panic: the more intense anguish is, the greater the fright the person feels. These mental currents provoke great wear on the nervous system and exhaust the person, who quite often suffers needlessly, *due to anticipation*. According to the intensity, the process can be classified as a psycho-pathological syndrome, a clear mental disease.

These self-induced mental currents constitute a phenomenon that affects all human beings, obsessed or not—perhaps due to atavism. Our prehistoric ancestors, living in dark and cold caves in the long winter nights, were in constant fear of wild animals, of the natural elements, and of other human beings. This terror, experienced over millennia through myriad generations, ended up *imprinted* on humankind.

During childhood we are afraid of the dark. And this darkness enlarges, becoming bigger and more important than only physical darkness. Among adults we find fear of the unknown. Fear of death. Terror of facing any kind of suffering. Anguish with the possibility of losing properties, or beloved creatures. Fear of becoming poor, (as we observe in some neurotics) and all the immense rosary of terrors more or less subterranean.

Obsessors take advantage of this fact, they terrify their victims—based on this atavistic foundation—in all imaginable forms, giving the most unbelievable excuses, aiming at the annihilation or suffering of their victims. In order to succeed, they use all kinds of means, from sophisticated hypnotic techniques (forming destructive mental images) up to the roughest ones and of physical effects, as raps, knocking (common in haunted houses), making the presence of the "other world" quite evident.

There are people who are very vulnerable to this kind of obsession. They are the ones who cultivate sickly thoughts, who, for instance, have pleasure in describing diseases they suffer from or that they imagine they suffer from. We could go on describing some unwholesome ideas that dominate people's lives or sometimes groups, but we would rather have the reader find and think about them. We mentioned only one or the other of these mental states, because they are very subtle and tremendously negative.

Very often we meet people who, facing any circumstances—even when the problem concerns faith and religion—are so vacillating that they make dubiousness an "anti-foundation" of their personalities; they allow doubt to influence their life more than the sound reality of certainty. They are mentally sick, but they do not know it. They might not have reached the point of clear imbalance. But they are always insecure, anguished, vulnerable and subject to the influences of people of strong personality. About these people and their diseases, André Luiz left clarifying pages for us. In his book *The Messengers,* for instance, we read the following in the chapter entitled "The Sick Mind":

> *Aniceto touched us slightly, and said:*

> > *See what sickly mind this man has. He is one of those curious incarnated sick people. He is of vast culture; however, as he has his feelings poisoned,*

everything that enters his reasoning, participates of the general poisoning. He is a researcher of surfaces as so many people are. He expects everything from other people, but he does not auscultate himself. He wants the divine accomplishment without any human effort; he complains about the divine favor, and formulates requests; he wants the wheat of truth, without participating in the sowing; he expects tranquillity through faith, without helping with the work; he values science, without consulting consciousness; he prefers easiness, without valuing responsibility, and living in the whirlwind of continuous libations, clinging to low interest and to the satisfaction of physical senses, in absolute manner, he is waiting for spiritual messages...

In all cases of obsession that we considered (and studied) these self-inducing parasitic mental currents, contributed to an appreciable parcel of frayed energy, aggravating the sick's state. In any treatment of obsession, therefore, it is necessary to consider this negative self-actuation.

Mental hygiene (so insistently recommended by religious guides of all times), well-conducted psychotherapy, and sound and loving moral support can make the sick take the safe way of cure, minimizing the effect of these animistic energies. Other kinds of medicine that we indicate include magnetic passes taken systematically, the study of the Gospels, outdoor life and well-oriented sports.

Let us see the analogies of these self-induced mental currents with the ones of physics.

We call this phenomenon "parasitic" currents, because, in their genesis, they behave the same as way as the currents of Foucault in an electromagnet. We know that, when electric currents circulate through an electromagnet, there is a formation of—parasitic—induced magnetic currents, in the iron nucleus. These currents become transformed into the form of heat. (In any electromagnetic current, if the frequency increases, part of the energy is transformed into heat.) The heat can be so intense that it can harm the device; due to this fact the iron nuclei of electrical devices are laminated to avoid the amplitude of these magnetic currents.

Exactly as in physics, many human beings have their psychism affected, "burned" by the "disease" that an electromagnet can suffer. Currents of animistic nature also overheat and destroy. An unrestrained egotism, a morbid liking for shocking news (criminal news, for example), "gossiping" about other people's low behavior, in short, a continuous *absence of mental cleanliness,* causes low frequency to the person, and is propitious to psychic confusion. Any difficulty that comes up in the life of these unwise people, a loss, pain or disease, can be enough to provoke an overheating and the self-destruction, followed by an annihilation of volition and a disorganizing of the personality values.

The phenomenon is of such subtlety that very often we do not give the necessary importance to it. And that is the danger. That is why we take more time and expose the result of our observations and studies. Nevertheless, we did not introduce anything new, except for giving more emphasis to it. Kardec, in *Posthumous Works* wrote:

> *Some sickly states and certain aberrations that are said to be due to occult causes, derive from the individual himself.*

PHYSICAL KARMIC STIGMAS THAT FORM OBSESSIVE NUCLEI

We all know people who were born marked indelibly by signs, scars, and other deformations that limit their psychomotor activities by giving them an ugly appearance—a fact that marks mainly women. Stigmatized individuals suffer very much from these deformations, for which they do not find any logical explanation. The anomalies generate more or less deep nuclei of anguishing states that evolve into a neurosis and, at the same time, produce repressions.

However, it is known that these marks always appear by the imposition of the Law of Karma. Their presence in this incarnation is a real good, showing the person the nature of a former mistake of his. The anomaly, therefore, is a guide to spiritual education.

These deformations may appear, for instance, in people who committed suicide in a former life. As the self-destruction deeply harmed the inferior bodies that they keep after death—somatic, etheric, astral and mental—injuries resurface in another life, an indelible sign of a committed mistake.

In 1979, we assisted a child (six years old) who suffered from congenital cardiopathy—mixing of venous with arterial blood—and a functional decompensation. Underdeveloped, sickly, and weak, always having a cold, the child had a limited relational life. Besides this he was always anguished and had constant nightmares. Before he was subjected to physical heart surgery, he came to the Garden House, to get prepared for it.

We studied the past of the boy, and discovered that the cause of the cardiopathy was a dagger driven deeply into his chest in the cardiac area. In a past incarnation, he killed a friend in an old mansion, where the two were wooing the same girl. Desperate because the girl preferred his friend, he decided to eliminate him. Therefore, when the two were visiting the girl (they had been invited for dinner) he took advantage of a moment when they were alone and, with the excuse of showing the friend a horse, he invited him to the stable. As they were going down the stairs alone, he suddenly turned to the friend and stabbed him in the heart. He jumped over the body and went out to the yard where he met other people with whom he started talking as if nothing had happened.

The criminal was not discovered, although there were some suspicions. As the two belonged to the high nobility, it was easy for the authorities to attribute the crime to a thief who was surprised by the victim before he could steal anything.

Time passed, but the criminal could never forget the dagger he had stabbed deep into his friend's chest, and the surprised look on his face at the moment of his death. As thought is a creative force in the astral, the criminal formed in his mind (through an ideoplastic creative phenomenon) a thought-form in which the dagger was continuously shining, stained with blood. The dagger became a *real* presence in every moment of the criminal's *spirit*.

In the course of time, the dagger was part of the criminal's astral body. When he disincarnated, the dagger went with him. Except that now the dagger was stabbed into his own chest, a consequence of the Law of the Return of Deeds Done—Good generates Good, Evil generates Evil.

The anomalous energy of the dagger, deeply dissociative in relation to the delicate biological equilibrium of the cells that would constitute the heart (during the embryonic formation), greatly disturbed the dynamism of the tissue formation, consequently provoking a congenital anomaly. The etiology of the cardiac pathology was, therefore, clearly of a spiritual order. It was totally different from the normal means of investigation and scientific treatment. The cause was, in the final analysis, based on the Cosmic Law of Harmony: following it, the criminal provided his own punishment; he was born sick, in just proportion to the evil he committed.

Due to divine mercy, however, the cardiopathy could be corrected through a difficult surgery. With this suffering, the cosmic pupil got to know, perhaps forever, that under no circumstance, should we hurt our brothers.

After three assistances at the Garden House, (at an interval of seven days) and with the removal of the fateful dagger, the boy underwent the programmed surgery, with relative success.

We assisted the victim of the past. In a process of simple obsession, the stabbed young man did not abandon the boy; he was sent to the place of recuperation in the astral.

In March 1987, we heard of the patient's situation. The cicatrization of the surgery took about four months. Over about five years (until 1984) he was still sickly; then he started to recuperate. Today he is perfectly well.

PSYCHIC KARMIC STIGMAS THAT FORM OBSESSIVE NUCLEI

Psychic stigmas have identical origins and consequences as the physical ones. The difference is that the physical ones are quite rare, while the psychic ones can be found everywhere once a large part of the incarnated must bear them, in the most varied degrees of intensity.

Vicious habits, for example, (not the clear and degrading vices) are stigmas difficult to be extirpated, because the scalpel of the surgeon does not penetrate to their roots. But there are also fixed ideas, radical and systematic opinions, unjustified hatred against people, races or institutions, that contribute to the increasingly large number of the psychically maladjusted ones.

The difficult in extirpating these stigmas is that the treatment requires, as we have already seen in other cases, a careful mental hygiene. The person has to actively control his ideas, modifying his way of behaving.

These flaws usually are only conquered through the arousing of a more profound consciousness, in respect to oneself, as well as to the reality that surrounds us. Individuals who, in the past, for example, exerted positions of command, (kings, rulers, despotic military officers) incarnate with twisted mentality, demanding immediate assent to their opinions, if not total obedience. Vices that result from economic power are also very common and difficult to eradicate; our physical existence is energized and controlled by money. There are also those important people and intellectuals, with messianic tendencies, who want to lead the crowd by means of forms of governments unacceptable for our historical moment; they usually are those politicians and demagogues that still are longing to be different from the common mortal, and who— according to them—have the right and the obligation to orient other people.

The number of these states of consciousness is so enormous that is it impossible to describe them in detail. We realized, however, that a good part of these stigmatized people (chiefly those who can have a certain influence upon others) is manipulated by the spirits of Darkness who, due to the lack of vigilance that characterizes them, tend to join in profound symbiosis of varied degrees.

All these individuals must *perceive* that the tonic note of their behavior is egotism. If they realize this and get convinced of the need for an antidote—evangelical renunciation—they will have their stigmas cured. They are not able to see that the cure *is in them,* in the One who said: I AM THE WAY, THE TRUTH AND LIFE.

MALADJUSTMENTS OF REINCARNATION

Maladjustments of reincarnation usually become the foci of anguish—ncurosis—which after some time gets transformed into psychosis. And psychosis characterizes the final and definite state of psychopathology, with serious risk to the personality structure, mainly in the evaluation of subjective values.

One of the causes of maladjustments of reincarnation is the change of sex. Seldom does a person live perfectly adjusted, when he incarnates to the opposite sex. The new state is going to be different from the habitual one, although he is living at a different time, with other customs and values, and in spite of the fact that his physical body isolates the new state from the experiences of the past.

We have seen many cases in which the previous gender appears in the present personality, causing strange disturbances, odd gestures and manners, enjoying values that are incompatible with the present personality. We have seen many other situations, tendencies and unusual attitudes, that harm the person including aberrations and vices in sexual practice.

The sexual maladjustments are more common because sex is ruled by atavistic tendencies, where instincts prevail and dominate. When the change of sex is due to karmic injunctions, the present situation overlaps with the deep experiences of former situations. These can, at times, appear in subliminal levels of consciousness, interfering with the individual's present existence. Consequently, there will be disturbances.

Although sex is a predominant factor in these maladjustments, all the other conflicts with former incarnated states can provoke irreversible emotional aberrations.

We have met people who do not appreciate social life. They are misanthropes. After deeper investigation we find that they had been hermits or monks who spent their whole lives running from living with other people because of a fear of the sins of the flesh. Usually these monks incarnate into the same sex, but they are always fleeing women. They are shy, naive and unable to live in brotherly togetherness. They lived as recluses for many years, imprisoned and coerced in conceptions that marked their personality for a long time. With these antecedents, they easily become maladjusted. They do not know how to live in society.

At other times, we have met formerly powerful individuals who today feel frustrated in their impotence since they incarnated without splendor and power. They now are poor and tied to jobs that they hate; and besides this, they are persecuted by their disincarnated enemies.

According to all this, we can understand the terrible drama of humankind.

Almost all human beings are spiritually sick. With a past full of mistakes and behavioral vices, man today is born maladjusted, with the heavy karmic burdens of yesterday. These burdens make a hell out of his life. Psychiatry also considers the majority of humankind neurotic. In effect, an individual rarely considers himself happy. Everybody presents some problems and a type of anguish, which sedatives do not solve. For this reason, religions recommend personal harmonization through prayer, meditation, the reading of the Gospels, etc. Without question, an internal renewal proportioned by a well-oriented spiritual education, is necessary for a cure of any of these psychic dysfunctions.

MENTAL-EMOTIONAL VICIOUSNESS

Any kind of mental viciousness indicates sickness of the spirit. These subtle vicious manifestations, in behavior or in addressing subjective values, all demonstrate some morbid abnormality of the character.

Whatever kind of vice it may be—smoking, alcohol, drugs, gluttony, extravagant sexuality, gambling, etc.—is first of all a vice of the mind, allied to emotional intemperance.

After some time, the morbid state of consciousness gets attached to the immortal individuality. It lasts then, along the incarnations, as an indelible stigma, that is necessarily lingering and difficult to cure. Mental vitiation, therefore, can have its origin in former incarnations, and its spiritual treatment requires investigation of the roots of the eternal past. The mental vices of the present life are much easier to extirpate, due to a relative inconsistency of their roots and of less profundity of the anomaly.

In all cases, cure is based on mental hygiene, honest living, the cultivation of noble actions and vigilant attitudes and words, in such a way that the individual is in a condition to leave the state of spiritual *inferiority* into which he sank.

We know that emotions give life and color to our acts. Therefore, controlling ourselves is the first step to an interior reconstruction. If someone is well educated, it is because since he as a child he is used to manifesting his emotions with moderation, without showy explosions and words of low level. (In synthesis, good education is obedience to more or less rigid ethical standards.) Correct behavior, consequently, is evidence of the efficiency with which individuals that are considered *educated* were molded.

If we control well our feelings, vices and character defects disappear. But it is necessary to be persevering, we have to constantly control what we feel, think of all our acts, attitudes and behavior. Only in this way can one achieve improvement of character, propitiating the elevation to higher plans.

The delimitation of this route to happiness and Spiritual Light has been shown by Masters of all epochs and civilizations. Buddha, the Illuminated, recommended that his disciples proceed correctly, following immortal rules that aimed at spiritual education through constant vigilance. In all religions, in spite of different words and labels, the basic orientation is the same. If this is so, why should we, on our own account, follow detours and short-cuts that take us to pain, vices and to the Darkness of nowhere?

UNCONTROLLED ANIMISM

As the word itself says, *animism* is everything that comes from the soul.

In mediumistic phenomena we sometimes detect an interference in the sensitive's psychism in spiritual communications. Many impressionable people—mainly sensitive women—simulate contacts with disincarnated spirits, transmitting messages and orientations that supposedly come from sublime entities. Usually they are maladjusted people, anxious for self-affirmation who, through this procedure, see a means to increase their prestige and standing within their communities. They use poor language to say trivial things devoid of content and thus show their lack of knowledge, the emptiness of the opinions they defend and their desire to exalt their personality.

Sometimes, mediums who are dissatisfied with the humble and evangelical language they normally use, emphasize their *personal* points of view. They include in the authentic message, creations out of their own minds, that although they are attuned to the gist of the message, distort it.

This phenomenon—i.e., conscious or unconscious deception—constitutes a plague, the tares in the yellowish wheat field. And, like the tares, it is difficult to eradicate this process because it implies a deep change in the medium's way of being.

Vigilance and determination are necessary to avoid deviation from authenticity, combined with strength and humility: these will show the safe route to a sincere medium, one who wants to serve with purity, discretion, and blessed charity.

Years ago, we had a very interesting case.

One of our fellows, a good mediumistic potential and with several years of work in our group, was receiving a higher entity whose function was the one of a physician in the Love and Charity Hospital, in the astral. She syntonized perfectly with the spirit and received from him safe orientation for the sick's treatment and also for the unfolding techniques.

In the course of time, however, she started dominating the supervisor, making her personal opinions prevail about the best way to treat the sick.

A person of domineering personality, our fellow medium, became intransigent and opinionated about faith, although she did not know the Spiritist Doctrine as deeply as others did.

At the beginning, we realized slight signs of animism in the disincarnated physician's communications—signs that suddenly appeared, in the exaggerated emphasis of concepts that coincided with those of the medium. At this point the message was not yet distorted. There was only a strong stress on the aspects that were to the medium's interest, with an emotion that did not come from the communicating spirit. The development of animism can be quite subtle as can be the trap in which a medium can be caught when not humble and vigilant.

Our fellow medium overlaid—only—on the real message, her own emotional opinion, reinforcing certain images and exaggerating some facets. But, as time went by, the undue interference got worse until there was a notorious mixture of her opinions with those of the spirit.

When the mediumistic-animistic jumble reached about 50% of animism, the unavoidable happened. The spirit, through the medium herself, (in an unquestionable authenticity) suspended the attention he gave to the sick because the assistance he was giving the medium was over. Consequently, we lost a worker who could still be in service if she had cultivated evangelical humbleness. Unfortunately, it was not the only case at the Garden House.

The animistic process, usually ends up in a clear parasitic obsession, if the medium (and now the patient) is not helped in time. Whenever personalism is present, the cult of the "ego" wants the "glory of the world" and transitory tinsel. Nothing good comes out of this. Soon, the inferior spirits that are jumping around us, try to create a symbiotic relationship with the unwary medium. And the medium often receives them, gratified and happy!

Animism is insidiously dangerous. It can cause upset in such a way that the sensitive individual ends up suffering from mental imbalance, be it from the unproductive parasitic mediumistic action, anomalous and possessive, or from the psychic exhaustion that overcomes him.

The treatment of uncontrolled animism achieves better results if it happens as soon as the *disease* is detected. To cure it, we employ the same procedures as are used for uncontrolled mediumicity.

PARASITISM

In biology, "Parasitism is the phenomenon by which a living being extracts directly and necessarily from another living being (called the *host)* the indispensable material for the formation and construction of his own protoplasm." The host suffers the consequences of the parasitism in varying degrees; it can even die.

Parasitism is largely spread among living beings—animal and plants. Great is the number of those that live at the expense of others, of the same or different kinds.

In the spiritual world the phenomenon varies only in the process of extracting the host's energies. There is, as the biological definition says, the dependence of the parasitic spirit; he becomes so specialized (over a long period) in living at the expense of someone else, that he loses any possibility of living on his own.

Spiritual parasitism implies—always—corruption of the parasite. The phenomenon does not have any support or origin in the natural tendencies of the human *Kind.* On the contrary, each individual always had the conditions for living by his own efforts. There is no natural compulsion to suction off somebody else's energies. Debasement makes many human beings used to living by exploitation, an anomalous condition that usually becomes aggravated when they disincarnate.

As common as parasitism is among living beings, it is also extremely widespread among spirits. There are cases in which the spirit is not conscious of what he is doing; sometimes he even does not know that he has disincarnated. Other spirits, living only a vegetative life, parasitize a mortal without knowing what they are doing; they do not have the faintest idea about it; they are sick, disincarnated spirits in painful situations. Most of the cases are of unconscious parasitism.

But there are also parasites that are placed by obsessors; unconscious, sick spirits are linked to the incarnated's astral body, to weaken him. These situations happen frequently in cases of complex obsession, chiefly when the patient is abnormally debilitated.

The first step of the treatment is the separation of the parasite from the host. Then the care of the spirit follows; during his treatment, valuable elements can surge, making the incarnated individual's cure easier. Finally, we energize the host, and indicate conditions and prophylactic procedures to him.

VAMPIRISM

Vampirism is the phenomenon in which a being, according to legends, leaves the tomb at night, to suck the blood of living people.

Let us see how André Luiz, a famous physician and disincarnated instructor, sees this phenomenon:

> *Without referring to sucking bats, the vampire, among men, is the ghost that leaves the tomb at night, to feed himself from the living being's blood. I do not know who the author of this definition is; at heart, it is not wrong. We only have to consider that among us a vampire is any idle entity, which uses unduly the possibilities of others and, if they are the kind of vampires that visit the incarnated, it is necessary to recognize that they are always ready for any sinister purpose, since they find shelter in the fleshy envelope of men.*
>
> — From the chapter "Vampirism" in *Missionary of Light*

Dr. André Luiz is right. We have seen all kinds of spiritual vampires. The most dangerous ones take the form of enormous bats like the ones in the legends—big Chiropteras (bats), with human heads. They are spiritually degraded human beings, totally transformed, in consequence of a long period of corruption. Dangerous creatures, of low vibratory frequency, great predators, these creatures inhabit the caves of the inferior astral. Like bats, they are enemies of light, and usually become active at night. They are totally conscious of their acts; they vampirize because they want to, and they know what they want. Many times they act by order of the princes of Darkness, who use them as devilish objects—to harm and annihilate people.

Vampirism, however, is not only practiced by beings that look like bats. There is a variety of vampires, from incarnated creatures to disincarnated parasites. All inferior spirits, idle and primary, can vampirize or parasitize dead and alive beings.

We can see the question that comes up in the reader's mind: "*What, then, is the difference between a parasite and a vampire?*"

In both parasitism and vampirism, the suction of other being's energies occurs. But the difference is in the intensity of the ominous action, determined by the consciousness and cruelty with which it is practiced. The parasite usually causes less harm because he generally does not know what he is doing. Now, the real vampire is totally conscious of what he is doing and never spares a vampirized victim.

In 1985, we treated a case of advanced parasitism, in which the parasite was so tied to the victim that the clairvoyants did not perceive his presence. His astral body was so tightly bound to the incarnated creature's body that he could not be distinguished by common clairvoyants. He was only discovered when we unfolded the patient apometrically. When he was unfolded, he carried the parasite with him—who, then, was immediately seen by the unfolded mediums.

We considered the case so interesting that we decided to investigate more deeply the spiritual problems. We induced the parasite to embody in a medium so we could question him.

It was an extremely long-suffering spirit, very hungry, since this was the state in which he disincarnated. So great was his anguish and fear, he could not eat anything, he clung to us looking for shelter, and asked us to allow him to stay with us as he stayed with the sick person. To make him feel relaxed we agreed. We even projected strong vital energy currents to feed him. He was very satisfied, but when we told him that he was going to leave the sick person, he clung more strongly to us, imploring us to allow him to suck our vital forces.

Some visitors who were present at our work became afraid. However, the spiritual parasite did not have any malefic intention. He felt very upset due to the lack of food, marked by a very painful incarnation. His primary vitiation obsessed him so; the only reason for his existence was the search for food. For him, disincarnated as he was, any vital energy was valuable, and he was going to get it from any incarnated being that would shelter him.

According to our understanding (and in congruity with our definition) he was not a vampire; he was only a sufferer. He would have been a vampire if he were determined to cause harm to others, by weakening and annihilating them.

Symbiosis

By *symbiosis* we mean an enduring biological association of living beings, harmonic and sometimes necessary, with reciprocal benefits.

Spiritual symbiosis can be defined using almost the same words, because it follows the same principle.

In biology the harmonic and necessary character derives from complementary needs of the species. There are authors who consider symbiosis an association that, primitively, used to be parasitism. In the course of time, the relationship evolved and was biologically structured; the one that was parasitized began to profit from the relationship.

Symbiosis exists between spirits as well as between incarnated and disincarnated beings. It is common to see groups of spirits near mediums, answering any of their calls. In exchange they receive vital energies from the mediums. Quite often mediums do not suspect that their spiritual "associates" are inferior spirits who join with human beings to live parasitically or symbiotically with them.

Most of the "fortune tellers" who have no prophetic gifts are only successful at reading the cards because they are inspired by the disincarnated that surround them. In exchange, the spirits receive from the medium—who is in a partial trance—vital energies that they absorb greedily.

In relation to this subject André Luiz makes interesting revelations about the spiritual world around the "real" world. Referring to a psychic who was more interested in money than in helping the sick, he writes:

> We would like to inform, that we have an enclosed place with a powerful mediumistic operator, without any special interior enlightening. He hired some tens of disincarnated Spirits, of incipient education, who absorb his emanations, and work blindly under his orders, for the good as well as for the evil.
> — From the chapter "Valuable Experience" in *Liberation*

Later in the chapter André Luiz describes the symbiosis between the material world and those disincarnated that used to help the psychic:

After showing his satisfaction with the financial agreement that he established, the clairvoyant fell in profound concentration and I noticed the flux of energies emanating from him through the pores, but particularly from his mouth, nostrils, ears and chest. This force, similar to a fine and subtle vapor, seemed to be dwelling in that small room, and I could see that the primary or retarded individualities who used to help the medium in his incursions in our plane were sipping it in long gulps, getting support from it in the same way as man supports himself from proteins, carbohydrates and vitamins.

In the Gospels there is some precious information about a symbiosis between dead and alive people with financial interests. In the description of Paul of Tarsus' preaching in the city of Phillipos in Macedonia (in Acts of the Apostles), Lucas says:

And it came to pass, as we went to prayer, a certain damsel possessed with a spirit of divination met us, which brought her masters much gain by soothsaying:

The same followed Paul and us, and cried, saying, These men are the servants of the most high God, which show unto us the way of salvation.

And this did she many days. But Paul, being grieved, turned and said to the spirit, I command thee in the name of Jesus Christ to come out of her. And he came out the same hour.

And when her masters saw that the hope of their gains was gone, they caught Paul and Silas, and drew them into the marketplace unto the rulers,

And brought them to the magistrates, saying, These men, being Jews, do exceedingly trouble our city...
                                                    — Acts 16:16-20

According to Lucas' description we see that Paul both expelled the communicating spirit from the young woman, and closed the channels (chakras) of communication between the spiritual and the physical plane. And this resulted in the servant's master accusing Paul and Silas, who were whipped and expelled from the city.

The report of the apostle shows that low-level mediumistic practices, (i.e., looking for financial profit), were as common in antiquity as they are today. Nevertheless, there is no excuse for this degradation of mediumicity. It must be outlawed. Venal mediums degrade the sublime faculties of the soul, and compromise themselves in front of the Divine Law, mainly those that take the abominable route of black magic. They harm themselves, their clients, and Humankind.

As we live in different vibratory worlds,[37] where we have to undergo our evolution, we only have the right to use the mediumistic exchange when the objectives are noble, charitable, or clarifying.

This is our conviction: it is better to close the door to mediumicity than to degrade it with low interests. Moses was right when he prohibited mediumicity among the Hebrews, who were unenlightened and ignorant about the high objectives of communication between the dead and the living.

---

[37] We live at the same time in the following dimensions: physical, etheric astral, buddhic, atmic and spiritual.

REPRESSED MEDIUMICITY

CONCEPTS

Mediumicity is the psychic faculty that permits the investigation of the invisible planes—the environments where the spirits live—through syntonization with their dimensional universe. A medium, therefore, is the *intermediate one*, the one who serves as mediator between the human and the spiritual, between the visible and the invisible, or who penetrates there, consciously or unconsciously, unfolded from his physical body.

Whenever we think of mediumicity we have to imagine a special, multiple, sixth sense which manifests itself in a very specific way—through sight, hearing, smell, premonition, intuition and any other form (external or internal) of perception. Whatever the *mode* in which it presents itself, it is, in essence, an internal sense. It manifests itself sensorially, but does not come from the *physical* senses. They just capture a phenomenon that emerges and develops out of the physical dimension.

This special sense can receive or record messages, visions or perceptions of the world of the spirits in the same way that a bridge connects distant locations. It can also be manifested as a form of intuition, without the help of the disincarnated. In these cases it is considered one of the famous *gifts* of prophecy or foreknowledge of an event—making known, therefore, unknown and invisible realities to the common mortal. This marvelous faculty made simple men, among the biblical Jews, the immortal prophets of the Old Testament.

MEDIUMS — MISSION WITH PROBLEMS

Every medium is an agent of *capture*. But he also transmits waves of radiant nature—the *noures* of Ubaldi. *Noures* are thought currents of the cosmic space that encircles our planet. Similar to common radio waves, they saturate the Earth's astral and can be picked up according to the sensitivity and psychic capacity of the receptor.

All men, and probably all living beings (chiefly the superior mammals), have this special sense in a latent state. But only a minority of men and women are conscious of the faculty and develop it. Considering the evolutionary steps that humankind has already taken, we can expect that, in the future, as humankind becomes more psychically refined, we will have this superior faculty from birth, as a natural and common state, in the same way as we have intelligence and memory, faculties that make us definitely different from animals.

However it is known that this special sense, when not disciplined, can cause great psychic perturbations (abnormal behavior, exaggerated sensitivity, fears, anguishes, persecution mania, etc.), that can lead to a complete disorganization of the personality, having even classic characteristics of psychosis.

This danger has an explanation. The medium is, before everything, a sensitive being and an individual who is apt to pick up radiant energies of different vibratory standards from the psychic world that surrounds us. If he does not *disconnect* himself from these emissions during his normal life, he will suffer successive shocks and energetic wear that will exhaust his nervous system, causing serious consequences to his psychic equilibrium. The conscious disconnection from the immaterial dimension is obtained through mediumistic education, indispensable to every medium. Syntony should only happen when he is doing useful work in the service of both Life planes.

(The malefic action of the disincarnated upon the incarnated—the so-feared obsession—almost always is installed due to mediumistic disorders. In the final analysis, every obsessed individual is a medium who does not know about his potentialities and how his special faculties work.)

To illustrate, imagine a poorly syntonized radio receiver, with the volume totally open, casting sounds *without stopping*. It is easy to understand that after some time nobody could stand the noise anymore. The bearer of unbalanced mediumicity behaves in the same way. After some time, the disharmonic vibration affects his nervous balance, making him psychotic.

Mediumistic education consists of controlling the radio in the above example, reducing the volume, adjusting the frequency and turning it on when we want or when it is necessary. This education requires severe discipline, almost the same that was required in the temples of the past—where the neophyte was subjected to tests over several years, until he was able to receive superior knowledge and powers. Under the dome of secret crypts, these practices had as their end the increasing improvement of the apprentice, in order to develop in him an intense notion of what was sacred, with such depth, that all moments of his life would be impregnated with religiosity. Today, in our civilization dominated by an absorbing materialism, the candidate that wants to be a mediumistic worker is not required to undergo an initiation like the one in antiquity.

As a result, we usually do not reach the outstanding spiritual knowledge that our ancestors attained.

Even so, we can operate as mediators between the Life planes with great results. To be successful it is absolutely necessary that the medium be aware that the correct use of mediumicity requires love for the sufferers and a sincere desire to serve. A medium is *a service instrument.*

There are workers, however, who, fascinated with their own possibilities, see themselves as having a halo of divine power, and become more conspicuous than their fellows. They consider themselves superior because they are mediums. Soon they will fail utterly. This is an inexorable fact.

BUILD UP ONESELF TO BUILD UP

At no time is one going to be a real medium, in one's spiritual plenitude, if he does not understand the sanctified and secret greatness that this psychic power bestows—a greatness that necessitates an ever-renewed humility and sense of responsibility. These are heavy responsibilities, of many and surprising facets, which require an extremely strong moral conduct.

To build a very high building in the physical world, it is indispensable that the base be broad and strong. In the same way, to conquer spiritual heights, a broad and solid foundation is necessary. Without this base, contacts will never rise up to the Superior Spirits. They will be restricted to psychic dealing with inferior entities who never bring anything good; on the contrary, quite often they become mere slaves of their low standard.

The building up of ourselves has to be as perfect and crystalline as the spiritual work we are going to *do* and that will happen through us.

Just as the volitional act, or the word, has the power to modify the world that surrounds us, so do the energies of thoughts and feelings, and the magnetic power of the incarnated spirit influence the invisible domains of the immaterial world— except they act in a more intense, more *precise* manner.

THE RIGHT WAY

The mediums who are fully conscious of their *duty* have profound reverence for the sublime function of mediumicity. They do not accept praises in order not to feed their self-conceit, neither do they lament their misfortunes, which only affect the external values of personality. The real initiated goes through life with his internal sanctuary untouched, be it by the applause or attacks of the profane. However, to conduct oneself in this way, one needs immense faith, an impregnable interior fortress fed by the stream of the Superior World.

If the pupil of Eternal Truth accepts, from the beginning, the mediumistic phenomenon as a divine gift; if he considers it an instrument of real apostleship and treats it so; if he practices his mediumicity, *feeling* that it is sacred; if he is able to become integrated with it, in his heart and mind; then, yes, the thresholds of the superior spirituality will open according to his will. Once this stage is transfused with crystalline polish and pureness, his psychic powers will enlarge, becoming transformed into an instrument of light. The medium's consciousness will then reach the threshold of the superior initiation. Mediumicity will be a divine prize for his efforts, allowing him to continuously develop his field of action and, at the same time, to offer, enriched by love, his psychic energies to the needy.

We would like to make clear that it is not our objective to exalt this psychic faculty and place it on a pedestal. Our intention is otherwise: we would like to emphasize the sacred character of mediumicity, with all its implications. The medium who does not feel this way, and who is not conscious of his responsibilities, does not deserve to be a medium. This is not only our opinion. All the great initiated, the Masters of all times, and the disincarnated entities whose function is to orient, always transmit these lessons.

MEDIUMICITY IN THE CONTEXT OF ETERNITY

Most of the time mediumicity represents a former spiritual evolution—i.e., a development of psychic faculties in religious cults of the past. Such development brings with it high responsibilities from a spiritual point of view, inherent to one's own superior experiences. If, in the present existence, the owner of this special faculty—be it by pride, vanity or egotism—degrades it through bad use, he will be responsible for it in front of the powers that rule the evolution of the planet, with serious consequences for his spiritual progress. Sooner or later, in this incarnation or in future ones, he will miss the magnificent opportunity of having contact with the world of spirits—an opportunity that will give him, if well-used, extraordinary conditions for his evolution.

In any of its forms, therefore, mediumicity has to be dedicated to service, in the great program to help evolution in all planes of life. It cannot be considered personal property, a disposable possession and a producer of profits and material advantages for the individual. Neither can it be a natural attribute of social sham, giving him the right to be distinguished among his fellows. A medium who thinks of material situations or personal honors is not going to be a real medium for long. If he loses the noble reasons for his mediumistic practices, it will soon be only a lever for egotistic and commercial exploration.

If the medium, in facing difficulties which may be immense and inherent in his human condition, and which may take the form of misunderstandings and attacks by his fellow beings; if he consecrates his faculty in the service of those who surround him—incarnated and disincarnated—he is fulfilling his sacred mission. The notion of responsibility and spiritual values will be a constant for him, the natural way of being a humble and well-formed medium. Hardly ever will he err or deviate. By upholding a strong, moral character, he will not lose the superior spiritual assistance—the only protection for a *useful* work. He knows that the loss of this protection will make him receive, automatically, the assistance of the low astral spirits, with great harm to himself and to the people he is to "assist."

ILLUSTRATIVE CASES

Case #1:
  Patient: M.E.L.A., female, white, single.
  Age: 22.

From the age of seventeen the girl presented strange symptoms: sensation of anguish, indefinable indisposition, a burden on her back, headaches, etc. These symptoms surged without any apparent reason, at the most varied times. After some time, she realized that the morbid state usually happened on the street, at parties, and when there were crowds of people.

In time, M.E. was living in constant fear, having the feeling that there was somebody close to her, like a brief and indistinguishable shade. Sometimes she had nightmares that made her feel uncomfortable; she used to wake up, wet all over by icy sweating. The patient was not able to work as a lawyer any longer, she, quite often came home to lie down, covering herself completely.

Treatment:

As the girl did not want, by any means, to work as a medium, (although she was Spiritist), it was necessary to convince her of the seriousness of her disease and of the harmful consequences to the structure of her personality, to make her decide on starting spiritual therapeutics—the only valid and safe technique in these cases. Therapeutics would consist in the education of her mediumistic faculty and in working on behalf of people in need.

We always helped her in cases of psychic crises. We removed the spirit that was inducing the disturbance, and transferred him to another medium. We treated the spirit's sickness and sent him to the Love and Charity Hospital. Some minutes afterwards the desperate girl was feeling perfectly well and went back to her usual tasks.

M.E. was suffering from the attachment not of obsessors, but of poor sick spirits, full of pain, anguish, and despair. They got close to her by chance, wanting only to enjoy the comfort of being near her uncontrolled energetic potential. Once they were removed and treated, they would not come back. But at any opportunity, they would be substituted for by others who were also sick who, by means of induction, passed their disturbances on to her.

After five years, M.E. has not presented any of the former symptoms. She is perfectly cured.

Case #2:
 Patient: R.L.A., female, white, single.
 Age: 20.

Her situation is very similar to M.E. in the previous case. At night, when she was sleeping, she had terrible nightmares, with the strange feeling that she was being choked. She felt the hands that grabbed her, dominating her so completely that she was not even able to cry out for help. Sometimes she woke from her sleep, hearing voices and groans that filled her with terror.

After some time she was so afraid to be alone, even when she was awake, that she avoided sleeping alone in the room. In spite of her extroverted temperament, happy and kind, her state was already deteriorating. She suffered from a disease that was not well known to physicians and the treatment had not been effective so far.

Treatment:

Right from the start, we realized that, in spite of the girl's good psychic sensitivity, due to problems caused by former experiences in a rigid Catholic environment (she had been a nun in more than one incarnation), she did not allow the flow of spiritual energies. In view of this, the spirits benefited from her energies when she slept.

The process started with a simple vibratory induction, going immediately to mediumistic embodiment, with the spirit's total possession of the medium. At the beginning it was induction, then it became vampirism and other inferior forms of obsession.

If a psychoanalyst had to interpret the girl's symptomatology, he probably would think of sex and the Freudian constellation of repressed sexual desires. However, in spite of the nice academic interpretations and a rosary of psychoanalytic sessions, the problem—certainly—would not be solved.

The cure was quite simple.

She underwent systematic spiritual treatment and did not have any symptoms again. The cure was simple because it was a consequence of an automatic phenomenon. Mediumistic education through ongoing work has, as a result, an automatic defense system. The medium had her corporeal chakras closed and only gave passage (this means, she syntonized with the world of spirits) at appropriate moments, on the occasion of spiritual work.

Case #3:

Patient: R.S.B., female, white, married.

Age: 20.

Biotype: Ectomorphic.

Religion: Catholic.

Date of birth: June 29, 1958.

For years she had been feeling fear, emotional instability, anguish, pressure in her chest; she had been seeing indistinct shapes of people, etc. And the symptoms had worsened since her marriage.

Treatment:

After the unfolding was done through Apometrics, the spiritual physicians verified that the patient had a large mediumistic energetic potential, with extremely sensitive chakras that worked like powerful antennas.

Close to the sick woman there was a disturbed spirit, but without malefic intentions. He did not even know that he had disincarnated; he just cuddled up with the young lade to receive human warmth and with it vital energy that kept him in a reasonable situation, but in this way he was devitalizing the medium/patient. He was sent to the Love and Charity Hospital.

The girl had her chakra activities reduced through special techniques to avoid the anomalous syntony with the world of spirits. (It is as if we reduce the volume of a radio until the sound was inaudible.) Afterwards she was sent to a group for mediumistic education, to have her energies controlled, and to use them at predetermined moments in assistance of the incarnated and disincarnated sick.

The psychic sick lady totally recuperated. She became an excellent medium.

Case #4:
   Patient: L.V.S., female, white, single.
   Biotype: Endomorphic.
   Age: 40.

She complained about indisposition, pains throughout her body, weakness (to such a degree that she could not sweep the house anymore), anguish, forgetfulness and dizziness. She had been under medical, clinical and psychiatric treatment for a long time—without results.

Treatment:

When the patient was subjected to an apometric unfolding, the physician realized that her astral body was entirely enveloped by plates of life material, a kind of thick movable and pulsating ooze, formed of a myriad of tiny larvae.

When we saw this kind of life material, we were able to make the diagnosis without fear of error; it was an obsessive case. Usually it is simple obsession; the obsessors try to weaken the victim in order to act more freely in the future. This primary vampirism is very common, mainly in black magic.

The presence of these beings of inferior biological level generally indicates that the obsessed does not keep watch over his thoughts. It provides sort of low level mental humus which feeds these low beings. In these cases the first step is to recommend the elevation of the thoughts through mental hygiene. It is necessary, for example, to avoid reading about crimes in newspapers, make comments about crimes, etc.

The sick woman was a medium but she did not know it. She exuded a large quantity of vital force that fed the larvae.

With some difficulty, the physicians cleaned the astral body completely. In the meanwhile we attracted the obsessors to a force-field, embodying them in mediums to discover the reason for the obsessive process.

The obsessors were weak spirits. They beset the victim to charge old debts, but without causing any great damage. They did not have sufficient magnetic strength to cause the victim irreversible harm. We sent these common sufferers to the L.C.H. for treatment.

As to the patient, we reduced the chakras, to decrease her mediumistic sensitivity. We advised her to energetically control her life style by cultivating sound thoughts, and forgoing her liking for morbid experiences. We told her to join a well-oriented mediumistic education group and to introduce the cult of the Gospels into her home.

She was totally cured.

Case #5:
   Patient: E.C., male, white, student.
   Age: 16.
   Biotype: Extreme ectomorphic (leptosomatic).
   Religion: Catholic.
   Date of assistance: June 4, 1977.

He complained about crises of absent-mindedness followed by loss of memory, real psychic "absences," long-lasting and pathological. Neurological exams, including several electroencephalograms, did not disclose any abnormality. The pathological process showed a tendency to get worse.

Exam:

The spiritual doctors verified the presence of a spirit linked to the patient by very strong affective ties, which started and were consolidated during his penultimate incarnation in England. This spirit, who did not have the merit to incarnate yet, was living in symbiosis with the patient in his present life. The symbiosis was well-developed. The patient wanted her presence so much that, while he was sleeping, his spirit detached from the body to meet her in the astral. The process became increasingly aggravated because, even when he was awake, the incarnated looked for the other. It was this that caused the psychic "escapes" (labeled by medicine as epileptic states).
   The boy was a medium and very sensitive.

Treatment:

We separated the fellow spirit, who was conducted to the L.C.H. for treatment. The boy himself, who was a good medium, was advised to have a mediumistic education. We did not hear from him anymore.

Case #6:
   Patient: A.S., male, white, a soldier.
   Age: 30.
   Religion: Catholic.

He complained about persistent insomnia. What sleep he had was frequently agitated as he saw himself fighting with an unknown enemy in desperate combat. He always woke up covered with cold sweat. He had frequent crises of tachycardia, always coupled with fainting and abundant sweating. Continuous nervousness was harming his military career. He had been in this condition for about ten years but recently he had gotten worse.
   No medical treatment had been effective.

Exam:

After the patient's unfolding, we realized the presence of an obsessor whose actuation was related to a distant past, when both were living in the Middle East. The spirit had been seriously harmed by the present victim, now suffering the reaction to his enemy. The obsessive process did not present any major problem because of the disturbing spirit's low energy potential. It could be classified as a case of simple obsession. The long harassment, however, caused the acceleration of the patient's psychic sensitivity.

Treatment:

Once the obsessor was separated from him, we sent the sick man for mediumistic education.

We followed the case for two years. The soldier is now perfectly well.

Case #7:
  Patient: D.E., female, white, single.
  Religion: Catholic.

She complained about unbearable anguish and a sensation of deep asthenia, which sometimes made her stay in bed for days. She had periodic crises of intense tachycardia, with manifestations of circulatory insufficiency. Cardiological checkups, including electrocardiograms, did not find anything pathological. She had been suffering from these problems for more than fifteen years. She had almost been taken to a psychiatric hospital during an outburst of schizophrenia (according to the physician's diagnosis).

Lately the patient had a clear impression of failure, one that she thought was a constant in her life, "because everything in her business went wrong" (sic).

Exam:

During the spiritual exam we could see that the sick woman had been guarded by an obsessor for a long time. In a remote past she had been a priestess in the Hittite civilization. At that time she had revealed **secrets of the religious initiation and of the State,** *amassing, therefore, powerful enemies. The present obsessor was her spiritual "warrantor": he who was responsible for her ascension to the priesthood. When she was judged for her crime, he was also punished. He lost his political power and was banished from the country.*

The just and wise Divine Law, however, makes enemies meet again during their long evolution so karmic readjustments can occur to dissolve the negative charges of the enemies.

As the sick woman had been a priestess, she had a great mediumistic energetic potential, which had been developed in the past. The spirit's presence irritated her sensitivity, activating the chakras in an anomalous way. Not only did she capture the presence of her obsessor, but also the auras of a great number of suffering entities who had come close to her, only to suck her irradiated energies as much as they could. This was the reason for her exaggerated asthenia.

Obviously, therapeutic medicine could not solve her psychic problem. It only lessened the state of her anguish.

Treatment:

Once the obsessor was removed, we suggested that the patient take care of her mediumistic education and that she have a spiritual treatment with passes and magnetized water. Some time later the patient told us that she had recuperated and joined a Spiritist group.

UNCONTROLLED MEDIUMICITY

In uncontrolled animism, a person may choose to express his or her opinion while receiving fake messages from disincarnated spirits. In uncontrolled mediumicity, this person does not control the aggressive psychomotor impulses emitted from the astral world.

Because of inadequate mediumistic education or an imbalance in the psyche, the sensitive individual is unable to balance all of these manifestations. The individual allows abuse and possessiveness by inferior spirits.

Attached to these mediums we have found powerful and enraged obsessors. They use every opportunity to persecute the mediums and attempt to destroy them. This may bring the medium to a state of psychic imbalance, seriously compromising the medium's personality.

Thus, it is easy to understand that the practice of mediumicity requires special attention and that the development of this ability requires great care. The medium usually establishes contact with spirits from inferior evolutionary levels. Because of such spirits are frustrated and repressed, they turn themselves against the medium by surrounding him with adverse magnetic fields.

The medium, therefore, must constantly monitor these communicating disincarnated individuals, search for their vibrations, control aggressiveness and allow the use of the body only in the amount necessary and sufficient for spirit manifestation. And the monitoring should not only focus on the communicating spirit. Everything that comes from the invisible world should be assessed and, if possible, filtered by the medium—without compromising truthfulness and legitimacy.

The treatment of uncontrolled mediumicity is summarized as follows:

First, cancel any mediumistic attempt of contact with the spirit world. To assist the medium, the activities of the frontal, cardiac and splenic chakras should be reduced to a minimum level.

Second, if it is desired to use the medium's services in the future, have the medium train in a school of mediumship, if possible. The medium should systematically study the foundations of the Spiritist Doctrine and practice controlled and progressive contacts with the spirits and their dimensional world.

Third, once the medium's education is completed, it becomes necessary to provide regular mediumistic work. This work is considered a donation (for the incarnated and disincarnated), as advocated by Kardec.

"THE DRAGGING EFFECT"
OF THE UNFOLDED SPIRIT

The spirit of the unfolded medium can suffer a kind of an attraction and follow the spirit that was embodied in him, when this spirit leaves him. After the communicating spirit gets out, the medium does not answer to commands any longer, he behaves as if he were not present, and he really is not. It takes some time until he comes back. And it might be necessary to project a force-field to bring him back.

Also unfolded, the other mediums tell us that their fellow medium went with the spirit. And that he is far away.

Though it is neither serious nor dangerous, it is advisable that the one who directs the work be attentive to this possibility in the mediumistic practice. If it is not known, it can cause fear.

The solution for this case, is simply to call the medium back, once, twice or three times. If he is he does not obey, we project a force-field, we touch his splenic chakra and we do a rather energetic counting. Almost always, it is enough to call the medium back and make him return.

This phenomenon has two causes:

1. The action of communicating spirits, chiefly the ones that have great mental and energy potential, as for instance, the black sorcerers. Due to evil, they attract the medium and take him with them even if they are already restrained.

2. The medium, due to his curiosity and his own will, wants to know where the communicating spirit dwells and, frivolously, is ready to go with him. (This cause is the most important one because of its implications, as we will see later.) The phenomenon is also common with superior entities. Due to their highly harmonic aura, they form a field of well-being that makes the mediums go with them, attracted by the feeling of peace they radiate.

This attitude of the mediums (second cause) reveals a certain immaturity and lack of discipline. Deviations of this type—giving attention to personal desires—are not in agreement with the nature of their work. It constitutes a transgression of a norm that may not have been expressed, because it is implied.

Only order and discipline bring good results in any kind of work, especially in spiritual work. Due to its nature, it requires the constant attention and vigilance of those responsible and—especially—of the mediums upon whom they depend.

No worker, therefore, should be seduced by curiosity, neither should he make any investigations in the astral world on his own account, venturing into the domain of the Umbral. We have already seen daring mediums who have come back terrified by an untimely thrust in the astral. It is necessary to understand that there are norms of safety, which, if violated, can endanger the whole work. The group is exposed to a sudden invasion of Darkness, invalidating the work plans so arduously prepared.

The "dragging effect" obeys spiritual laws similar to the physical laws, whence we got the definition. "Dragging" in physics is the phenomenon of motion and conduction of a body in consequence of forces coming from outside.

Fixation Of Mental Imbalances

Mental imbalances are pathological alterations of psychism. They are the result of a degenerative state of the mental faculties, with diverse etiologies. They can be the consequences of long obsessive processes or of a disorder of the patient himself, due to self-obsessed animistic phenomena.

Whatever the origin might be, the final state is always the same. Once the imbalance is established, it gets fixed as a second nature. Besides this (and what is even worse), it has the tendency to be repeated in other incarnations, if there is no effort to improve the character, or if there is not any violent karmic imposition that shakes the individual.

The positive acquisitions, as we know, get stored up in each person's memory bank of the spirit—as part of an inalienable inheritance. But the vicious experiences, by the same process, accumulate and augment the negative load that has to be purged by the individual for all eternity.

The more we practice self-control the stronger and brighter we become, and, consequently, we will be more able to defeat disorderly forces. In the course of time, due to continuously repeated positive experiences, we will acquire strength in the educational process that *is our Life*, and of which we must take advantage. It constitutes a slow but conscientious completeness of the Christic state of each individual, spiritualizing and enlightening him.

We should never forget that we are on the Way. Our cures, our futures and our horizons depend on us. Only on ourselves.

MALEFIC EFFECTS OF "WAVE FRINGES" UPON THE INCARNATED

Quite often we see sensitive people—*mainly young people*—suffering from low level obsessive processes (including black magic) that had not been directed specifically against them. They were affected only because they were near the true target.

These people become disturbed, anguished, stop working, feel sick and, in short, suffer the whole malefic action of the negative vibrations discharged against another person of their family, their home or their environment. The true targets, however, are immune to that kind of spiritual attack or they are only slightly affected. The cause of this phenomenon is the great sensitivity of these extemporaneous receivers, who, without wanting to, enter in resonance with the negative torrents. In this way, they are used as a protective shield for the main target of these forces who usually is the head of the family.

The destructive effect, even if it does not totally hit the sensitive (and direct) target, will be proportional to the energy potential of the evil deed, to the type of evil "work," to the spiritual defenses of the home and to the merit of the family members, according to the Divine Laws. We also have to consider the degree of sensitivity of the disturbed person as well as his spiritual condition and karmic problem. The last is of primary importance: karmic anomalies are *gaps* through which negative forces filter.

* * *

If it is a process of black magic, the situation is not so easy and involves many details. We consider two situations:

First: The mobilization of natural forces chosen, manipulated and directed to harm the victim. This is done by skillful artisans of Darkness, specialists in producing disharmony and suffering. Their objective is to destroy the victim, mentally or physically, through disorderly vibration of magnetic fields of extremely low frequency.

Second: The presence of one or more members of a group of low mental, intellectual, or spiritual level entities, some of who behave as slaves, constrained by other forces; others freely and

260

conscientiously enjoy serving—with perverse ferocity—the "Dragons" of Evil. These low level entities are linked to the "evil deeds" of the technicians of Darkness, incarnated or disincarnated. The slaves are used to watch the negative field and to whip the victim's astral body occasionally, besides leading those recently disincarnated (suffering and desperate) spirits close to the victim, transforming them into enormous vampires that the victim has to feed with his already meager energies.

Intense vampirization, concentrated continuously on only one part of the organism, ends up weakening the area in such a way that it becomes easy to tear the buddhic web. When the main defense of the physical body is torn, the victim is at the enemy's mercy.

Normally, it is this inferior gang that shows up at kardecist sessions, making noise and terrifying people with works of black magic; however, they are the most harmless *ingredients*. Their removal (when possible) does not mean much. If we do not capture the technicians and chiefs, the problem is not solved.

Once the technicians and chiefs of the gang are captured, it is necessary to deactivate their bases in the Umbral.

The bases shelter many creatures and sometimes they are so big that they constitute a real citadel of Darkness. There are schools with regular classes to create technicians. It is there that they elaborate, well and safely, their plans to harass the incarnate. Very well-protected, these bases have abundant materials (often very sophisticated) to act directly or indirectly upon their victims—by means of all kinds of electronic devices, chiefly an arsenal of potent electromagnetic emitters, used to torment and annihilate human beings. Their sources of energy are nuclear power plants situated deep under the constructions, placed there to avoid any outside invasion. These nuclear power plants provide energy for the various laboratories, specialized in all the imaginable and unimaginable branches of scientific experimentation.

We found, for instance, bases that specialized in the nervous system. They had models of brains of human beings and other primates, in large sizes, which were technically perfect and would be the envy of researchers on Earth. Some time ago we found a base that was specialized in...Cardiology! It was the only one we found, so far, with this kind of specialization. In one of the many meeting rooms there was an enormous heart on a table. The heart was made of diaphanous material, where one could very clearly see the venous and arterial nets, and the whole nervous structure. The two mediums who had gone down to deactivate the base were surprised at the perfection of the model. Specialists, the technicians of this umbraline model, used their knowledge to disharmonize and to destroy. They were able to provoke heart attacks and other pathological cardiac states with ease.

Once the bases are deactivated and the obsessors gathered, it is still necessary to undo the magnetic fields, which, otherwise, will go on vibrating for an indeterminate time.

For this process of annulment in the spiritual world we use many techniques. From simple "lifting"—(i.e., the removal of the magnetized amulets) to the destruction ("undoing") of the whole *muamba*[38] (or "works"), which can be at a cemetery, at one's residence, or at the place where the victim works. Once the fields are undone physically, or undone in the astral plane, the evil is annulled.

All works of black magic, (and we have been repeating this), besides being complex, usually present one or two different surprising facets, even for experienced workers.

* * *

We focused on this subject again, when we referred to "the effects of the wave frills," to alert the reader to what can be found through deeper investigation. *Not always*, however, is this investigation necessary. Since it is an *indirect* effect of black magic "work"—and, consequently, diminished—the syndrome of "wave frills" is usually easily removed. It is enough to raise the vibratory standard of the patient (and of those indirectly bewitched) to make him immune to the evil deed.

We call these effects "wave frills" because they behave, in everything, like the external edges of radiant magnetic fields.

---

[38] Malefic works.

"EFFECT OF WAVE REFRACTION"
OF MALEFIC NATURE

In physics, "refraction is the deviation that the luminous ray suffers when it passes from one transparent means to another transparent means, contiguous, but of different density."

In a magnetic field of spiritual nature, a similar phenomenon happens.

A magnetic emission of black or mental magic, which is projected upon an incarnated individual, has consequences that vary according to the victim's levels of defense and evolution. If the target is in an inferior vibratory band (consequently without any natural defenses), be it due to lack of vigilance, because he enjoys evil, or even because he is not in a normal condition of evolution, the aggressive wave can reach him fully. In these cases we can imagine that the victim will be an easy prey for the predators of Darkness.

But it can happen that the victim is in a good evolutionary condition, a reasonable harmonization and an above average vibratory frequency. In this case the projection can be totally or partially refracted and consequently deflected. It is quite common, according to what we have observed, that the negative wave is deflected by the positive field of the target person and usually reaches one or more members of the family, who are sensitive to these attacks. Without defenses they suffer more or less intensely the effect of the evil projection.

Therefore, as we see, there are spiritual diseases caused by negative charges that were *not aimed against the sick*, but against another person.

There are also special, and rare, cases in which the incarnate being totally deflects the malefic wave, in complete refraction, a phenomenon that happens only to very highly spiritually developed beings.

The consequences of the "effects of wave refraction" are very similar to those of the "effects of wave frill," that we discussed in the previous chapter.

Although these classifications seem to be ornamentations to the investigation of psychic phenomena, they really help to make very precise diagnoses and allow a better systematization of researchers.

HYPNOTISM USED IN OBSESSION

Hypnotism is an induced state of a somnambulistic trance, in which the person's volition is totally or partially dominated by the hypnotist.

Although the techniques for inducing this state of trance are extremely old, it was the Austrian physician Anton Mesmer, (1733-1815) who used this method in a more or less scientific way under the denomination "animal magnetism." Mesmer treated the sick in Paris at the end of the 18th century in sessions that became famous. Some time later Braid, a British physician, created the word "hypnotism," by which this type of psychic treatment would become known.

Mesmer believed in a kind of energy of a magnetic nature. He believed it to be an agent that caused sleep and might cure the sick. Subsequently, other researchers formed a school which defended the concept that *suggestion* and not magnetism was the main factor that provoked the somnambulistic trance. The theory was greatly reinforced, in recent times, by the Reflexological School of Pavlov.

Without considering the theories of hypnotism from a deeper point of view, we understand that the positions of both schools are valid. The techniques of both can be conjoined, with much more success in the treatment.

Within the therapeutic framework, hypnotism follows a sequence of levels of various intensities. The hypnotic subject starts in a light state of suggestion and later may attain, by steps, a deep level of catalepsy. Several factors contribute to these differing levels: resistance to hypnotic induction, environment, the emotional state of the person, and the magnetic potential of the operator, among other conditions.

A sensitive person can be dominated in such a way that he will fall deeply asleep. If he receives orders from the operator while he is sleeping and unconscious, these orders will be performed after the somnambulistic period and will be executed by him. He will obey an internal compulsion when he is awake, unaware of what happened during his hypnotic sleep.

There is, obviously, an imposition. The actuation of the operator upon the patient's (technically called the "subject") psychism is notorious. A kind of conditioned reflex is formed in the "subject," independent of his volition, that makes him carry out the orders he received when he was asleep, although he does not remember them.

This state of partial domination is more common than we imagine. Those of strong personality—domineering egotists— create around them a state of hypnotic fascination, thus exerting a despotic domination over weak individuals or those of poorly structured personality, especially if the "subjects" depend financially on the domineering individuals.

Leaders of great masses usually possess this faculty. They use it (and even abuse it) over those they lead. A classic example: the charismatic leaders of World War II who led thousands to sacrifice in the name of foolish "ideals"—people who did not realize they were standing at an abyss.

These mass magnetizers, however, do not realize that they are hypnotists. They act naturally, with positive results, without knowing the least about hypnosis—without knowing they form a very powerful magnetic field around them that is a result of the mental action and of volition (Mesmer's "animal magnetism"). This field is independent of any kind of suggestion, and has a coercive effect on sensitive individuals who have fragile characters—those who are always easy prey for incarnated and disincarnated obsessors.

If we imagine the creation of this magnetic field, a creation of the operator's mind and volition, combined with the directed energetic suggestion, we can understand the subject's submission and subservience.

The strongest factor is, perhaps, *suggestion* which gives origin to the cortical conditioned reflexes (according to the Pavlovian School, the only one accepted by science). But hypnosis depends on "animal magnetism" and suggestion.

If it were only due to suggestion, everybody would have the same hypnotic power, because there are many people who use words quite well. Not everybody, however, gives his words enough energy to affect or modify the behavior of an audience.

The hypnotic phenomena to which we refer do not constitute any surprise. They have been occurring in the normal life of men since prehistoric periods. But there are few incarnated human beings who exert a sound influence upon others. Most people live coupled to others of the community, but in a harmful situation, suffering coercion, pressure, and even mental enslavement from relatives, bosses, leaders, etc.

This also happens in the world of the disincarnated.

Disincarnated leaders of inferior moral evolution exert a very domineering action upon the disincarnated of their communities. And the malefic action goes to the world of the living, harming them mainly when they are tied to long-lasting obsessive processes. These disincarnated leaders of inferior morality can possess great mental potential. They can possess extensive knowledge of the Laws of Psychism including Physics, Chemistry, Anatomy, and the Physiology of the Nervous System. These predatory beings are dangerous enemies for the incarnated who can syntonize with the frequency of the Umbral. They use sophisticated techniques to dominate others, make beings suffer, or destroy the physical body of those who fall into their obsessive nets. One of these techniques, perhaps the most simple and generalized, is the practice of hypnotism. They induce situations of suffering, cause people to deviate from moral behavior and come to erroneous conclusions, and, what is worse, terrorize people in all possible ways.

André Luiz showed us how this happens when he described cases in which the obsessor applies suggestive-magnetic induction. In his book, *Liberation,* he reports dramatic scenes from a long-lasting obsessive process. The sorcerer of Darkness subjected a young girl to an intense hypnotic-magnetic process to weaken her moral defenses, then subjugateed her and, finally, disincarnated her:

Penetrating the room in which Margaret was resting, there were the two hypnotists in activity.

....

....

The two disincarnated, possessed of frightening faces, were bent over the sick woman's breast. She was trusting and they were domineering, and they subjected her to a complicated magnetic surgery. The strange situation was astounding.

Margaret looked exhausted and embittered.

Once the cerebellum's path of equilibrium was dominated and the optic nerves were involved by the influence of the hypnotists, her frightened eyes gave an idea of the hallucinatory phenomena that were going on in her mind, signaling her impaired ability to see or hear.

The obsessor in charge of the action, who was close to the patient reveals:

We have been actively working here for exactly ten days—he clarified resolutely. The prey was fully hit, and fortunately there was no resistance at all. If you came to collaborate with us, we are sorry to tell you that there is nothing to do now. In a few days, we will see the result.

The guide's comment:

The story of satanic geniuses who attacked zealots of different creeds is, in fact, absolutely real. Perverted intelligences, unable to receive celestial advantages, are transformed into passive instruments of rebellious intelligences that are interested in the ignorance of the masses, with a lamentable disregard for the superior spirituality which governs our destinies. The acquisition of faith, therefore, demands very persistent individual work.

Additionally, he describes one of the obsessors:

What did that psychological mask of the magnetizer of darkness mean? He was lying down, almost blind, totally insensible. He answered the long and important questions with vague monosyllables, and demonstrated an irreducible insistence, in relation to flagellating the victim.

Hypnotized by the owners of disorder, anesthetized by numbing rays, he temporarily lost that capacity of seeing, hearing and had feelings of imbalance and dizziness. Like a common man, he was going through an affective nightmare, in which Margaret's laceration became a fixed and obsessing idea.

Magnetism is a universal force that assumes the direction we dictate. Opposite passes applied to the paralyzing action will bring one back to normality.

(Quotations from chapters IX, XIV and XV of *Liberation.*)

Part III

Operational Techniques

INTRODUCTION

We have used many of these procedures and techniques over many years in the treatment of incarnated and disincarnated sick spirits. Some of them are classic and old, and of well-known efficacy. Others, more complex and tested with recently corroborated success, are the result of a continuous investigation and learning process.

Some of these techniques and procedures include:

1. Apometrics
2. Coupling of the unfolded spirit
3. Dialymetrics
4. Pneumiatry
5. Depolarization of the memory's stimuli
6. Astral trips under command
7. Technique of psychic syntony with the spirits
8. Embodiment among the living
9. Dissociation of space and time
10. Technique of mental magnetic impregnation with positive images
11. Regression in space and time
12. Technique of energy mobilization for the operator spirits
13. Technique of mediums revitalization
14. Theurgy
15. Special treatment for black sorcerers
16. Treatment of the spirits in temples of the past
17. Use of the spirits of nature
18. Spiritual sterilization of the working environment
19. Technique to conduct the incarnate, unfolded spirits to the astral hospital
20. The medium as a modulating transducer
21. Psychic diagnoses—telemnesis (thoughts projected at a distance)
22. Imposition of hands—curative magnetism
23. Magnetic passes
24. Cure of lesions in the disincarnated spirits astral body
25. Mobilization technique of cosmic energy
26. Technique of energy emission at a distance: $\vec{\Sigma} = \vec{K}.\vec{Z}$
27. Astral surgeries

28. Technique of the destruction of malefic astral bases
29. Technique of inversion of the "spin" of the astral
    body's electrons of disincarnated spirits
30. Materialization of objects in the astral plane
31. Burning of objects in the astral plane
32. Chromotherapy in the astral plane
33. Study of mediumistic phenomena according to
    Quantum Physics
34. Fields-of-force $\begin{cases} \text{tetrahedral} \\ \text{gravitational} \end{cases}$
35. Archecryptognosis

Most of these techniques are, in some way, seen in this book.
While it is not possible to present them in as much detail as
we would like, some deserve special attention because of the
importance of the benefits they provide. They are:

1. Depolarization of the memory's stimuli
2. Pneumiatry
3. Dialymetrics—Etheriatrics
4. Utilization of Nature Spirits
5. Archecryptognosis

Each of these will be explored in the following chapters.

TREATMENT OF THE SPIRITS

More important than all these techniques, the treatment of the disincarnated is paramount. Throughout these pages we have emphasized how much we have to cultivate the flame of Divine Love through the practice of charity. Charity is naturally transformed into Universal Fraternity, and peace will consolidate the awareness of love and of the willingness to serve. TO SERVE—not because it is an obligation, an imposition, a rule or a *convenience*—but due to pure love and gratitude to life and to the light of the world that life contains; to serve blessedly and humbly, not only our brothers on this side, but also those *on the other side.*

The dead also suffer. They also feel pain. They have diseases that are life-reflections of the pain, suffering, and physical diseases they had to face when they were alive. If the disincarnated do not have the energy and understanding that allow them to go beyond this state, they cannot get out of it and consequently, neither can they get rid of their anguish.

But we can help them, giving them the energy they need to enjoy the relief from their pains and peace of spirit. We cannot forget that they live. They live! And we, on this side of the river of life, have to offer them our charity, since we can cure and console them almost instantaneously. The spiritists themselves, accustomed to treating the disincarnated, ignore these extraordinary possibilities of distributing cure, light and peace.

When we operate in the free energy world of the astral, with our minds vibrating in this dimension, it becomes extremely easy to project curative energies. As the spirit does not have a material body, the harmonization of his tissues requires less energy. A sufficiently strong stream will flood his fibers giving complete and instantaneous improvement. According to what we have realized, these energies, projected by the mind, are of very high vibratory frequency. They have an immense power of penetration, similar to that of x-rays of high potency, or of radioactive isotopes. It takes only a few moments to recompose an amputated member, serious lesions, extirpated organs, and even some deeper diseases that, sometimes, accompany the disincarnated brother over several incarnations.

The workers in Spiritist sessions have to be attentive to this point: the "treatment" of spirits is not intended only to send

273

them away. No! We have to recuperate them. And this is easy, incredibly easy.

When we face one of these unhappy spirits, with signs of great suffering (caused, for example, by serious lesions of his astral body), we project all our volition upon him to cure him. We place him in the field of our intense desire so his diseases will be cured, his pain relieved, or his members reconstituted. While we talk to the spirit, we insist that he is going to be cured. At the same time we project cosmic energy, condensed by our mind's power, onto the injured area. This is easy since he is embodied in a medium. It is enough to project energies upon the sensitive's body, counting slowly up to seven. We can repeat the procedure as many times as necessary—usually once or twice is enough to attain the objective.

We recommend to those who are interested, and to the instructors who attempt this, to do it early, in the spiritist sessions. Cure! Cure through a direct and conscious action, through a firm, energetic, and harmonizing volitional action. Do not forget that, for the spirits, the treatment will be experienced physically in their reality.

This same treatment can be applied directly upon all spirits present at the sessions, even if they are not embodied in a medium. Believe it and try it. Once the energies are projected, all of them will be cured. We have the ability to treat a large crowd of suffering spirits all at once.

In the chapters on *Dialymetrics* and *Pneumiatry* the reader may find some interesting material. But, basically, it is in the principle of Apometrics that we find the essential thing we need—Love. Love is the essential and prime component.

DEPOLARIZATION OF THE
MEMORY'S STIMULI

From the studies of physiology and biochemistry we are beginning to understand the innermost functioning of our bodies. We are still far from controlling innumerable organic functions, especially those of the nervous system. But we have already advanced a great deal.

The determination of the "Krebs Cycle,"[39] for instance, gave us an understanding of the metabolism of the assimilable organic substances and their use by the living organism. But we do not know the why of most of the vital phenomena because we have not yet fathomed what life really is. We detect it through the phenomena that life *causes*, not through its *nature*. The phenomenon of life cannot be measured by the tools of Medicine—by the surgical knife or the microscope. It occupies a dimension beyond physics.

If our bodies, which are touchable and measurable, still have mysteries indecipherable to investigator's intelligence and to the sophistication of their instruments, what should we think in relation to the soul's physiology? Its immense and mysterious complexities are out of the reach of science (at least, in the way that science goes about its investigations)—scientists block in a radical and primary fashion: they deny the existence of the soul. Medicine, therefore, becomes shortsighted when the phenomenon of the soul is touched. It sees only the somatic body, *under* a materialistic view that Quantum Physics has shown to be inconsistent, if not confused. Even psychiatry, which deals with (or should deal with) the soul's manifestations, digresses from the patient's cure when it treats the sick only with chemical substances that have exclusively physical actions.

Freud tried to treat the mentally sick person by considering the disease in a mode more compatible to its reality. But he failed when he did not consider the immortal spirit as the seat of individuality. Consequently, he should not have even

---

[39] A series of enzymatic reactions in aerobic organisms involving oxidative metabolism of acetyl units and producing high-energy phosphate compounds, which serve as the main source of cellular energy.

considered or *investigated* reincarnation, let alone, admit it: reincarnation is a phenomenon of the spirit. And, if we do not consider the eternal *continuum* that man is, then it is not possible to understand him or his diseases.

It is truly lamentable that the interpretation of a person's innermost world is up to the analyst's intellect which, along with his conclusions, are so distant from pathological reality that they can only be unreal. Therapies naturally are inefficacious even if the analysts are close to the etiology of the nervous disturbance; but simple methodology is not compatible with the Spirit's reality.

It is exactly because of this—and only because of it—that they were not able, for example, to discover and apply an objective scientific method, which can be used by any operator, to penetrate the intimacy of human remembrances, with the possibility of altering them.

DISCOVERING THE LAW.
DEVELOPMENT OF THE TECHNIQUE

This is, however, what we achieved with the "depolarization of the memory's stimuli," a powerful weapon in the treatment of innumerable foci of neuroses and psychoses.

According to the theory of Pavlov, the learning process is the result of stimuli repetition, in a systematic and progressive manner. In the neuronal tissue structure, the stimulus record is always polarized; the neuron allows the electric current of the stimulus to go in only one direction. We can suppose, therefore, that when recorded in memory, the stimuli obey a stratigraphic polarization, similar to that of a common magnetic recorder.

Apometrics, which has already opened so many doors to us, could also be the key to penetrating memory.

We stated the research. Concentrated magnetic fields were projected upon the cerebral cortex until we reached the memory areas.

And there was the unexpected success.

The experience was repeated several times, always successfully. So we came to the Law:

> *Whenever we apply specific energies of a magnetic nature upon the cerebral area of the incarnated or disincarnated, with the objective of annulling the electromagnetic stimuli recorded in the "bank of memory," the stimuli will be erased due to the effect of the neuronic magnetic depolarization and the patient will forget the event related to the stimuli.*

In recorders which use ferromagnetic tape, the electromagnetic stimuli take the form of a small magnetic field in the magnetizable material of the tape (e.g., iron or chromium), according to the intensity of the current's variation as it passes through the recording heads. The process obeys a regular sequence of space-time factors distributed along the tape. Microscopically, the surface of the blank band is modified, forming clusters that are oriented according to the magnetic field.

We have reasons to believe that the process of memory depolarization *works* similarly, at a microscopic level. The cerebral neurons of the astral cerebrum (or physical, in case of the incarnated), suffer spatial alterations due to the flux effect Σ (sigma) of the magnetic charge emitted by the operator. And so, it modifies the electric passage of the neuron net that corresponds to the storage of the stimuli; this means the memory is altered.

When we intend to erase a recording on a magnetic tape, it is enough to pass it through a similar field, but of a stronger and of a more regular intensity. In this case there will be a complete depolarization of the force-field previously formed and the tape is *erased*. In human beings, the erasing of the magnetic stimuli (which organized the electric fields of the neurons) follows the same law: *mutatis mutandis*.

As we can see, it is very simple: in a few seconds we can totally erase from the disincarnated's memory the harmful emotional charges (i.e., hatred, vengeance, humiliation, rancor, etc.), which polarize the patient's attention and obstruct the altruistic ideas and feelings that he would have if he could enjoy normality.

As far as we could observe, the disturbing event is not totally erased from the incarnated, but the patient no longer *feels* it as it had been previously—i.e., the emotional aspect has disappeared. Once the mind is depolarized, the person usually does not care about the event that worried him so much before. We believe this happens because the image was strongly recorded in his physical brain. The remaining magnetic field is too strong, and too intense to be defeated in a single application. Now, the emotion that was recorded in the *astral* cerebrum, is easily removed.

TECHNIQUE

(Application Upon the Embodied Disincarnated Spirit)

We spread the hands on the medium's cranium, along the cerebral hemispheres and command a strong energetic pulse; 1!

Afterwards, we change the position of the hands, so they will be on the opposite hemispheres. Then we project another pulse: 2! We go back to the first position and count 3! And so we go on, always changing the position of the hands.

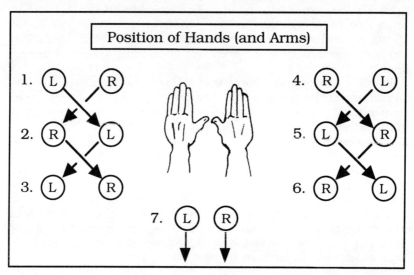

Since 1973 we have been using this technique with *complete* success in the treatment of obsessors with the incarnated, and in some other cases as a therapeutic intervention for drug addiction, for example. The changing of the positions of the hands is necessary. Each hand represents a magnetic pole that *has to be inverted.*

During the experimental phase, we faced an unforeseen fact: when we applied the depolarization on a disincarnated spirit, he jumped, automatically, to the previous incarnation. The phenomenon is odd, but constant. It seems to be the effect of the operator's potent magnetic field, which, being of an isotropic nature, embraces, at once, the present incarnation and the memory of the others that are recorded, in an unknown way, in some dimension of the cerebrum. Be that as it may, if we have another depolarization, it jumps again to a former incarnation. And so it goes on successively—always—at each depolarization.

RESULTS & CONSIDERATIONS

In practice, the technique has already given extraordinary results. We have become used to seeing the obsessing spirits— full of hatred against their victims, wanting to destroy them and make them suffer—return from a depolarization, totally calm, and even denying that they knew the victims who they had hated so much just a few moments before. A whole drama that sometime lasted for centuries is erased totally from the spirit's memories.

Before we bring the depolarized back to the incarnation in which he is situated, we impregnate his mind, magnetically, with kind, altruistic, fraternal ideas using the same technique—only now our objective is polarization. To achieve this, it is enough not to change the position of the hands; we are polarizing the cerebrum. We count slowly, saying in a loud voice, the idea to be imprinted in the disincarnated's mind. For example:

My friend, from now on you will be a very good man, a friend of everyone's...1! very good... 2!... 3!... friend... 4!... good... 5!... very good... 6!... always a good friend... 7!

In another counting we can imprint the following:

My dear, from now on you will be very hard-working... 1!... very hard-working... 2!... responsible... 3!... you will do your duties... 4!... hard working... 5!... very hard-working... 6!... 7!

In another counting we can imprint:

> *...you will like your family very much...*
> *...you will be happy, very happy...*
> *...you will be a joyful person... etc., etc.*

Once the spirit is depolarized and brought back to the present, we cannot just free him and leave him in erraticity. It is necessary to send him to a hospital in the astral to complete his recuperation and reintegrate into his evolutionary route.

The depolarization of the memory might not be successful in spirits that are mentally very strong, as for example, the black sorcerers. As they receive initiations in temples of the Past (from which they deviated), they still have magnetic fields which make them powerful. For them the procedure has to be different.

We would like to inform the investigators who come after us, that the treatment is purely magnetic. It does not make use of any kind of suggestion, and it is infinitely superior to suggestion. The effects of hypnotism usually do not last long because the stimulus is superimposed on another one, without erasing the first. Therefore, the older stimuli come up again very soon in the patient's consciousness, dominating the new ones, and within a short time everything is back to the former situation. In depolarization, however, we erase the older stimuli, and all others that refer to this subject. The cerebrum is now ready to receive new positive stimuli.

To finalize or complete the treatment of the incarnated and disincarnated, we look for an incarnation in which they experienced a good time, happiness, peace, and joy, so that, when they come back, they will have the best memories. If a treatment takes the spirit to a dramatic incarnation, full of painful events, we repeat the polarization until we find a better one. And only then do we bring him back to the present.

We have used depolarization successfully in the treatment of the incarnated's vices—chiefly those that have to do with the addiction to drugs of young people. As the technique erases the emotions that feed the vice, a cure comes naturally. It is even faster if the patient, at the same time, undergoes a well-oriented therapy, or if he becomes a member of any sound anti-vice movement.

IMPORTANCE OF SPIRITUAL ASSISTANCE

Because we discovered, experimented with and developed this technique, we feel very responsible for the consequences that it has for our human brothers.

The work in the Garden House happens according to a plan to help the sufferers, elaborated by the Superior, and it is followed by all workers, both incarnated and disincarnated. Therefore, the ideals and lessons of the Gospels guide us more than the Hippocratic oath. Scientific achievements, studies and research are only a by-product of our activity on behalf of our fellow beings.

We recommend care—rigorous care—in the application of this Law and technique. Before anything else, spiritual works have to count on the assistance of the Superior World, without which, any kind of success can be endangered, even if it may not appear so initially. Besides this, we should not frivolously treat rebellious and powerful spirits and the crowds that they command. Without special assistance, this can be dangerous.

ILLUSTRATIVE CASES

Case #1:
   Patient: I.C.C., male, white, student.
   Age: 19.
   Date of assistance: July 1984.

Clinical story:

For two years the patient took "sedatives." Together with a group of friends, he began by smoking marijuana. Some time later, that drug did not satisfy him anymore, and he started using cocaine whenever he had some money to pay for it.

He interrupted his studies and started working to get money for his vice. The drug became an inseparable part of his existence, an ever-increasing need. For this reason, he began using other kinds of drugs. His friends, all addicted to drugs, discovered a place near the stables of the Jockey Club in Port Alegre, where there was a special type of poisonous mushroom growing on land that had been fertilized with horse manure. They prepared an intense tincture with these mushrooms, and took this liquid in small doses with black coffee.

Within a short time, the action of this drug (probably psilocybin), together with the others they had already taken, produced its deleterious effect. The young man stayed more and more by himself—usually at home—and went out just at night to join his friends. He quit his job. He did not study any longer, he was unable to comprehend the most simple mathematical equations. From the happy and communicative person he had been, he became an introvert, totally absent-minded and uninterested in everything, even the most urgent family problems. His relatives (mainly his mother) were desperate. They watched, helplessly, as the young man stood ready to fall into the abyss.

Treatment:

*When we opened the frequency of the man we had a surprise. We did **not** find the presence of a black sorcerer who are usually behind cases of drug addiction. There were only some poor disincarnated drug addicts, that joined the group in a sad exchange of gross sensations gotten from the effect of the drugs. The obsessors, in an awful state, used the opportunity to vampirize the vital energies emanating from the incarnated. Since they were sick and weak spirits, without any major objective except for the vice, it was easy to remove them through powerful fields-of-force. They were conducted to the Love and Charity Hospital to undergo treatment.*

*It was a case of **simple obsession.** The disincarnated's parasitism looked like a case of symbiosis, in which they and the young man, unconsciously, exchanged among them the sensory experiences common in this kind of relationship. Once we had diagnosed the case, we started treating the patient.*

The young man was at home, according to the two mediums who went to his place to examine the environment.

We unfolded the sick fellow, at a distance, bringing his spirit to our work place. We embodied him in a medium, as if he were disincarnated; he was in a lamentable state. He just wanted some drugs, he only wanted to be "well" using the sad language of the nihilist youth of today.

*We immediately applied depolarization of memory to erase the
desire for drugs, as well as the vicious image and habits, from
his mind. With the depolarization shock, he jumped to his previous incarnation, when he was a sturdy peasant in Germany,
working as a woodcutter in the Black Forest. He had been very
active, extremely strong, and ignorant. His life, however, had
been very healthy; in contact with nature, he absorbed the natural simplicity of the woods and the mountains, which was
reflected in the naiveté and pureness of his habits.*

*We used this characteristic of the past as a therapeutic factor,
and made him stay firmly in this phase of evolution. We polarized his cerebrum positively with sound ideas of love of work,
goodness, fraternity, love of nature, etc. When we finished the
treatment, we brought him back to his body which was in a
daze—usual in these cases. Then we coupled him firmly to his
body and activated his chakras quite a bit.*

*Some days later we got news from the patient. His behavior
had changed; from an almost robot-like state, he was now feeling well and unusually active; he started painting his room, then
the kitchen and finally he painted the whole house! He resumed
working and intended to go back to his studies. Following his
mother's advice, he started going to church. He quit his vices
totally, and had a positive attitude.*

Discussion:

*Addiction to drugs at an initial stage, the result of a perversion
of customs. Very young, he was as curious as any adolescent;
without any solid and experienced religious basis (this means,
without any safe orientation), he was easy prey for the vice
exploiters. He fell into their hands as so many do. Under simple
obsession, he had his memory depolarized, the obsessors
removed and treated. He was in resonance with his former
healthy life and, at the end he received positive polarization.*

He was cured.

NOTE: *The treatment of drug addicts is almost never as simple
as the reported case. It tends to be difficult, very difficult—even
the spiritual treatment—because it usually requires facing the
black sorcerers, with all their dense and sophisticated malefic
action.*

Case #2:
   Patient: A.J.P., male, white, businessman, living in
   Buenos Aires, Argentina.
   Age: 30.
   Date of assistance: At a distance, on August 28, 1976.

Clinical story:

*After getting married, A.J.P. suddenly started having neurologi-
cal disturbances, something similar to epileptic seizures (though
weaker), that left him able to work only one or two days a week.
He felt a sensation of numbness in the extremities. Dizziness,
headaches, vomiting, prostration, etc. His tongue quivered and
he felt drowsy all the time.*

*Initially the episodes were frequent, the intervals short; later,
the episodes became less frequent, until they reached a three
month interval. He has been suffering from this problem for
three years.*

Treatment:

*He was assisted, at a distance, in answer to a letter his wife
had sent us.*

*On the day set for the treatment, we sent two mediums to the
patient's home. They were apometrically unfolded and accompanied by the spiritual staff headed by Dr. John—a disincarnated Canadian physician who was taking his internship at the
Love and Charity Hospital. When they arrived the patient was
in bed, very depressed, as if he had just come out of a crisis. On
his night table were several kinds of medicine, one specifically
for epilepsy. Spiritually, the patient was encircled by dense
vibratory bands (similar to fish scales), that were more compact
around his head. The treatment began by removing these scales
very carefully. Then they revitalized his cerebrum, and next the
whole nervous system.*

*After carefully examining the material removed from the sick
man, they tried to discover the origin and the probable obsessors, although they had not identified the presence of disincarnated entities. There was only a rather intense vibratory field
oscillating in the room.*

*They tried to find the station that was emitting the signal and
realized that ten kilometers from the place there was a house
where a young woman and her four-year-old child lived. The
young woman was the emitting focus of the magnetic field.*

*Through investigations, they found out that the young woman
was living an intense affective drama. She had had a love affair
with the patient (before his getting married) from which resulted
the birth of the little boy. Despite his promise of eternal love,
A.J.P. abandoned her to marry someone else.*

*Shocked and frustrated (chiefly after her son was born), she
constantly thought of her beloved and of the dreams that had
been destroyed. And so she vibrated intensely with the remembrances of those happy moments she had lived with her love.*

At this point the disincarnated doctor explained that the problem was the constant emission of her thoughts which reached the patient, although the girl did not have the intention to harm him. His image in her cerebrum, influenced greatly by the frustrated feeling (the emotion fed the image and the image fed the emotion in a positive feedback loop), she created a thought-form of enormous intensity (vector Σ of the magnetic flux) which interfered in the physiology of the cerebral neurons of her beloved, causing him serious disturbances.

First we treated the girl, the pivot of the drama. We unfolded her at a distance, by Apometrics, and embodied her mental body in a medium, as if she were a disincarnated spirit. Next, we depolarized her mind. We imprinted positive ideas of peace, hope, and joy, focusing chiefly on her little son. We showed her the brilliant future that he would have in the future, and the happiness that her son would certainly give her, chiefly in her old age. Charged with these positive ideas, we conducted her back to her home, into the kitchen where she was almost asleep. We coupled her to her physical body and activated her chakras.

She woke up pleasantly surprised (the mediums were observing everything). She straightened her hair, then her apron, without knowing what had happened to her. At this moment the boy came running in her direction from another room. She hugged her son, kissing him while she cried, as if she had not seen him for a long time. The ideas imprinted in her astral cerebrum were already showing results.

The erasing of her memory stratification did not make her totally forget the drama imprinted in her physical cerebrum. But it was erased from her astral cerebrum. Therefore the emotional state became lighter: it was there as a remote remembrance, almost forgotten, not able anymore to be the focus of neurotic or emotional problems. Due to the positive polarization, the past was only a distant nightmare.

Discussion:

A case of magnetic interference of malefic characteristics, caused by strong action of a magnetic polarized (vector Σ) flux, emitted by the powerful mind of an incarnated person. It is the action of an incarnated person upon another incarnated one, without interference of the disincarnated.

*The inopportune action provoked the victim's **spiritual unfolding**. The magnetic field forced the spirit to leave the physical body violently. This was the reason for the patient's disturbance, dizziness, headaches, etc. The situation would go on until the unfolded spirit was naturally attracted back by his* *physical body in a spontaneous coupling (as always happens in these cases).*

Although the author of the magnetic field did not have any desire for vengeance, her mental conditions were strong enough to cause the disturbance; the ardent desire, influenced by constant emotion, created the field.

If the inopportune unfolding was the main cause of the disturbance, there was also a group of destructive energies that joined the perturbation itself; the parasitic, self-induced currents, a result of the fear that surged in the patient himself. This conjunction would take A.J.P. to a mental state resulting in dissociation of his personality, a typical state of schizophrenia.

Number of assistances: One.
Duration of treatment: Thirty minutes.
Diagnosis: Pseudo-obsession, by unfolding at a distance.
Prognosis: Very favorable. Once the cause stops, the effect also stops—as happened in this case.

Final Observation: *Although there was a logical explanation for the clinical situation, and the treatment had been successful, we had not confirmed, at that time, that a simple woman had energy enough to interfere, with such an intensity, in the life of a healthy man. We informed Dr John about this incongruity and he agreed with us. He told us he would study the girl more deeply. After some minutes he informed us, smiling, that she had been a priestess in a distant past, when she acquired extraordinary mental powers. So, the mysterious disease of the Argentinean patient was totally explained. The scales that covered him were nothing other than the materialization in the astral of the magnetic fields around him.*

* * *

The reader should notice that this patient would have been one more of the unhappy beings who augment the statistics on mental diseases, diagnosed as a case of schizophrenia. In past centuries, medicine prescribed bleeding for several pathological manifestations—including anemia. We hope that, in the future, the diseases of the spirit will no longer be treated with chemical medicine—the modern equivalent of bleeding.

Case #3:
   Patient: W.S.C., white, single, high school teacher.
   Age: 27.
   Date of assistance: October 12, 1987.

Clinical story:

For years he had been feeling a strange disturbance: he did not know why, but his life had been luckless (sic). Everything went wrong. In his studies, it was difficult for him to fulfill his duties; not because he was intellectually weak, he was almost always one of the best among his colleagues. In his love affairs the situation was not very different. There was always something wrong with the girls; when he was close to getting married, everything was over. In his work the situation was even worse; it had been very hard for him to get a position as a teacher.

He felt he was a failure and discouragement was overtaking him.

Treatment:

We had hardly opened the man's frequency when an obsessor presented himself, raving against the patient and against whoever wanted to help him. We asked why he was so furious. He said that he wanted W.S.C. to suffer as much as possible, in the same W.S.C. had inflicted suffering on others. He introduced himself as "The Avenger," saying that this is how he was then known in the inferior environment of the astral. He revealed that in the past he had been one of W.S.C.'s victims, and that W.S.C. had ruined his life. Now he was taking his revenge; his enemy had to return tit for tat.

In spite of our conciliatory approach, "The Avenger" did not care to relinquish his quest for vengeance. We decided, therefore, to erase those painful scenes of the past from his memory.

First we carried out the depolarization, and "The Avenger" automatically jumped into his former incarnation. It was the existence where he suffered the evil actions of his enemy—now incarnated and now our patient. In the incarnation to which the jump took him, the obsessor did not show very good feeling; his situation is equal to, or even worse, than that which his enemy was living at the time. When we come across a situation of this kind we have to use a second depolarization—and even additional ones—until we find an existence in which the general situation is positive, marked by good feelings and virtuous procedures. At that point, we fix the spirit, apply magnetic currents with high-minded advice and evangelical teaching on his cerebrum, and then bring him immediately back to the present. As we see, there is no violence used against his spirit— everything is perfectly compatible with his way of being—we only stress the positive ideals and ethical postures that were his own at that time.

In the second polarization "The Avenger" was a monk and we had a very interesting dialogue with him:

Dear friend [we said], we can see that you are a priest, a very devout monk, aren't you?

Thank God, I am very devoted. I love God and Our Lord Jesus Christ.

My dear brother, could you tell us in which year we are?

Well ... we are in 1564!

For some moments the monk seemed to be confused. He held his head between his hands and said:

But what is going on with me? Where am I? Did I leave the monastery? It...is it possible that somebody came to fetch me, as there are so many crimes happening there, this...this... I do not even enter there...These are the Prior's orders and of those that are over there. Probably the superior ecclesiastic authorities finished with everything there... His Holiness, The Pope, must have ordered the necessary intervention.

Realizing that the monk was confused, we tried to make him feel relaxed.

Listen, dear friend. You did not leave the monastery, you just came to talk with us a little. By the way, we would like you to meet a friend of ours; we are almost sure that you know him.

He looked attentively at the incarnated patient (whom he had wanted to strangle some moments before) and then he shook his head:

No, Sir. I do not know this man. I have never seen him in my life. [And soliloquizing] And also... I seldom go out...

He became startled:

Oh! I want to warn you. Be careful with the Prior and with those who are around him. For nothing do they torture the prisoners and have them burned in a bonfire.

We released all the prisoners, who were in lamentable conditions; confined in underground dungeons, they looked like walking skeletons. Afterwards, we imprisoned all the monks, and brought them to the present in a powerful force-field, sending them to spiritual groups for selection (they all belonged to a terrible community of the Spanish Inquisition). The monastery was demolished to prevent other spirits of the Umbral from taking shelter there.

As soon as we finished this part, we conducted the monk to the small chapel of Domrémy-la-Pucelle, where Joan of Arc used to hear the voices that oriented her in her mission. We took him *there to arouse in him the flame of devotion and vivid faith, in contact with the vibrations of Joan and Saint Catherine, both of whom were still active in this place.*

When the monk entered the chapel he fell into a state of ecstasy. He also heard the voices that advised him to practice goodness, to love his fellow beings, etc., so much so that he betook himself to pray fervently.

*Finally, we brought the spirit back to the present, where he appeared totally renewed spiritually, eager to follow the target that he had glanced at. He abandoned any idea of vengeance because his hatred was erased by the gorgeous experience that was **imprinted** in his mind.*

Result:

The patient did not ask for another assistance. At the end of the month (when we were finishing this book) we heard that he had improved quite a bit.

Dialymetrics — Etheriatrics

Cures Near the Lake

And Jesus departed from thence, and came nigh unto the Sea of Galilee; and went up into a mountain and sat down there. And great multitudes came unto him, having with them those that were lame, blind, dumb, maimed and many others, and cast them down at Jesus feet; and he healed them. Inasmuch that the multitude wondered, when they saw the dumb to speak, the maimed to be whole, the lame to walk, and the blind to see; and they glorified the God of Israel. — Mat. 15:29-31

Cures in the Land of Gennesaret

And when they were gone over, they came into the land of Gennesaret. And when the men of that place had knowledge of him, they sent out into all the country round about, and brought unto him all that were diseased. And besought him that they might only touch the hem of his garment; and as many as touched were made perfectly whole. — Mat. 14:34-36

The Cure of a Leper

And, behold, there came a leper and worshipped him, saying, Lord if you wilt, thou canst make me clean. And Jesus put forth his hand and touched him, saying, I will; be thou clean. And immediately his leprosy was cleansed. — Mat. 8:2-3

The Cure of a Maimed

Now Peter and John went up together into the temple at the hour of prayer, being the ninth hour. And a certain man lame from his mother's womb was carried, whom they laid daily at the gate of the temple which is called Beautiful, to ask alms of them that entered into the temple. Who seeing Peter and John about to go into the temple asked alms, and Peter, fastening his eyes upon him with John, said, Look on us. And he gave heed unto them expecting to receive something of them. Then Peter

*said, Silver and gold have I none; but such as I have
give I thee; In the name of Jesus Christ of Nazareth rise
up and walk. And he took him by the right hand, and
lifted him up; and immediately his feet and ankle bones
received strength. And he leaping up stood, and walked,
and entered with them into the temple, walking, and
leaping, and praising God.*   — *Acts 3:1-8*

SOME REFLECTIONS

How is it possible for us, men of the 20th century, high-level
scientists, and rationalists *par excellence,* to accept piously
these fantastic descriptions that are atavistic and have the
taste of oriental legends?

How is it possible that today somebody cures certain tumors,
operating on the physical body without any anesthesia, without the least aseptic care. On the contrary (on purpose and
only as a demonstration), he puts earth from the ground on
the surgical wound or even saliva from one of the onlookers,
without causing any sign of postoperative infection?

Science does not believe in miracles; therefore, it does not
believe in supernatural cures. It is right about the first item:
there are no miracles. Everything follows Laws; we do not know
the Laws that rule unusual circumstances, therefore we reject
these facts. Neither does the supernatural exist as a mystery,
because all phenomena are natural and can be repeated, once
we know the Laws that rule them.

These reflections are necessary to understand the importance of *Dialymetrics,* a subject we will now examine. It is a set
of phenomena which obey immutable Laws; Laws that may
have been used by Christ and His sanctified followers at the
beginning of Christianity.

* * *

At the beginning of this century we had individuals who were
able to cure, not only when in somnambulistic trances (Edgar
Cayce, American) but also through prayers (The Worral couple,
Americans). In England, Harry Edwards became internation-
ally famous as a medicine man. Those who have studied paranormal phenomena in recent times have met many individuals
able to cure a great variety of diseases, some considered incurable by "accepted" medicine. This unusual faculty became
outstanding with the strange, bloody surgical operations practiced by medicine men in the Philippines—men such as Tony
Agpoa, Muratore, José Mercado and Marcelo Agular. In Brazil,
we had among others, the famous José Arigó who, embodied
as Dr. Fritz, did revolutionary surgeries. Now they are repeated

by the same Dr. Fritz embodied in the medium and doctor Édson Cavalcanti de Queiróz.

How can we explain these unusual facts, facts that seem to be a violation of the biological laws, since these medicine men do not use any kind of anesthesia or asepsis?

The most probable answer is that there is the projection of a kind of power, or energy, from the medicine man to the patient—an unknown magnetic force, perhaps "animal magnetism" as Mesmer called it. These people are supposed to have the faculty to project modulated cosmic energies by the power of their minds, a power of high harmonizing content which interferes directly in the forces that join the tissues.

CURE & ENERGY

In the miraculous cures done by Jesus and his apostles, the operational process was based on a direct and instantaneous interference in the tissue structures of the ailing organisms. In other words, the energetic stream of the Master acted on the innermost parts of the tissue's molecules, rapidly dissolving excrescences, calluses, anomalies that characterized the mal-formation or the disease. Strengthened by the energies that came from outside the body, the Laws of Equilibrium attenu-ated and harmonization was regained; the injured tissues recovered their vitality and form immediately, returning to their normal standard of health. That the paralyzed could walk, the blind could see, the leper became clean—among other miraculous cures—shows that it is possible to harmo-nize, in a few minutes, all kinds of unbalanced biological tis-sues. The first problem is the necessary energy. Next, we have to consider what kind of energy has to be used; it has to be specific, according to the conditions of the tissue and of the anomaly that is to be cured; the projection of forces has to be done in such a way that it does not harm the tissues, but only modifies the structures.

Up to now, we have not known of any kind of energy that, in a moment, is able to *dissolve* living tissues without also destroying the phenomenon "Life". Therefore, we can imagine the complexity of the subject.

What kind of energy is it then?

Are the frequencies of radiant energy (x-rays, gamma rays, cosmic rays) or any similar force known to science, modifiable and modulable by the action of thought?

For many forms of energy, the laws of their *manifestations* are well known even though their "innermost" qualities are not fully understood. These include electricity, the phenomena of iron magnetism, electromagnetism, gravitation, etc. We also know that thoughts are energy, but we do not know the nature of this energy, nor do we know how the transmission, called *telepathy*, happens. But the *power*, the *force*, the *energy* responsible for the phenomenon of curing is what most puzzles us and galvanizes our attention. In effect, this phenomenon existed in the past (even in the extremely remote past), was repeated many times by medicine men throughout the centuries, and is repeated in today, under our eyes. Nobody can deny it. We are in the presence of facts, and exactly because they are facts they *can be repeated*, once we know the conditions and causes of their occurrence.

For over ten years we have been studying all kinds of paranormal cures. At the same time we have evaluated the effects of the application of magnetic energies (through thought) at a cellular level. For this we created a technique— *Dialymetrics*[40]—which includes a set of phenomena and laws that constitute the basis of the medical treatment for applying specific magnetic energies. It is based on the knowledge and the laws about the mental energies which modulate cosmic energy of high vibratory content.

DEFINITION. *MODUS OPERANDI*

We could define Dialymetrics, therefore, as a form of medical treatment that combines the magnetic energy of mental origin (perhaps in the form of a "vital force") with energy of high vibratory frequency coming from boundless cosmic space, conveniently modulated and projected by the operator's mind upon the patient.

The potential of cosmic energy is unlimited but, in practice, it is limited by the operator's mental power. When the operator's potential is able to reach sufficient vibratory frequency to defeat the intermolecular cohesion,[41] this force will be diminished momentarily. The body or the target area will become plastic and malleable for some minutes, the molecules will be separated, according to the energy that was projected upon them. The process starts in the etheric body and, if sufficient energy was used, will reflect on the physical body.

To understand what Dialymetrics consists of, it is enough to consider the states of matter. For example, in its normal state, water is liquid; its molecules are separated, allowing an extreme mutability of form. If its temperature is reduced suffi-

---

[40] From the Greek verb *dialyo* (dissolve, dissociate), to which is added the word *metrics* (relative to "measurement"—or in our case, magnetic pulses).

[41] "Cohesion" is defined, generically, as the property of the bodies to maintain a stable form, once they are not subject to deforming forces. It results from the attraction forces between molecules, atoms, or ions that constitute matter.

ciently, it becomes solid and its molecules become more structured. But, when water evaporates due to the heat of the sun,
it is transformed into a gas and the molecules separate so
much that the water loses its form.

The same thing happens in Dialymetrics. The extreme molecular separation makes any solid body vanish completely. This
"miracle" has been performed countless times by mediums of
"physical effect." Among those who have become famous, we
mention Daniel Douglas Home, Eusápia Paladino, Florence
Cook and Madam d'Espérance (who went so far that her own
body suffered a partial and momentary dissolution in front of
the scientist Alexander Aksakof). The history of Spiritism is
rich in the phenomenon of sudden disappearance of objects
which reappeared at distant places. During some of these
incredible sessions of "physical effects" famous scientists were
present (William Crookes, Alexander Aksakof, Zollner, Wallace
and others) who gave public evidence of these facts.

In all of these cases one finds the interference of the molecular cohesion of the bodies, a phenomenon that also explains
the famous physical surgeries of Jose Arigó and of the medium
and physician Édson Cavalcanti de Queiróz. The loosening of
cohesion allows deep incisions; consequently it is possible to
remove internal tumors with almost no bleeding. The bleeding,
in effect, has to be at a very low level; the tissue is not integrally cut as it is in a classical surgery. The surgical opening is
more an incised separation of the body's components (skin,
subcutaneous cellular tissue, aponeuroses, muscles, etc.) than
a real cut. These tissues become locally plastic and malleable,
allowing cutting instruments or even the operator's bare hands
to penetrate the body without major traumatic consequences
or painful manifestations.

This property—the plasticity of biological tissues—can be
used in curative treatments, considering the rapid recomposi-
tion of the etheric body. At the beginning we were surprised
when we realized, even in treatment at a distance, that in a
state of plasticity, the organism becomes *malleable*, allowing
the action of the physiological laws to be immediate, complete,
and surprisingly fast because the tissues are less resistant.
Physical lesion can be easily healed by means of natural internal forces, which are able to recompose any affected or injured
area, regardless of the size or the type of lesion. Cure happens
automatically and from the inside to the outside according to
the laws of tissue growth.

It is without any doubt an extraordinary phenomenon, totally
new for classical medicine. But that is easily explained by the
laws that rule Life. The healthy state—the state of well-being—

results from the action of laws (biochemical, physiological, vital, etc.) which have only one goal: to keep Life in perfect balance. This balance is better known as *health*. A disease, or any lesion caused by an external attack (independent of its nature), is an *accident*. When, for example, traumas happen, physiological laws start acting automatically: *some days afterwards the lesion is healed* and health is regained. But if we apply Dialymetrics to the injured area, the laws of physiology will act more freely, and therefore, more rapidly. Only *a few seconds or minutes* are enough to make the recuperation *ad integrum* become real.

We have seen, in cases where the lesion is very serious, the disincarnated physicians use the body's significant plasticity to treat the lesion through the astral body. They perform extremely delicate and complex astral surgeries and, after some time, transfer the reconstituted part to the fleshy body. This spiritual treatment can easily be understood due to its similarity to the "principle of communicating vessels" in physics. When we connect vessels of the same size containing liquid at different levels, as soon as the communication is established, the liquids will have the same level in all vessels. As the astral body integrates our being and is intimately linked to the other corporeal structures, its cure is transmitted to the etheric body and then to the physical body.

With this technique we see new horizons for medicine. We feel that there are so many possibilities that we are not able to evaluate all of them. We are only outlining our research, the first steps in this investigation that—with God's Grace—will provide to humanity the access to a divine and inexhaustible source of all sorts of cures.

Dialymetrics gives us the conditions to successfully treat all types of harmed, sick, maimed and injured spirits. In the physical plane, however, we feel that we are still very far from having complete control of this technique, although we already have had good results. For the incarnate, we use apometric unfolding to treat the patient's *spirit* with Dialymetrics (as if he were disincarnated) and, finally, we couple him again with his physical body. Simple and tiny cosmic energy *transformers*, we do not have the conditions necessary to overcome the energy barrier of matter and act directly upon the dense body. For the time being we act upon the etheric body; as a result the physical body gets cured, too. But this is only the first step; it is only a matter of time. We will enter the third millennium with medicine using Dialymetrics, as we apply it today to the sick of the astral. Cures will happen—*completely*—in a few seconds.

THE TECHNIQUE

The technique is very simple. In a way it is similar to that of Apometrics.

We concentrate strongly on the body of the sick, focusing on the diminution of molecular cohesion, to receive adequate energy treatment. The counting has to be firm and the pulses slow, but charged with energy. We repeat the counting two or three times. The physical body does not show the least change in form or texture. But the etheric body becomes soft, less dense, and ready to receive the treatment. The sensitive clairvoyants and the disincarnated physicians who are treating the sick, register the phenomenon immediately. (The physicians immediately take advantage of the new situation to intervene, more deeply and more easily, to treat the astral and etheric bodies.)

While we intervene in the molecular cohesion of the physical and etheric body, we project energy upon the etheric body to dissolve the compact masses of low vibratory frequency (they are almost always of dark color), energies that quite often are the root of the disease. Next, we apply vitalizing energies to the injured areas, making them circulate through the tissues by means of local magnetic passes of small extension. In morbid processes, circulation of vitality along the body is endangered, similar to the inflamed state of the tissues—where lymph and blood circulation become stagnated, causing pain, edema and swelling of the affected tissues. Once these stagnant energies (which look like dark stains to the clairvoyants) are dissociated, the tissues become more permeable to the vitalizing energies which accelerate the process of cure.

THE FUTURE & DIALYMETRICS

From our studies and research, we have developed a systematic approach, thanks to our experience with hundreds of cases treated and observed in Porto Alegre and in the groups of Brasilia, Pelotas[42] and Santa Maria, Dialymetrics clearly represents a *technique of the etheric body's treatment*, with safe and effective results.

At the same time, an understanding of the way in which certain cures happen (cures that up to now have been considered miraculous) is becoming clear. The "new" technique points to a large field, practically unexplored by medical science: that of the etheric body, its constitution, properties, physiology, and its interrelations with the physical and astral bodies. The

---

[42] We owe an extraordinary debt for their contribution in the field to the group of our brother Prof. Althen Teixeira from Pelotas (RS).

horizon is vast. The phenomena that Dialymetrics takes care of represent only a segment of *Etheriatrics*—a word used to describe medicine that takes care of the etheric body.

Our research, observations, and studies are improving day by day as we dedicate ourselves to the assistance of the sick and to the dialymetric treatment. Our knowledge of the etheric body—this invisible structure of pure energy and, at the same time, quintessential matter—has grown step by step. Lifting the veils that made things mysterious, this new field is illuminated by a fascinating light. However, we know that we are only beginning. We are taking the first steps, those allowed and supported by our spiritual mentors. For the time being, we are accumulating data and experience which, perhaps at some future time, will be revealed to the public.

Something now seems to be definitive—the *results* of our experience. All of us, all of the "Garden House" group, feel that we are working on the cusp of a new vision of medical science, a medicine stratified in *dimensions*, *levels* or *horizons* of Energy. To define and delimit the levels we can consider them in the following way:

Pneumiatrics	Dimension of the spirit
Psychiatry	Dimension of the astral (soul)
Etheriatrics	Energetic dimension (etheric body)
Classical Medicine	Physical body

As one can see, our persevering work of almost a quarter of a century, with research and discoveries that were guided by our brothers of the Superior World, points to an integrated medicine in which man is seen as an eternal *continuum.*

We will go on. We hope that we will be surpassed by even more competent people on this route that belongs to all human beings.

ILLUSTRATIVE CASES

Case #1:

In 1978, in an evening of spiritual work at the Léon Denis Spiritual Center, we received the visit of a psychiatrist who was trying to solve a family problem. Anguished, feeling visibly uncomfortable because he had to resort to a Spiritist center, he asked us for help.

His father was about to undergo surgery: he was going to have one of his legs amputated since it was affected by a disease that hindered his blood circulation, and there was the imminent possibility of necrosis. Medicine was incapable of healing this case, in spite of all its resources. Not even a precise diagnosis had been given.

The simple fact of the necessity for amputation showed the existence of a serious, irreversible pathological process. We asked our colleague about the patient's state, age, the complete story of the disease, etc.

The sick man was 59 years old and, up to that time, had been very healthy. He had never had any symptoms of circulatory problems, either generally or of the extremities. Blood tests were normal. He did not have diabetes. The disease had started a short time before and became worse despite the intense treatment he was undergoing.

We asked our colleague if he was Spiritist. He became rather red in the face. "No," he answered, he did not know anything about Spiritism. He had never had been in a Spiritist center.

We invited him to enter the small room to attend the development of our works; he sat in a corner. We asked him not to become frightened by what he would hear, because we never know, when we start a session, what kind of spirits will manifest themselves. We advised him with great emphasis: we do not do miracles, neither do we do miraculous cures; if there would be cure, it would be due to divine mercy. His father was suffering from a physical disease; consequently the treatment belonged to classical Medicine. Our work was of a spiritual order. But we were at the disposal of our friends, the disincarnated physicians, to help them. If the cause of the disease were spiritual we would feel freer to assist the case.

Once he understood these premises, we began our work and started assisting the incarnated sick man. We wrote the name of the person on a piece of paper and, when it was time, we pronounced it in a loud voice. We opened his vibratory frequency through the emission of energetic pulses (counting up to seven). Then, we waited for some moments until the first manifestation of the entities that obsess the sick turned up.

As soon as we opened our colleague's father's frequency, a spirit embodied in one of the mediums, crying in pain, saying that they had amputated his leg. He was so anxious, suffering from intense pain, that he was not able to answer our questions.

To shorten his suffering, we projected a strong jet of energies to make him feel relaxed and, mainly, to reconstruct completely, his amputated leg. After three energetic projections, with slow counting to seven, the disincarnated suddenly became calm. He was surprised that his pain had stopped, but he was still afraid of touching the stump of his leg.

As we always do in these cases, we affirmed that he was cured. There was no need to be scared; never again would he feel any pain. We insisted. We asked him to palpate the leg for a long time, to be sure that it was there, perfect and sound.

Astonished, the spirit could not believe what he was feeling and seeing. More relaxed, he revealed his name and his story.

* * *

He had been a very good friend of the psychiatrist's father. He had had his leg amputated, after a long painful disease.

He told us that, after a long sleep—he did not know how long it was—he woke up feeling very weak, in a strange place, where the strangers there did not care about his need for help. Feeling abandoned, he wandered around for some time, until he met a "pilgrim" (sic) wearing a long garment, who tried to help him: he took him to a nice place where there was a creek flowing among very green, small and scarce bushes. The pilgrim advised him to look for a hospital to get adequate treatment.

When he heard the word "hospital" he tried to escape: he had just left one, where he suffered a great deal without any result. However, "what a strange thing!" (sic), as soon as he started to speak about his disease, he felt the pain in his leg again. He also felt weak, extremely weak. He began to experience breathing problems.

The pilgrim wanted to help. He took him in his arms and laid him on the grass telling him incredible things. They had a long talk. The pilgrim tried to convince him that he was already dead, and that he was in this condition because his spiritual situation was not very good. That place was not adequate for an individual in his condition because it was infested with pitiless beings.

All these revelations sounded fake to our friend. As a Catholic, he refused everything energetically. Since when does a dead person have pain in his leg? And what kind of story was this, that he was already dead, if he was still wearing his clothes? If there was any pitiless person in this place, it surely had to be the pilgrim (or the monk, or whatever he was). He turned his back and crawled, with all the energy he still had, to a faraway place. He only stopped when he could no longer see the other man.

He does not know how long he lay there.

One day, already an unbeliever, he remembered his former devotion to the Holy Virgin and he felt like praying. He prayed. He prayed again. To his surprise, a feeling of total well-being overcame him, and he heard the soft murmurs of angels which made him meditate. He remembered, then, his distant childhood, the kind of life he had, the problems... He cried, lost in his recollections. He remembered his friends, those who had helped *him so much in the last years of his life. He felt drowsy. Tired and weak he fell into a deep, long sleep.*

When he woke up, he felt that he was being moved by a strange force which lifted him up and was taking him slowly to a busy city, full of people and vehicles. He soon recognized the city; it was his old Porto Alegre! The memory of his friend got stronger. It was enough to think of him for him to be able to move faster. Almost immediately, he was in front of the house that he knew so well; he entered without hesitating.

His friend was reading the newspaper. He felt moved and went close to his friend. For a long time he hugged this man who he considered a brother. He talked to him energetically, but—what a strange thing! (sic)—the friend went on calmly reading his newspaper. He only waved his hand over his face as if he wanted to remove an annoying insect!

Shocked with this inexplicable indifference, he sat on a chair in front of the friend, waiting for what was going to happen. The friend did not pay attention to him, but he also did not expel him from the place and that was good. Not having a place to go, sick and in no condition to move by himself, he decided to stay in that home, which used to be so hospitable.

Although he was reasonably installed, his pains went on. He only felt some relief when he got close to his friend: these were moments when a warm wave invaded him, making him feel comfortable. He realized that his friend also started to have problems with one of his legs—he knew so well the symptoms. He was desolate when he came to know that his friend also was to be subjected to an amputation.

Suddenly, however—he could not understand why—he was at a place that was not a hospital, and where they recomposed his leg, in a surgery without pain, without anesthesia, openly and rapidly.

This was the long report of the spirit.

Now, it was our turn to assess what the spirit did not know.

* * *

We explained his state and his present situation to him. We also revealed that if he had accepted the suggestions of the "pilgrim" (who had helped him as soon as he woke from the sleep of his physical death), he would now be in much better spiritual condition and probably would be walking around in the garden of a hospital.

Understanding well now what had happened to him, he agreed to be conducted to the Love and Charity Hospital for a definite treatment. He lamented for having been, unwillingly, the cause of his friend's disease. He promised that as soon as he could, he would do everything to repair the evil that he had unconsciously caused his friend.

* * *

When he disincarnated, he was in a barren place of the Umbral. He went there due to the Spiritual Specific Weight Law: when he detached from his physical body, he floated, unconsciously, to the place that was most compatible with his magnetic density. When he arrived there, he woke up. As he was not a bad person, there were no enemies waiting for him; therefore he did not suffer any attack from disincarnated predators. But, since he did not know the reality of the spiritual world, he did not accept the suggestions of his protecting spirit ("the pilgrim") who had helped him; he had to learn the truth by himself, because, in the spiritual world, free will is law and is respected.

When he thought of his friend, he was attracted. The rest we know. His presence caused a state of vibratory resonance that became stronger with time. The disharmonic magnetic action disturbed the physiology of the tissues in the same area where the friend had had his problem, and so started the disease. We described this syndrome—unknown to medicine in 1975—calling it "spiritual induction."[43] It is, as we have already seen, a process by which a disincarnated spirit can cause a disease to the incarnated, simply by his continuous presence, even if he does not want to cause harm.

It was a simple case. It was enough to remove the inductor for the patient to feel better.

Result:

One week after, the patient was considered out of danger—the surgery was canceled. In two months he was totally cured.

We had the opportunity to meet the patient in 1984. He was then in perfect health.

This case shows us the enormous possibilities of the use of Dialymetrics in the treatment of disincarnated spirits.

For us it was very interesting. It was the first case, and it showed us the way and sharpened our curiosity to reach, with the help and the permission of the spiritual world, the laws and techniques of the use of Dialymetrics.

Case #2: Dialymetrics applied to an incarnated patient.
  Patient: F.R.S., female, white, 29, married.
  Date of assistance: December 6, 1986.

---

[43] See the Illustrative Case in the section "Vibratory Resonance" of Part I.

Clinical story:

Chronic salpingitis in the left fallopian tube, with a tumor involving the large ligament, ovary, etc. Surgery was scheduled for the coming days. Even a superficial examination of the abdomen presented a palpable and painful tumor in the left inferior quadrant. A persistent purulent discharge—when it got stronger—alleviated the abdominal pains. The patient was given antibiotics.

The pathological story started after a uterine curettage some years earlier when the endometrium was drained to remove the remainder of a spontaneous abortion.

Treatment:

When we opened F.R.S.'s frequency, we saw that her etheric and astral bodies were involved in a greenish, fetid glue, a consequence of sexual disorder. Our first step was to clean carefully these two bodies.

We started treating the physical body.

We applied Dialymetrics to get the largest possible separation between the molecules of the etheric body (with the maximum loosening of molecular cohesion). The treatment was completed with intense projections of sterilizing energies of green color.

After the first application, we applied two more at an interval of one week.

Result:

The patient started improving after the first application.

The physician suspended the surgery due to the patient's recovery.

Case #3: Dialymetrics applied to an incarnated patient.
   Patient: E.S.B., male, white, 26, single.
   Date of assistance: May 5, 1987.

Clinical story:

The patient came in on crutches. He had been suffering for years from extensive coxofemoral osteomyelitis of the left leg, where he had an intense suppuration which came out of some fistulas. He had already undergone four surgeries, which gave him some relief, but they did not eliminate the disease.

Exam:

When we opened E.S.B.'s frequency, we realized that there were no obsessors present at the time. As we always do in these cases, we opened the frequencies of the young man's past. (This means we investigated his former incarnations.)

His past was turbulent, chiefly the penultimate incarnation, when he seriously hurt his enemy, causing him a lame leg. In this earlier existence he was violent to those around him. And all of his victims were paralyzed in time, still carrying the whole charge of their sufferings.

Treatment:

We looked for all of his victims of the past and treated them, relieving their pains. As a consequence, E.S.B. also alleviated the consequences of the resonance with his own cruel and aggressive past, which had been full of hatred, suffering and disharmony. This—always—causes disturbances, anguish and other serious consequences to the guilty.

Only after we had treated the sick's past did we start the real work on his body.

We applied Dialymetrics on the injured segment of the left leg, and projected strong jets of green light to sterilize deeply the affected area. In the meanwhile, E.S.B., unfolded, was assisted at the Love and Charity Hospital by disincarnated physicians who treated his astral body.

The treatment was repeated every fortnight for three months.

Result:

Immediate.

The few purulent foci healed and the pains vanished. He started walking firmly and, in a short time, he did not need crutches when he was at home. He continues with the treatment.

Case #4: Dialymetrics applied to an incarnated patient.
   Patient: M.R.A., female, white, 28, married.
   Date of assistance: June 28, 1986.

Clinical story:

Since she was married eight years before, she had intense pain in her breasts, which were always swollen, hardened, and painful when palpated. Symptoms were worse during menses.

The medical diagnosis was "chronic mastopathy" (pathology of the breast) due to a hormonal disjunction, caused by the action of contraceptives taken indiscriminately. Mammograms showed only swelling of the lactiferous glands, without any malignant neoplastic tumors.

Treatment:

Without interfering in the medical treatment M.R.A. was undergoing, we applied Dialymetrics on the affected area. In the mean time, spiritual physicians applied physiotherapy on the client, who, unfolded, was taken to the Love and Charity Hospital.

Results:

After the second application, her pains disappeared and the glandular swelling vanished. She had three applications at an interval of fifteen days.

PNEUMIATRICS

INTRODUCTION

If man were fully conscious of the enormous potential of the energies he has contained within his own physical body, he would be astonished by the power he has always had but did not take advantage of. Does this mean, then, that he could make use of all this potential if these energies were transferred and put to work in the astral world? This, however, is not everything. This energy stream of the physical body also exists in the quintessential state, in the astral body of all human beings. There are many kinds of energy at our disposal.

Inside ourselves, in the pigeonhole of our cosmic consciousness, we keep latent divine powers. It is necessary that we wake them up, to become conscious of this fabulous *natural* reality, a consequence of the Divine Presence in us, in Life. We are a sacred source of infinite energies that are *inherent* in our beings: they are part of our *essence*. Our whole evolutionary journey is directed to this source—so we can reach it and then release and use these energies. When this happens, when we are one with the target that this source is, the liberated Christic energies do miracles that are as powerful as those that Jesus did. It was not in vain that the Divine Master told us: *"You are gods..."*

When incarnated, the spirit is involved in dense vibratory bands that constitute the physical body—this fleshy diving suit that all of us dress in when we incarnate and that gives us the ability to mold, modify and act upon it as we like. As a counterpart, however, our consciousness and our perceptions are limited by the solid horizon of everything that is physical, dense and material.

Spiritual evolution, therefore, is a process of extraordinary complexity, in which the spirit wanders through unending spaces for an immensely long time. Ascension is only completed after millennia of polishing: the human diamond, when polished, will have the shine and transparency of the infinite Light. All this time is spent, actually, in a slow dematerialization, since evolution implies a separation from physical matter: the more the spirit is evolved, the less materialistic the person is.

This degree of dematerialization can only be realized and measured in the astral dimension. In the physical plane we are all equal in our fleshy body suits, and we are in a constant effort to get rid of them, through the slow acquisition of eternal values. But all of us have an appointment with the definite enlightening of consciousness, which will result in a permanent and unmovable syntony with our own essences, with the consequent understanding of our cosmic destinations.

In this state we start assimilating eternal values. And we enter, automatically—as we progress to each step on the *Way*—into a gradual Christic completeness that involves us in natural and clear wisdom: Knowledge, that at this level is more Love than Knowledge, and that is why it provides immense happiness.

At this stage, matter has lost the value that most of our human brothers value so highly; and we kindly understand our brothers who have not yet penetrated into this awareness sanctuary that reveals a peace made of love, harmony, hope, and happiness.

This is the precious light of all men, whether they know it or not. However, how much effort does our ignorance waste until we recognize it? How much time do we waste?

It is interesting that there is no use in showing the *Way* to individuals who are still immersed in the whirlwind of passions: they do not believe in it. Neither are they ready to follow it. When they enter it they have to pass through the "narrow door" where our voluminous luggage of illusions and the egotistic knickknacks that feed our love for feelings do not fit. Only when we learn to feed ourselves from the Spiritual Light will we be in a condition to evaluate the importance of the Way *that is* each instant of our lives—and follow it happily.

We usually are blocked—tied to matter, interests, and the things of our daily lives. We do not realize how we can rise up to the height of the spirit. But there will be a moment when a vivid flame penetrates us, animated by an unknown kind of energy—sometimes by the paths of the heart, frequently by mental or moral pain, rarely by the cerebrum (because no one turns to God by following cool reasoning), or through an enlightening perception of our cosmic *reality*. This vivid flame opens gaps in our Egos, it throws down our junk, barriers and prejudices, it transforms, it fulfills, it converts us into believers. This sudden "brain wave" characterizes the experience of something transcendental, which lifts us from the ground of the material to the sacred planes of the spirit.

Living Religion, we *live* spiritual values. Nobody, then, can change the course of our lives. And the nearer we are to the light, the stronger becomes our faith, and the firmer are our steps on the Way. Together with Paul, the apostles, the mystics and the martyrs of all time, we will be ready to lose everything, the purest affects, our own body, in order not to renounce the divine flame of truth that is lit in us.

Once he sees this Flame, any spirit—incarnated or disincarnated—will turn his back on material interests and search only for the peace and happiness of Christic light.

In the disincarnated, this process of consciousness awakening can be easier, not because of more or less interest of the spirit (which, in most cases, does not know anything about it), but because we can intervene in a decisive manner, helping him to find in himself, his Way. It is not even necessary to take him to a sacred place that would awaken in him strong emotion and religious devotion (as we sometimes do successfully). It is enough to guide him in the search for the Way in himself, making him look for—*and find*—the Christ that is in himself.

The result is always marvelous. The completeness of the momentous action of the Christic flame—*which is* He himself—constitutes a vivid, real and imperishable experience. The spirit takes a new direction as a being in evolution, he accepts the kind orientations and invitations from the Superior. We have always had more success with a simple trip to the Christic essence than with hours of kardecist dialectics. This technique we call *Pneumiatrics*, which means the cure through the spirit (in Greek, *pneuma)* Himself. Pneumiatrics, however, cannot be used for all the disincarnated since syntony with the cosmic "I" is only possible from a certain degree of harmonization on. It should be applied only on those who are not vengeful, perverse, obstinate persecutors or black sorcerers—who are already detached from material interests and have at least a little bit of good will.

THE TECHNIQUE

Once the disincarnated is prepared and shows a favorable disposition, we project upon him a very intense field of luminous energy (mainly upon his head), counting slowly and longer (up to 21 or 33), in which we use all the energy of our will to have him taken to the Christic planes in Himself. We achieve this in one or two attempts. The spirit tends to fall into ecstasy; he usually does not want to leave this luminously pure place of peace and well-being that he had never expected (a state he would experience normally and definitely, after a long evolutionary process). In this state of absolute and indescribable happiness he might cry with joy or kneel down, thanking Our Lord for what he sees and feels.

We use this moment to indoctrinate him. This, in fact, is easy now: the words become vivid, indelible, of a spiritually illuminated meaning. Right afterwards we make the spirit return to his normal vibratory state. Ecstasy from then on will be a constant objective for him: he will miss it. The glimpse of the goal, an unforgettable light imprinted in his memory, will make him persist in the direction of the light.

As we see, the technique consists of raising momentarily and artificially the vibratory state of the spirit, taking him to Christic levels by the action of powerful energetic fields, *discharged* by the operator's mind and, obviously, potentiated by the Superior World. As it is an artificial situation, one to instruct and enlighten the spirit, it will last only while the supporting energy actuates the spirit. He will return to his natural state even without the operator's intervention.

Again, we would like to alert the reader: we should not attribute any magical property or mystic connotation to the counting or to the numbers that are pronounced in a loud, slow tone. At each number we project a jet of energy in the same way that people utter sounds to make it easier to lift or push something heavy.

There is no magic. No mysticism. The energy is, in the final analysis, the one of Christ in us (the same that *lives*, in this very instant, in the reader himself).

THE UTILIZATION OF
THE SPIRITS OF NATURE

In all the kingdoms of nature dwell immaterial living beings, that guard and give life to these vibratory dimensions which constitute their habitat. Orientals have known of these entities since antiquity: they called them "spirits of nature." The literary sagas of the non-Latin countries in Europe—mainly the Nordic countries—are full of reports of goblins, gnomes, fairies, sylphs, etc., and their relationships with mortals.

As far as we know, these beings have their evolution in the astral; they do not incarnate among human beings.

In Brazil, Umbanda and our folklore tell us about the existence of *saci-pererês*[44], *iaras*[45], *boi-tatás*[46], *caiporas*[47] and other spirits of nature. There is *Iemanjá*,[48] who is worshipped in the sessions of Umbanda: she presides over the "people of the sea." There are spirits of nature called sirens, undines and others. Even fire, an irresistible dissociative energy, contains the well-known salamanders, extremely active beings that were very much invoked by the medieval alchemists, as a source of transforming energy.

In principle, all spirits of nature can be utilized by men in the most varied spiritual tasks, for useful purposes. For example, the cleansing of a Terreiro[49] of Umbanda of "heavy environments" (this means infested with malefic objects and substances, destined to harm people), is well-known in Brazil. On these occasions the old black invokes *Iemanjá* and asks her for permission to have the people of the water clean these infested environments (homes, offices, "terreiros", etc.) taking the evil burden to the depths of the ocean. Clairvoyants perceive when the sylphs arrive in enormous ocean waves and collect, with their fine nets, everything that is evil. In spiritual

---

[44] In slave time, a little black boy with only one leg.
[45] Indian-Brazilian siren.
[46] An Indian-Brazilian genie that protects the fields against fire.
[47] A fantastic entity that could be a one-legged woman, a child with a big head or a giant sitting on a wild pig—Indian-Brazilian origin.
[48] The Queen of the Sea—Afro-Brazilian origin.
[49] A place where Afro-Brazilian cults are celebrated.

works we tend to utilize this sound practice chiefly at the end of our work.

The spirits of nature are—all—naturally pure. They are not contaminated with dissociative doubts, egotism, or envy, as happens with men. Innocence and simplicity are predominant among them. Always ready to serve, they come immediately when we call them, eager to perform our commands. However, we should never use them for less meritorious tasks or in the service of mean, degrading interests. Whatever they do wrong due to our deceptions will inevitably return to our detriment (Law of Karma). Besides this, we can only use them for a special purpose: we should never enslave them according to our wishes and interests. We cannot forget that they are free beings who live in nature and have their own evolution. We can invoke them to help us in services that is for the best of our fellow-beings—since this accelerates their evolution. But we have to respect them very much. If we use them as slaves, we will be responsible for their destinies, because, in this case, they will not abandon us, demanding support and protection as if they were little pet animals. By doing this, they may harm us, even if they do not want to.

The Divine Laws have to be observed. Once the spirits of nature finish the task we ask them to do, we have to set them free immediately, thanking them for their collaboration and asking Jesus to bless them.

ILLUSTRATIVE CASE:
UTILIZATION OF A SPIRIT OF NATURE

In 1984, a woman who was extremely anguished about her husband's financial situation came to see us. She also mentioned that her husband had been feeling sick for four months.

She said that everything "was going wrong" in her husband's business. That the great amount of money the couple had was dwindling away, lost in businesses that failed without any special reason, although everything had been favorable and well-planned. Even the new car they bought was demolished in an accident. But her greatest concern was her husband's health problem which had grown worse and worse.

Treatment:

When we opened the family's frequency two deformed spirits presented themselves. They were **exus,** *cursing and challenging us. We reduced them immediately to impotence and conducted them away to the recuperation colonies.*

Once the **exus** *were removed, there came the chief of the legion of Darkness. Calm and very sure of himself, he chal-*

lenged us to undo the work that he had been asked to do. (The malefic work had been done in two parts, one in Rio Grand do Sul and the other in Bahia.)

We invited him to undo his work and he laughed at our naiveté. He said that even if he wanted to undo the work he could not, because it had been carefully prepared and then thrown into the sea. "Now, who would find it in the deep sea?" he asked, and laughed disdainfully.

We tried to show him that he was mistaken. When we operate for the best, everything is easy. In this case, it would be enough to call the spirits of nature who would come immediately to help us.

From words we passed to action. We invoked **Iemanjá** *and asked her to authorize the people of the oceans to bring the evil deed to us. We begged her not to allow such a negative focus to remain in her domain. It was enough to match the vibratory syntony of the sorcerer's mind with the life forces of the ocean to make the whole "work" jump into the astral, brought by the mermaids in front of the amazed eyes of the sorcerer.*

Terrified, he saw a shell full of objects belonging to the victim (including some hair), bewitched papers covered with words, ribbons, and the name of the victim on a paper covered with wax. The shell was also covered with a thick coat of wax to insulate it from the salty water.

The sorcerer was obligated to undo everything; we burned the remainder immediately. As soon as the sorcerer finished, he was reduced to impotence and sent, unconscious, to an appropriate place for his recuperation.

As we see, we can—in theory—undo any black magic work in any part of the world with the help of the spirits of the kingdom where the evil was placed. It is only necessary to know how to call them. Normally, unfolded mediums accompany the undoing of black magic works and help chiefly with the cleansing.

There is no mystery in these actions—any person can prove it. We use the Laws that God created for all beings; in our work we are frequently helped by undines, mermaids, gnomes, salamanders, *sacis*, and other spirits of nature. We use salamanders, for example, to burn the malefic material of the sick, mainly substances and excrescences of cancerous tumors. Everything is easy, easy to do. However, even most spiritists do not believe in these beings.

ARCHECRYPTOGNOSIS

The word is of Greek origin and means *the knowledge of something ancient and hidden in time*. It is, more precisely, concerned with the unveiling of ancient texts, of a remote past that disappeared into the whirlpool of the ages.

Archecryptognosis was uncovered, by chance, when we treated a patient during 1980.

A woman came to see us looking for help because her home had become a hell (sic) after the death of her husband, a well-known physician. The youngest daughter had become addicted to drugs, which worried her very much. Influenced by the general dissolution of morals today, the daughter declared her premature independence and started spending many days away from home. The oldest son also deviated from the right path. He exchanged his studies for bad company. Even the house in which they lived, in spite of being new and well-built, showed inexplicable signs of aging, losing great pieces of its internal plaster. The contractor was astonished; he said he could not understand this unusual phenomenon. Besides this—the most important fact—the lady told us that she *felt something heavy in the air*—a sensation of despair, of anguish and powerlessness—and had the feeling that everything was rotating around her.

While she reported, over the telephone, the evil things that were afflicting her—mainly the moral anguish and terror—we came to the conclusion that it had to be another case of black magic, due to the similarity with other cases.

On the day of the appointment, the patient was there and we opened her frequency looking for the bands of black magic. However, we found none.

Puzzled, we opened the doors to her past. As soon as we fixed the frequency, two mediums found themselves in an intense sandstorm that hardly allowed them to breathe. The violence of the wind and sand was so intense that they were not able to identify the place where they were.

We tried to calm them by giving them confidence and quieting their fears. They, then, started to perceive a tomb of stones in the open desert, with an inscription on one of the sides. They were not able to find out the origin of the tomb, neither the meaning of the unusual inscription, which, according to their information, was composed of "silhouettes of little ducks, some different style of feathers, rope circles, broken lines in the form of saw teeth, etc." It was obviously a hieroglyphic inscription.

We asked the mediums if they could translate what was written there. They thought it funny, because they did not have the faintest idea about the Egyptian language, let alone about reading hieroglyphics.

We explained to them that it should be very easy to know the meaning of the signs of any type of writing. They constitute the objective part of the subjective meaning, linked to the form and position of the symbols. Therefore, to understand the meaning, they had to penetrate this subjective reality.

We asked them to stay at some distance from the tomb, and look attentively at the inscription. They should not eye the signs fixedly, but look at the contents. In the meantime we would project energy to get them syntonized with the subjective meaning, by frequency resonance.

Suddenly and simultaneously both mediums started reading the inscription as if it were written in their native language:

> *Anyone who is going to surpass his Destiny will have a tempestuous future.*

This inscription seemed so strange to us that we decided to investigate the causes of the warning. We then discovered the origin of our patient's reverses.

At the time of Ramses III (1197-1165 BC), at the margins of the Nile and near Tebas (Upper Egypt), there was a beautiful young girl who lived in a miserable shack, and who fed herself from fish, water birds, and the products of a meager farm. It was the same life for all the girls of the village. But the aggressive exuberance of her youth, her satiny tanned skin, her rustic beauty, made her surpass all the other girls.

One day, when she was at the edge of the river, walking between the fishing rods, the pharaoh's boat passed by, very slowly, near the shore. The sovereign saw her surrounded by the riparian vegetation and was so impressed with her beauty, that he ordered one of his men to invite her to live at the palace, in his harem.

Feeling very happy that destiny had placed her in this new kind of life, she started enjoying life with all her fire and unlimited egotism. Free, powerful, surrounded by servants, she went to visit her humble village as soon as she could. Not that she was feeling homesick; she wanted to show her former enemies the power she had now. She had already gained the friendship of the lower officers of the royal guard, who took her, escorted by three men, to the extremely poor village. As soon as she arrived, she ordered the soldiers to stab some of her former enemies with a sword and to burn down their shanties. The executioners took the opportunity to show that they were good soldiers and fulfilled the orders right away— while the girl sat comfortably in a litter and laughed at the poor people. The naked little children, terrified and crying, were running in all directions. The girl's purpose was not to kill these people, but to show her power and punish them for minor squabbles that they had had. For some time, she went on with these visits, always doing the same: causing pain, running about and trampling on her victims who cursed her with growing hatred.

A long time after these events she disincarnated.

As she did not belong to the royalty, she did not have the right to be buried in the Valley of the Kings. She was buried in the desert, in a simple tomb. She received a terrible sentence from the priests, who had been silently observing her behavior for a long time.

In reality, because of her violent acts, she surpassed her destiny. She should have been the equal of the other anonymous fish-girls who lived at the margins of the great river. Since she was a simple plebeian without any official position, she could not have any executive power, even at the social level to which she had been taken. All the evils she had sown were returning to her surroundings as negative life forces, exactly as the Holy Writings advise:

> ... *be sure your sin will find you out.* — Num. 32:23

Probably the patient's spirit had already had the opportunity to redeem, in former incarnations, a great part of the evil she had sowed in the past. The disharmonic vibrations that were haunting her now had been left for the "end of times"—the present time.

As a treatment, we involved her in positive vibratory fields, fixing her in a harmonic frequency. We erased from her cerebrum, (using depolarization of the memory's stimuli) the anguishing remembrances of the past to prevent her from syntonizing with them in vibratory resonance. We advised her to follow the evangelical standards of behavior, and to keep positive thoughts and constant vigilance. We oriented her for a better understanding: karmic debts of any kind can only be paid with love—through the practice of charity and through dedicating ourselves to goodness with all our energies. (It is a mistake to think that karma has to be paid with suffering.)

Following our instructions and receiving passes regularly, the patient gained peace. She recovered confidence and was blessed by the light of vivid faith. She was cured.

This lady, however, could never have imagined that, due to the need to assist her deeply, we discovered another animistic technique, one of great importance, chiefly in the cultural field. Our new *instrument* would allow us to investigate the past, even the remote past, through the readings and translations of inscriptions. The moment we dive into the Past, we are really entering another equation of Time, reviving eras that were buried during the passing of centuries. Everything becomes transformed again into the Present, due to the dimensional conditions. These conditions are new, but they are ruled by mathematical laws which make them amenable to reduction to equations.

We decided to investigate the subject because of its historical interest.

We achieved astonishing results. We could translate some extremely old texts, painted on the walls of temples. Here are some that were read in one of the crypts of the temple of Karnak (about 1500 B.C.), a temple that had disappeared:

The Good and the Evil walk together, he, who trails on of the routes, hardly ever will trail the other one.

We do not have any other alternative, because in this wandering one gets either the crown or loses the head.

This one was seen in front of the image of a pharaoh:

You are the King because you have always been the King. You are the blessed of the gods, who protect your destiny, like the Moon controls the achievements of creatures.

Unfortunately, with our work totally dedicated to the assistance of the sick, we are not able to do a systematic investigation in the past, to explore its lost cultural richness. It is our intention, however, to search the old Egyptian temples more extensively, as soon as possible.

We hope that other investigators will apply themselves to this vein, with more technique and time, to call up those lost treasures of wisdom out of the past.

CONCLUSION

Everything we saw, everything we showed, solved, commented on, revealed, studied and analyzed is of vital importance to human beings—we are sure!—and, therefore, fascinating. The scientific aspects of the presented phenomena are important and valid, as we know. The well-applied mathematical equations on which our research and findings are based represent Truth in its logical coolness; but all this is not worth it (and neither is this book) if there is not Love as the cause and Love as the objective.

Love has to be the Alpha and the Omega of human action, because only Love gives eternal consistence.

Based on this principle, we programmed our work that has lasted for more than twenty years, during which we tried to stay with the essence of the Gospels and the most important of the commandments: Love. This book is only a by-product of our essential work; it was only written because this work has to be enlarged to involve, if possible, all the people in need on the planet—both incarnated and disincarnated.

It is not important, therefore, what this book may present. Independent of its value, it will be surpassed by others that come after. It is necessary that it be this way because its aim is charity, and the charity it creates will be inexhaustible. The apostle Paul said: "charity will never vanish."

But covet earnestly the best gifts: and yet shew I unto you
a more excellent way
Though I speak the tongues of men and of angels,
and have not charity,
I am become as sounding brass, or a tinkling cymbal.
And though I have the gift of prophecy,
and understand all knowledge;
and though I have all faith,
so that I could remove mountains,
and have not charity, I am nothing.
And though I bestow all my goods to feed the poor,
and though I give my body to be burned,
and have not charity, it profiteth me nothing
Charity suffereth long, and is kind; charity envieth not;
charity vaunteth not itself, is not puffed up.

Do thee not behave itself unseemly,
seeketh not her own, is not easily provoked,
thinketh no evil;
Rejoiceth not in iniquity, but rejoiced in the truth;
Beareth all things, believeth all things,
hoped all things, endureth all things.
Charity never faileth: but whether there be prophecies,
they shall fail; whether there be tongues,
they shall cease; whether there be knowledge,
it shall vanish away.
For we know in part, and we prophesy in part.
But when that which is perfect is come,
then that which is in part shall be done away.
When I was a child, I spake as a child,
I understood as a child:
but when I became a man, I put away childish things.
For now we see through a glass darkly;
but then face to face: now I know in part;
but then shall I know even as also I am known.
And now abideth faith, hope, charity, these three;
but the greatest of these is charity.

— 1 Cor. 12:31–13:13

All the words of this book were written to become instruments of charity in the hands of those that work in Jesus Christ's grain field. They were born from charity, and to charity they must return.

BIBLIOGRAPHY

Aksakof, Alexander, *Animismo e Espiritismo* (Animism and
  Spiritism), Ed. Federacao Espirita: Rio de Janeiro, 1956.
Baraduc, *La Force Vitale*, Paris, 1912.
Bozzano, Ernesto, *Unfolding, Bilocation Phenomena*.
de Chardin, Pierre Teilhard, *O Fenomeno Humano* (The
  Human Phenomenon).
Crookes, William & King, Katie, Clarin: Sao Paulo, 1975.
Dellane, Gabriel, *Les Apparitions Materialisés de Vivants et
  de les Morts*, Editora: Paris, 1911.
Durville, Hector, *Le Fantôme des Vivants*, Vol. 1&2, Editora:
  Paris, 1909.
Freire, Antonio, *Da Alma Humana* (Of the Human Soul), Ed.
  Federacao Espirita: Rio de Janeiro.
Guerney, E. & Meyers, F.W.H., *Visible Apparitions*, Ed.
  Cidade: Rio de Janeiro, 1972.
Gurney, Meyers & Podmore, *Phantasms of the Living*,
  Editora: London, 1886.
Hansel, C.E.M., *ESP and Parapsychology*, NY: Prometheus
  Books, 1980.
Isaiah (Prophets) (The Old Testament).
Koestler, Arthur, *O Fantasma da maquina* (The Ghost of the
  Machine) Zahar Editora: Rio de Janeiro, 1967.
Levi, Eliphas, *Dogma and Ritual of Black Magic*, Ed.
  Pensamento, 1924.
Luiz, André, *Workers of the Eternal Life*, Ed. Federacao
  Espirita: Rio de Janeiro.
— *Liberation*, Ed. Federacao Espirita: Rio de Janeiro.
— *Missionaries of Light*, Ed. Federacao Espirita: Rio de
  Janeiro.
— *The Messengers*, Ed. Federacao Espirita: Rio de Janeiro.
Macedo, Horácio, *Dicionario de Fisica* (Dictionary of Physics).
de Miranda, Manuel Philomeno, *In the Background of
  Obsession*, Ed. Federacao Espirita: Rio de Janeiro, 1972.
de Rochas, Albert, *L'Extériorisation de la Sensibilité*, Paris,
  1912, Trad. Edicel, 1971.
Rohden, Huberto, *The Man*.
The Gospels (The New Testament).
Tyrrel, G.N.M., *The Personality of Man*, London: Pelican.
Ubaldi, Pietro, *Noures*, Ed. Herder: Sao Paulo.
Vierira, Waldo, *Projecoes da Consciencia* (Projections of
  Consciousness), Ed. Lake: Sao Paulo, 1982.

ABOUT THE AUTHOR

Dr. José Lacerda de Azevedo was born on June 12, 1919 in Porto Alegre, Brazil, the capital of Rio Grande do Sul. He descends from an upper-middle class family that came from Portugal in the middle of the 19th century. As an adolescent he faced great adversity due to his father's economic ruin.

He is the oldest of four brothers, three of whom graduated from University by their own effort.

Although his family followed the Roman Catholic religion, they were never particularly religious. During his adolescence his maternal aunt provided Dr. Lacerda with a firm orientation in the religious field of Spiritism. As she did not consider Spiritism a religion, but rather a cosmic reality infinitely superior to any religion, her instruction did not include any exaggerated mysticism or fanaticism. Since then he has tried to make Spiritism known from this aspect.

His aunt was instrumental in teaching him how to make choices in relation to life—including his professional activities and the metaphysical problems of existence.

Early in life Dr. Lacerda opted for medicine, a choice with which he has always been satisfied. He entered Medical School in 1945. After a six-year degree program, he completed an additional four years of training in surgery and gynecology.

In 1965 he began working at the Spiritist Hospital of Porto Alegre, a 700-bed charity institution famous throughout Brazil. For twenty years he was the head of the Psychic Research Division. This book is the result of much of the research conducted during that time.

Today he continues his research on Apometrics at the Spiritist Center Ramiro d'Avilo where he assists mainly those with psychic problems.

He was married in 1947 and gives significant credit to his wife for her motivation and support for all of his undertakings.

He has two daughters, both mediums.